P9-CLO-763

63P

TRANSITION
from
SCHOOL
to
WORK
for
PERSONS
with
DISABILITIES

TRANSITION
from
SCHOOL
to
WORK
for
PERSONS
with
DISABILITIES

Dianne E. Berkell
Long Island University—C. W. Post Campus

James M. Brown
University of Minnesota

Longman
New York & London

Transition from School to Work for Persons with Disabilities

Longman Inc., 95 Church Street, White Plains, N. Y. 10601

Associated companies:
Longman Group Ltd., London
Longman Cheshire Pty., Melbourne
Longman Paul Pty., Auckland
Copp Clark Pitman, Toronto
Pitman Publishing Inc., New York

p. 112 *Tomorrow's Teachers* (A Report of the Holmes Group). The Holmes Group, East Lansing, MI, 1986. Reprinted with permission.

p. 147–148 *Third Annual "Looking Ahead" Parent Training Workshop*, The Association for Retarded Citizens in Dane County, Madison, WI (ARC), Wisconsin Association for Children and Adults with Learning Disabilities (WACLD) and Cooperative Educational Services Agency Number Two, March 1987. Reprinted with permission of ARC and WACLD.

pp. 142–143 "Discover Exceptional Parents: Barbara Geer," *Counterpoint*, February 1987. Counterpoint Communications Company, Fairfax, VA. Reprinted with permission.

pp. 149–150 *Parents Needs Assessment Instrument*, Madison Metropolitan School District, 1987. Reprinted with permission.

pp. 151–154 Memorandum of Understanding Between the Division of Vocational Rehabilitation, the Division of Developmental Disabilities and Washington Parents Advocating for Vocational Education (PAVE). Reprinted with permission of Washington PAVE.

p. 155 *Individual Transition Plan*, The School Board of Leon County, Florida, Exceptional Student Education. Reprinted with permission.

Executive editor: Raymond T. O'Connell
Production editor: Dee Josephson
Cover design: Susan J. Moore
Production supervisor: Eduardo Castillo
Cover Art: "Sky and Water I" © 1988 M. C. Escher Heirs/Cordon Art—Baarn—Holland

Library of Congress Cataloging-in-Publication Data

Transition from school to work for persons with
    disabilities.

    Bibliography: p.
    Includes index.
    1. Vocational guidance for the handicapped—United
States. 2. Vocational rehabilitation—United States.
3. Handicapped—Employment—United States. I. Berkell,
Dianne E. II. Brown, James M.
HV1568.5.T7 1988   362.4'088055   88-12757
ISBN 0-8013-0228-5 (pbk.)

88 89 90 91 92 93 94 9 8 7 6 5 4 3 2 1

Contents

Preface

This book was designed to serve as a reference book for professionals, as well as for advocates for persons with disabilities, and as a textbook for students in the fields of special education, vocational education, and rehabilitation. It is intended to fill the vacuum created by the lack of practical, comprehensive references designed specifically to address current issues, trends, and concerns related to the transition from school to work of persons with disabilities.

Federal funding initiatives during the past decade have encouraged the emergence of a wide variety of secondary and postsecondary activities designed to prepare individuals with special learning needs to enter the work force and the adult community. During this period the U.S. Department of Education has been instrumental in initiating and supporting efforts to improve school curricula by emphasizing the need to prepare persons with disabilities to complete their education and to become productive members of society.

One of this book's most important attributes lies in its comprehensive coverage of a broad array of topics that examines crucial aspects of successful transition programs and services. Since we believe transition concepts transcend issues related only to specific types of disabilities or service providers, we have elected to address issues related to program development and service delivery rather than to focus on the particular disabilities of those served. This book's chapters, therefore, focus on topics viewed from a broad, generic perspective.

After deciding to write a book about transition issues, we focused our initial activities on identifying major issues related to the book's topic. As existing transition models, programs, and related issues were analyzed, a broad schema of transition emerged. The major components of this schema were then described in terms of their potential importance in the transition process, with special emphasis directed toward their impact on quality-of-life issues. Next, these descriptions were used to develop the first outlines for this book's chapters. Only then did we seek out persons with expertise in these specific areas and invite them to help create this publication.

Viewed broadly, this book focuses on the following transition issues:

1. A new perspective on the identification, assessment, and program placement of persons needing transition assistance
2. Transition enhancement viewed from the perspective of career development theory
3. A discussion of issues and processes that affect educators' roles in transition activities
4. An examination of current and emerging factors affecting employers' roles in transition processes
5. A discussion of job development and placement efforts, issues, and recommended strategies
6. A synthesis of important interagency collaboration activities and a discussion of the roles, rights, and responsibilities of parents
7. A unique analysis of transition concepts from the perspective of a labor economist
8. An epilogue that examines each of these factors within the total framework surrounding the concept of transition and discusses the developments and changes that lie ahead.

We believe that readers should be encouraged by recent improvements in the nature and extent of services for persons with disabilities. However, a close look at current conditions in our society will disclose that the true integration into our society of persons with disabilities has been only partially achieved. In addition, when we look into the future it seems likely that current transition programs and processes will be subjected to increasingly threatening scrutinization. As public awareness of the costs of transition-enhancement services grows, it will become necessary to provide convincing evidence of the economic benefits of these services to both service recipients and society. Clearly, we are faced by many serious challenges and a never-ending series of difficult tasks. It is hoped that recent developments and successes, as well as failures, will provide the insight, motivation, and mechanisms to attain the increasingly difficult objectives ahead.

The successful production of an edited book depends upon the efforts of many individuals, especially the chapter authors. The contributing authors have filled the pages of this volume with innovative, practical, and creative information to facilitate the transition to work for persons with disabilities. Their contributions to this text as well as to their respective fields are acknowledged and appreciated.

We also wish to express our gratitude to Ray O'Connell, Longman's Executive Editor. Without Ray's professional and personal advice, support, and friendship, our efforts to develop this book's conceptual framework and to turn those concepts into a printed document would have been much more difficult and far less personally rewarding.

Finally, we wish to thank our families whose confidence and encouragement motivated us to pursue this project. They were extremely supportive as we spent the hours necessary to convert our ideas into reality. This book is lovingly dedicated to Arthur, Kelly, and Jacqueline; Kathy, Jessica, Christian, and Mollie.

Dianne Berkell
Jim Brown

Foreword

William Halloran

The transition for youths with handicaps from school life to adult and working life has become a critical concern for parents, professionals, and policy makers. There are many reasons for placing increased emphasis on transition services. At the present time, youths with disabilities face an uncertain future when they leave public school programs. Parents, advocates, and educators are coming to realize that the only service mandated for persons with handicaps is public education, but some students reach the end of their public school experience poorly prepared for competitive employment or independent living. As students approach the end of their formal schooling we frequently ask what they will be doing after school ends. Unfortunately, when we look back to determine what preparations have been made for students to live and work in our communities we often see a series of disjointed efforts lacking a focus on the skills necessary to confront the new expectations and demands of adult life.

Qualification for employment is an implied promise of education. However, 50 to 80 percent of working-age adults who report a disability are jobless. Outcome and follow-up studies of students who have left special education programs indicate that many school leavers experience major difficulties in making successful transitions from school to community work and living. High unemployment for school leavers exists even when the leavers have participated in special education programs tailored to their individual needs. Approximately two-thirds of handicapped school leavers continue as adults to live with their parents. Of students enrolled in secondary special education programs, large numbers—over 30 percent—drop out. Of those who remain in school and graduate, fewer than 15 percent obtain employment with a salary above the minimum wage.

Serious implications from the results of outcome studies have been addressed in the 1986 revisions to the Education of the Handicapped Act (Pub. L. 99–457). These amendments draw specific attention to the need to improve the scope and quality of transition services and service planning efforts. In response to Congressional authorization for new initiatives for transition services, the Office of Special Education and Rehabilitative Services defined the critical components of transition planning and set in place new model demonstration programs throughout the country. The critical components of transition include

1. Effective high school programs that prepare students to work and live in the community
2. A broad range of adult service programs that can meet the various support needs of individuals with handicaps in employment and community settings
3. Comprehensive and cooperative transition planning between education and community service agencies for the purpose of developing needed services for completers, leavers, and graduates

Although isolated programs have demonstrated that the technology and strategies needed to accomplish these three activities are available, responsive transition services are the exception rather than the rule. Publications, dissemination activities, and replication efforts are needed to provide the background and direction to agencies, professionals, and organizations interested in making our nation's schools more responsive to the transition needs of youths with handicaps. The guidance and direction provided in this book should make a major contribution to this effort.

Effective transition services for all youths with handicaps is a laudable goal. However, the prevailing thinking of many education agencies stops short of the ultimate measure of effectiveness. Have our efforts demonstrated that youths who leave our programs become well-adjusted and suitably employed members of our communities? I believe educational responsibility must go beyond the preparation phase to the actual placement and follow-up phase necessary to complete the initial transition. We have to extend the notion that transition is merely the passing along of youths to the community or adult service agencies. Completing initial transitions will require education agencies to take more responsibility for ensuring successful adjustments for youths exiting their programs and also require significant adjustments of programs to meet the desired outcomes.

Isolated programs throughout the country are demonstrating that public education can assist youths with a variety of disabilities and levels of impairments in making the adjustment to adult life in their communities. Studies of effective programs have led me to believe that three essential components are necessary. First is the need for families of youths with handicaps to be included as partners in the development and implementation of purposeful activities that maximize independence. The family is a major facilitator of transition. Second, transition programs must be community-based, and opportunities to experience and succeed in employment and other aspects of community life must be provided. The third component is the need for working partnerships with employers to ensure that efforts of the schools are consistent with employers' needs. Programs that prepare youths with handicaps for employment should include measurement of employers' and employees' satisfaction. Additional strengths in effective programs that merit significant attention include measures of program effectiveness and systematic coordination of agencies, organizations, and individuals from a broad array of disciplines and professional fields.

Development and improvement in transition programs and services can be enhanced through the identification and replication of effective practices. However, among successful efforts there are components that can be attributed to the unique differences that exist in local areas. Often attempts to replicate successful programs do not take this component into account. Each of the successful programs I am aware of has utilized the resources of its community and has therefore developed a strong sense of local ownership. The more this sense of ownership is dispersed among agencies, organizations, and individuals, the greater the likelihood of commitment to the goal of ensuring that students exiting the program will become well-adjusted and suitably employed members of their communities.

Although responsive education programs are rather scarce, there are several signs of optimism in terms of the provision of transition services:

- Special educators are starting to perceive a responsibility to prepare youths with handicaps to live and work in the community.
- Advances in technology in teaching employment skills are enabling a much broader population of youths with handicaps to enter the job market and obtain competitive employment.
- Demographic changes and population shifts are causing employers to consider youths with handicaps as a contributing solution to the dwindling working-age population.

I frequently hear that there is nothing new in transition, that it is just a new term applied to old practices. Others claim that transition is a new and different approach designed to compensate for the poor performance of previous efforts to assist individuals in making the adjustment to adult and working life. I believe the current focus on transition has evolved from an expanding state of the art, in which the development over time has enabled the field to become more precise in its efforts on behalf of youths with handicaps. It will continue to evolve as our educational technologies improve. However, individuals working on the cutting edge of advancements must respect the historical evolution of training and employment services for these persons. It is not necessary for us to denigrate the previous effort of others to enhance the status of our contributions. Agencies, organizations, and individuals from a broad array of disciplines and professional fields must effectively and systematically coordinate their efforts to meet the individual education and employment needs of adults and youths with handicaps.

The transition from school to work for persons with disabilities enables them to participate in a major aspect of community life. Work, domestic living, and leisure and recreational pursuits are the major areas of focus for community integration. This book will provide the reader with a background in transition programming and a basic framework for developing and implementing responsive programs to facilitate the transition from school life to adult and working life.

CHAPTER 1

The Concept of Transition: Historical and Current Developments

Dianne Berkell and Robert Gaylord-Ross*

It has been estimated that there are about 4,339,000 children and youths through age 21 enrolled in education programs for students with handicaps in the United States (Human Services Research Institute, 1985). Approximately 300,000 youths with handicaps leave high school each year, the majority of whom are faced with unemployment and underemployment.

Today, despite improved public awareness and significant improvements in the education and adult service systems for persons with handicaps, hundreds of thousands of these potentially employable individuals remain idle (Wehman & Kregel, 1985). The U.S. Commission on Civil Rights (1983) reported unemployment rates between 50 and 75 percent among persons with disabilities, and a 67 percent unemployment rate for Americans with handicaps was found in 1986 by a Harris telephone survey with a cross section of 1,000 persons with handicaps, aged 16 and over.

A literature review on unemployment rates among adults with mental retardation by Hill and colleagues (1987) clearly indicates the negative financial and societal impact of the current high unemployment rate for this group. In contrast, the economic benefits of placing and supporting handicapped indi-

*Dianne E. Berkell is chairperson of the Department of Special Education and Reading at the C. W. Post campus of Long Island University. She received her Ph.D. in educational research from Hofstra University. She has published extensively in the areas of autism, developmental disabilities, and supported employment.
Robert Gaylord-Ross is the coordinator of the Vocational Special Education Program at San Francisco State University. He received his Ph.D. in educational psychology from Mississippi State University. He has published numerous chapters and monographs.

viduals in competitive employment are significant (Rusch & Phelps, 1986), leading to reductions in social service costs and a national increased productivity capability. Also, a study by Schneider, Rusch, Henderson, and Geske (1982) examined the cost effectiveness of support to individuals who had handicaps as they made the transition from school to work, projecting improved financial outcomes when adequate support was available.

The need for improved transition services is clear. Adequate programming through systematic vocational training and provision of the needed support services can substantially reduce the high unemployment rate for persons with disabilities. It can also lessen the enormous federal financial burden created by their unemployment, and most important, it can improve the quality of life possible for these individuals.

THE RIGHT TO WORK

Earning a decent wage in a regular job is an important part of our lives. In fact, a person's status in our society is often determined by the type of job held and the salary earned. Our work defines how we appear to others and how we view ourselves. Besides providing economic support, it offers opportunities for social interaction and a chance to use and enhance skills in a chosen line of work.

Work is especially important for persons with disabilities. It generates the respect of others (Terkel, 1974) and can be a source of pride, self-satisfaction, personal fulfillment, and of course, income. In a 1985 Harris survey, 67 percent of all the unemployed persons who were handicapped stated that they would like to work. Yet despite all the currently available education programs, youths with handicaps are leaving our schools ill equipped for work, lacking the skills and behaviors, and equally important, the support services needed to secure and maintain competitive employment.

Integration of handicapped citizens as full members of our society with the right to hold a job and earn a decent living should be a national priority. Toward this end, educators will need to take responsibility for preparing all students to join the nation's work force. To do this, we must begin to evaluate the effectiveness of our own efforts by the quality as well as the demand for our product—our graduates.

THE CONCEPT OF TRANSITION

In the past two decades, there have been major changes in the delivery of education and social services to persons with disabilities. These changes reflect an increased public recognition of the fact that the service needs of these individuals extend beyond school boundaries (Hasazi et al., 1985) to include preparation, training, and support for community integration. One of the most crucial and complex components of community integration is the transition from school to work.

A successful transition from school to work and adult life is the ultimate indicator of effective schooling and service provision (Bellamy & Wilcox, 1981). The objective of transition is to provide training and support that will enable individuals to enjoy successful adult living with the maximum degree of independence and community integration possible.

The transition from school to work encompasses a period that includes high school, graduation, postsecondary education or adult services, and the initial years of employment. It is a process that requires preparation and support throughout secondary school and follow-up services after employment is begun.

For youths with handicaps there are three major goals for transition to adult working life (McDonnell, Sheehan, & Wilcox, 1983). The first goal involves providing opportunities and services that will support quality adult living. Second is the need to maintain community integration with nonhandicapped persons in all living and working environments. Finally, it is important to maximize the productivity and independence of students leaving the school system.

Defining Transition

Wehman and colleagues (1986) have defined transition as

> . . . a carefully planned process, which may be initiated either by school personnel or adult service providers, to establish and implement a plan for either employment or additional vocational training of a handicapped student who will graduate or leave school in 3–5 years; such a process must involve special educators, vocational educators, parents and/or the student, an adult service system representative, and possibly an employer. (p. 114)

This is a good definition because it identifies the goal of transition while highlighting the need for interdisciplinary cooperation and parental involvement. Such cooperation is the cornerstone of effective transitional programming.

The transition to working life calls for a range of choices about career options, living arrangements, social life, and economic goals that often have lifelong consequences. As Madeline Will, Assistant Secretary for the Office of Special Education and Rehabilitative Services, has defined this process (1984), it is a bridge between the security and structure offered by school and the many responsibilities and choices of adult life.

Transition is a shared responsibility of all involved parties (student, teacher, vocational counselor, parent, and employer). It has been conceptualized as a process of movement through life's phases (Ianacone & Stodden,

1987). This process encompasses activities that lead to independent living, employment, and other productive life situations.

An Example of a Current Transition Program

In response to recent federal initiatives, research and demonstration efforts on the delivery of transition services have attempted to identify (1) critical elements of education programming (Ianacone & Stodden, 1987), (2) necessary linkages between service delivery agencies (Caparosa, 1985), and (3) means of gaining services that can facilitate the transition from school to work (Elder, Conley, & Noble, 1986).

The READDY Program (Real Employment Alternatives for Developmentally Disabled Youth) on Long Island, New York, is an example of a federally funded project that has continued even after the funding period terminated. The purpose of the READDY Program is to prepare severely handicapped autistic students, through a community-based vocational training program, for competitive employment. The program represents a cooperative effort between university and field-based personnel. The primary grant recipient was Long Island University. The Nassau Center for the Developmentally Disabled was, and still is, the demonstration facility, which all the participating students attend. In addition, representatives from several state and local service agencies participate in an advisory capacity.

Students in the READDY Program receive instruction at community-based work sites. They learn how to perform actual work tasks, as well as how to interact with co-workers. Two-thirds of the students are currently earning the minimum wage at their jobs, and several have received salary increases.

Both consecutive and concurrent instruction in school and nonschool environments is provided. Program staff includes a project director, a field coordinator, two certified special education teachers, an administrative assistant, and ancillary support staff. To illustrate the work potential of students who have been classified as severely handicapped, a case history of one student who has participated in the READDY Program follows.

JOSEPH: AN OFFICE CLERK

Joseph, a 21-year-old man, is a graduate of the READDY Program. He has a diagnosis of autism and mild mental retardation. On the Weschler Intelligence Scale (WISC-R), Joe achieved a full-scale IQ of 70. Speech-language pathological reports indicate that Joe exhibits a language disorder characterized by delays in receptive and expressive language, cognitive abilities, and social interaction skills. He exhibits self-stimulatory behaviors in the form of head and body rocking and has exhibited self-abusive behaviors when frustrated, including hand biting and body pinching.

Joe received three years of vocational training in the READDY Program. Initially, he was placed in a supermarket, where his work consisted of collecting carts and reshelving unpurchased items. At first, Joseph required full physical prompting to

Figure 1.1 Courtesy Paul Gravina and the Nassau Center for the Developmentally Disabled.

complete his job tasks. Written task analyses were developed to help teach him the skills he would need and to assess his progress.

After one year of community-based instruction given only two mornings per week, Joe had surpassed all the goals established at the outset of instruction. He was accepting directions from the store manager rather than from his vocational trainer, just as were the other workers in the supermarket. By the middle of his second year of participation in the READDY Program, Joseph was considered to be functioning independently at his job in the supermarket.

As Joe entered his third year of vocational training, and his final year of school, the program staff members began to direct their efforts toward finding him a placement at which he would be able to earn a living following graduation. The central office of a large retail chain was selected as a good work site for Joe because of its proximity to his home, as well as for the supportive attitude of the company's executives and other personnel.

Joe began training as an office clerk, receiving instruction and supervision directly from his vocational trainer. His job responsibilities included data entry on the computer and preparation of checking account statements for bank reconciliation. The cooperation and patience of the office staff were cultivated gradually through the friendly overtures of the trainer. As Joe demonstrated increased competence in his job, his parents were invited to visit the office and to observe him at work.

A meeting was arranged for Joseph's parents to develop communication channels with the local adult service agencies with whom they would need to interact after Joe was no longer in the educational system. Persons who attended this meeting included a teacher, a school administrator, a counselor from the Office of Vocational Rehabilitation, a caseworker from the Office of Mental Retardation and Developmental Disabilities, a representative from the Social Security Office, and a legal advocate. With the cooperation and assistance of all these parties, Joe was able to make a smooth transition from school to work.

A GENERIC PERSPECTIVE

The READDY Program is just one example of the many successful transition programs across the nation for youths with handicaps. There are currently over 100 such programs supported by the U.S. Department of Education. The range of students served through these new programs includes youths between the ages of 16 and 21 with all types of handicapping conditions and levels of ability, from individuals with mild handicaps to those who have severe developmental disabilities.

When the wide range of recently developed programs and the wealth of new research studies that have emerged as a result of the federal initiatives are examined, it is apparent that educational goals and transition support services needed by persons with disabilities are generic and, in fact, transcend traditional education and diagnostic categories (i.e., type of handicapping condition). Although adaptations and modifications in transition programming may be necessary to accommodate specific disabilities, the general types of support services required, such as job skill training or transportation, tend to remain constant regardless of the type of disability.

For instance, although a person who uses a wheelchair may require a special vehicle with an access ramp to transport himself to and from work, and someone who has severe autism and mental retardation may need an attendant on her bus, both these persons share the common problem of obtaining a suitable means of transportation to their work site. Many of the available options, such as utilizing a vehicle that has been adapted to meet particular needs, enlisting a co-worker to drive, or hiring a taxi, are identical for both parties.

This is also true with regard to job coaching needs. A client who has severe mental retardation may require more support in learning to perform a particular skill, whereas another with a language and communication disorder may need extra assistance dealing with personal interactions at the job site. Both clients have different types of problems; however, both require some form of on-the-job coaching.

These two examples illustrate the point that transition is a process that needs to be considered from a broad perspective with regard to services. Rather than focusing on specific disabilities or the needs of special interest groups, it is necessary to look beyond disability labels and to begin to address transition as a generic topic. As universally encountered problems—such as (1) wage and benefit issues, (2) availability of job training and follow-up, (3)

access to transportation, and (4) co-worker and employer attitudes—are resolved, all disability groups will benefit.

FUNCTIONAL ANALYSIS
AND CATEGORICAL DIAGNOSIS

Different types of disabilities may result in different learner characteristics and needs, and the preceding argument for a generic service viewpoint is not intended to negate the importance of understanding student and client abilities and limitations. An awareness of learner characteristics and needs is always necessary in program planning.

Disabilities can be viewed from two perspectives: categorical diagnosis of specific disabilities, which results in the assignment of diagnostic labels, and noncategorical analysis of functional characteristics, which identifies ability level and instructional needs. Through categorical diagnosis, a traditional perspective of persons with disabilities is provided, which focuses on the etiology of cognitive, behavioral, and physical impairments. This type of diagnostic information has been used most frequently in determining treatment and placement decisions, such as the type of school program in which a student is to be enrolled.

Noncategorical analysis of functional characteristics, on the other hand, is not concerned with causality, as is the more medically oriented diagnostic model, but rather considers how disabilities affect the intellectual and behavioral functioning of individuals. Degree of impairment (mild, moderate, severe) across intellectual and behavioral functioning areas is analyzed, along with the assessment of specific skills, leading to the development of individualized educational goals and instructional programming.

The major benefit of the functional approach lies in its focus on individual ability levels and learner needs. Through this approach instructional programming may be tied to actual learner needs in selected performance areas (Gollay, 1981), resulting in measurable behavioral gains.

This is not to say that professionals in the field all agree with this viewpoint; many still question the utility of the noncategorical approach, claiming that the reduction in labeling and its diagnostic and prescriptive potential have yet to be realized (Summers, 1981). There are also a number of implementation concerns related to this approach (Kiernan, Smith, & Ostrowsky, 1986) because of the lack of clarity that arises when diagnostic definitions are not available. In spite of these concerns, however, a noncategorical functional model of disability is advocated here because of the generic nature of the transition process and the need to understand learner characteristics and abilities. (See Figure 1.2.)

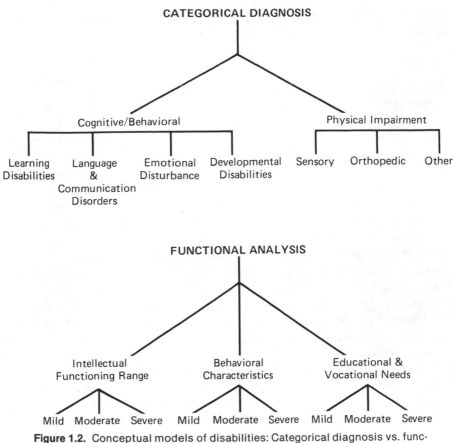

Figure 1.2. Conceptual models of disabilities: Categorical diagnosis vs. functional analysis.

Diagnostic Labels

When addressing issues related to transition programming, educators should avoid focusing on traditional diagnostic labels that inherently emphasize persons' disabilities or deficits. However, along with an awareness of the functional analysis of behaviors and skills discussed earlier, some familiarity with these labels and definitions will still prove necessary in dealing with many existing service systems (e.g., school districts and state and federal funding sources) and in communicating with other professionals.

For this reason, a list of diagnostic categories (Heward & Orlansky, 1980) and definitions are provided on pages 9–10. The reader should note that each of these diagnostic labels represents a major field of study and that the definitions are intended only to distinguish superficially between categories. This categorization of the factors inherent in our planning efforts on behalf of indi-

viduals with disabilities is fundamental. It will be new to neophytes in the field and provides a brief review for those of us who daily utilize these concepts.

1. *Mental retardation:* Significant subaverage general intellectual functioning (IQ 70 or below) existing concurrently with deficits in adaptive behavior and manifested during the developmental period (Grossman, 1983), which is considered to extend from conception to age 18. Mental retardation exists in varying degrees of severity and is the outcome of interaction between constitutional and environmental factors (Clarizio & McCoy, 1983).

2. *Specific learning disabilities:* A disorder in one or more of the basic psychological processes involved in understanding or in using language, spoken or written, which may manifest itself in an imperfect ability to listen, think, speak, read, write, spell, or do mathematical calculations (Lerner, 1985). As stated in Public Law 94–142 (U.S. Department of Education, 1977), the term includes such conditions as perceptual handicaps, brain injury, minimal brain dysfunction, dyslexia, and developmental aphasia. This term does not include children who have learning problems that are primarily the result of visual, hearing, or motor handicaps; mental retardation; emotional disturbances; or environmental, cultural, or economic disadvantages.

3. *Behavior disorders:* A condition exhibiting one or more of the following characteristics over a long period of time and to a marked degree, which adversely affects educational performance: (a) an inability to learn that cannot be explained by intellectual, sensory, or health factors; (b) an inability to build or maintain satisfactory interpersonal relationships with peers and teachers; (c) inappropriate types of behavior or feelings under normal circumstances; (d) a general pervasive mood of unhappiness or depression; or (e) a tendency to develop physical symptoms or fears associated with personal or school problems (Wood & Lakin, 1979).

4. *Language and communication disorders:* Difficulty in understanding language or in expressing oneself through language (Heward & Orlansky, 1980). Such communication problems may be classified as either organic or functional. Organic problems are the result of a physical impairment, whereas functional communication problems are exhibited in the absence of an underlying physical cause. Speech and language impairments may be severe enough to impede education (Suran & Rizzo, 1979) or to cause problems in social development.

5. *Hearing impairments:* Includes the two more specific subsets of deaf and hard of hearing (Meyen, 1982). According to Public Law 94–142, *deaf* is the term used to describe a hearing impairment so severe that the child is impaired in processing linguistic information through hearing, with or without amplification, which adversely affects educational performance. *Hard of hearing* is the term used to describe a hearing impairment, whether permanent or fluctuating, which adversely affects a child's educational performance but is not under the definition of deaf.

6. *Visual handicaps:* Impairments in the structure of functioning of the eye, regardless of the nature of the impairment, which causes a limitation that even with the best possible correction interferes with incidental or normal learning through the sense of vision (Barraga, 1976). Three categories of visual handicaps may be diagnosed: (a) blind, (b) low vision, and (c) visually limited.

7. *Physical and other health impairments:* All persons within this categorical group have a physiological impairment or chronic health condition that affects normal acquisition of skills or interferes with the ability to process information. Persons with physical impairments have a diverse range of characteristics and are different by virtue of their disability (Hardman, Drew, & Egan, 1987), and it is impossible to include these individuals under a single set of descriptive characteristics.

8. *Severe and multiple handicaps:* Those persons who function intellectually in the lowest 1 percent of the population (IQ 50 or below) and may have been diagnosed as autistic; psychotic; moderately, severely, or profoundly retarded; trainable level retarded; physically handicapped; multiply handicapped; or deaf or blind (Powell et al., 1985). Such persons have specific needs that go beyond traditional education and social services to include lifelong training, therapies, and support services.

A substantial amount of overlap is evident in these definitions; there are no sharp delineations between the categories of handicapping conditions. The systematization gives us a working diagnostic classification system, or taxonomy, to direct our efforts when working with other professionals. In combination with the functional analyses discussed earlier in the chapter, this information can serve to facilitate educational planning.

HISTORY OF TRANSITION

The concept of transition may also be examined historically. Although transition may include the domains of community living and social interpersonal networks (Halpern, 1985), we will focus on the transition from school to adult employment. One can go back to different eras in history and find writings dealing with youths and work. Yet a true history of vocational education appears to have emerged in the nineteenth century (Phelps & Fraser, 1988). In reviewing these historical developments, one should attend to the different fields of vocational education, rehabilitation, and special education.

Also, the general historical developments for youths with mild handicaps versus those with severe handicaps are different. Mildly handicapped individuals were indirectly affected by developments in vocational education for the general population. Severely handicapped youths and adults were largely served by segregated facilities, which offered no promise or opportunity for nonsheltered work. Yet there have been developments in the past ten years that have brought great attention to the transition of disabled youths. Let us examine the historical backdrop for these recent developments.

Vocational Education

The first major development in vocational education centered around efforts to provide preparation for agricultural and industrial workers. The Morrill Act of 1856 and the Land Grant College Act of 1862 established land grant colleges in every state of the nation. Thus, initial vocational education focused on college-level preparations.

Subsequently, the focus was extended to include programs designed to prepare youths for work. The Smith-Hughes Act of 1917 placed a priority on preparing skilled workers for employment before they left school. It also mandated that federal, state, and local agencies form partnerships in vocational education efforts.

The federal role in vocational education grew with the passage of the Smith-Sears Act of 1918. The Smith-Sears Act and the Vocational Rehabilitation Act of 1920 began rehabilitation programs and offered funding for disabled war veterans and disabled civilians, who were attempting to return to the work force. Subsequently, the federal role in vocational education continued to grow into the 1960s.

The George-Dean Act of 1936 stimulated states to offer training for personal and public service occupations and distributive (marketing) occupations. Furthermore, the George-Barden Acts of 1946, 1956, and 1959 funded vocational guidance programs and construction of vocational facilities. Finally, the 1956 amendments to the Health Act gave monies for the training of practical nurses.

As is often the case, a major political event stimulated the growth of an education program. The Soviet Union's launching of Sputnik and the subsequent space race between the United States and the Soviet Union stimulated a demand for trained personnel at all occupational levels. The need for skilled technicians and engineers resulted in the National Defense Educational Act (NDEA) of 1963. This act encouraged an important shift from training for specific occupations (e.g., agriculture or home economics) to an acknowledgement of the diverse needs of youths to be served by vocational education (Phelps & Frasier, 1988). It funded projects for curriculum development, research, and teacher training, and model programs. Of great import, the act appropriated 10 percent of its federal funds for handicapped students and 15 percent of its funds for disadvantaged students.

The act also adopted a flexible view for course offerings. That is, based on a needs analysis of marketplace demands, it encouraged the development of curricula and course work in the high-demand areas. Our current vocational education legislation conceptually emerged from the NDEA.

Public Law 94–482 (1976) was passed to assist states in improving planning in the use of available resources for vocational education. It involves a wide range of agencies concerned with education and training within the state in the development of vocational education plans.

The Carl Perkins Act of 1984 (P.L. 98–524) provides federal funds to be passed on to local school districts for equipment, staff, and buildings. It earmarks 10 percent of its funds for handicapped students and 22 percent for disadvantaged students. A total of 57 percent of its funds are allocated for special needs populations. The Carl Perkins Act also encourages vocational education in least restrictive settings and the inclusion of vocational education as a component of each student's Individual Education Program (IEP). This requirement has set the tone for work experiences in real employment settings. It also encourages social interactions at the work site between workers with disabilities and their co-workers.

Besides providing work experience opportunities, vocational education funding has developed a network of occupational training courses in such fields as automotive mechanics and computer operation. These courses and certification programs may be offered at the secondary level at comprehensive or vocational-technical high schools. They may also be provided by vocational programs in community colleges and by adult education. Students with mild handicaps have often participated in such programs through a mainstreaming approach. Often resource specialists work with vocational educators to adapt curricula and socially integrate disabled students into instructional programs.

Special Education

Special education programs began to appear in public schools in the 1930s and 1940s. Students with severe handicaps, though, tended to be institutionalized or to stay at home with their parents. In collaboration with vocational rehabilitation agencies, some high schools began to have work experiences for mildly disabled youths.

During the 1960s the federal government began to exhibit a growing interest in handicapped students. The Education for All Handicapped Children's Act (P.L. 94–142) was passed in 1975, and it is a significant milestone that should not be underestimated. Besides providing a free education for all handicapped students, it encourages instruction to take place in the least restrictive, most integrated setting. This legislation, as well as the development of models for career education (Brolin, 1982), encourages work training for mildly and moderately handicapped students in real employment settings. Also, this federal legislation has led to the education of an increasing number of students with severe handicaps in integrated public schools. The integration concept was soon extended to nonschool community settings (Brown, Nietupski, &

Hamre-Nietupski, 1978). Students with disabilities, even those with severe handicaps began participating in work experiences at real employment sites in the community (Sailor et al., 1985).

As school integration, occupational training, and work experience developments grew, a question arose concerning what would happen to these students after graduation. As educators surveyed the adult work opportunities for handicapped individuals, they found the future prospects for their students to be dismal. There were no mandated adult services, as was the case for school-aged students. The unemployment rate for disabled adults was dismally high—ranging between 50 percent and 75 percent (U.S. Commission on Civil Rights, 1983)—and those disabled adults who were employed tended to be employed for too few hours of work per week or to be employed in sheltered work settings.

The federal government attempted to change these circumstances by passing Public Law 98–199 in 1984. The law amended Public Law 94–142 by placing a priority on the transition phase. It funded model transition demonstration and research programs throughout the nation. It called for school districts to begin planning for the transition of their students for adulthood. This often took the form of Individual Transition Plans, with transition objectives being added to the students' IEPs. Of great importance, the transition initiative encouraged school districts to form interagency links with adult service agencies. Such interagency links enabled students to continue to receive services (i.e., not fall between the cracks) and to increase their chances for employment.

Vocational Rehabilitation

The federal and state rehabilitation agencies have traditionally been the main service providers for adults with disabilities. Rehabilitation agencies have given particular attention to matters dealing with employment.

The historical emergence of vocational rehabilitation services in the United States is similar to their appearance in Europe (Gaylord-Ross, 1987). That is, after World War I, society and government were greatly concerned that injured and disabled veterans received proper care. As a consequence of the concern for veterans, similar concerns were generalized to the needs of all persons with disabilities. Therefore, the federal government passed the Vocational Rehabilitation Act of 1920 to assist disabled veterans and other disabled citizens in returning successfully to the labor market.

Rehabilitation funding continued over the years, but the 1959 amendments to this act gave greater emphasis to employment issues. Services to be provided by local agencies included job counseling and job placement. The Rehabilitation Act of 1973 (P.L. 93–112) further addressed employment-related problems often encountered by individuals with disabilities. Section 503 of the 1973 act required companies with federal contracts to have affirmative action hiring policies. It also asserted that these employers must make reasonable job accommodations. The 1974 amendments to the act (P.L. 93–576) went further in encouraging severely disabled persons to be trained and employed in actual work settings.

In general, vocational rehabilitation programs have provided effective employment services for a number of persons with disabilities. Since services can be provided to individuals as young as 16, rehabilitation can play a key role in enhancing the transition of school-aged disabled youths to adult employment. In fact, some work experience programs like Project Workability in California (Semmel, Cosden, & Konopak, 1985) have effectively linked rehabilitation with education to provide employment and permanent job placements for disabled youths in transition.

A problem with many traditional rehabilitation programs is that they have excluded a number of persons with disabilities from their employment services. Based on vocational assessment findings, an individual may be judged to be incapable of competitive employment. For most persons with severe handicaps, this has meant, at best, being employed in sheltered workshops. Yet as more severely handicapped youths in secondary school programs have been trained on actual work sites, there has been a call for the shift to nonsheltered settings for severely handicapped young adults. It would seem regressive to go from nonsheltered work experience in school programs to segregated employment as adults.

Thus, a supported employment movement has emerged that offers nonsheltered employment options for adults with serious vocational handicaps. Supported employment assists those individuals who previously were deemed to be unemployable. It provides such services as job development, on-the-job training, family support, and follow-up maintenance. Without such services these individuals would not be capable of nonsheltered employment. The supported employment movement has just emerged in the 1980s, but it offers much hope for the wide-scale employment of persons with disabilities.

The supported employment model has been demonstrated to be effective in a number of instances (Rusch, 1986; Wehman, 1981). Because of this success and the need for adult employment options, the federal government has passed the Rehabilitation Act Amendments of 1986 (P.L. 99–505). The act seeks to promote the employment of persons with a wide range of disabilities. It legally permits the nonclosure of supported employment cases that need lifelong service delivery. The act established a $25 million state grant program. Award recipients have made a commitment to convert their adult programs from a sheltered to a nonsheltered mode. The grants "will enable the states to plan, develop, and expand supported employment programs through authorized demonstration projects, technical assistance, and training of personnel in this area in order to compliment existing vocational rehabilitation services" (Weicker, 1987, p. 8).

ADULT EMPLOYMENT OPTIONS

There are a number of types of employment options for adults with disabilities. Although there has been a large movement toward nonsheltered work in the 1980s, the vast majority of adults with severe handicaps who are working are doing so in sheltered workshops. Although it is expected that there will be a gradual shift of persons and funds from sheltered to nonsheltered employment during future years, sheltered workshops will probably continue as a work option.

Competitive Employment

The primary option for nonsheltered employment is competitive employment. In competitive employment an individual handicapped person works in an actual work setting with nonhandicapped co-workers. The person is paid at least minimum wage and is considered to be a regular employee.

In the past, many adult persons with disabilities have been placed by rehabilitation agencies in competitive employment situations. These individuals usually had mild handicaps like learning disabilities or cerebral palsy with normal cognitive functioning, so that little was required in the way of extra on-the-job training. Usually these individuals learned their job tasks informally under the direction of supervisors or co-workers. Sometimes there was a need for adaptations in equipment or job responsibilities to secure the position.

Will's (1984) model of three bridges to transition notes that a person may find and learn a job with no specialized services. In fact, Hasazi, Gordon, and Roe (1985) found that mildly handicapped youths most frequently found jobs through personal networking with friends and families, and not through employment agencies. A second bridge to transition involves "time-limited" services. Here, an employment agency may open a case upon receiving a referral. That agency might vocationally assess, counsel, place, and train the individual. After the person has successfully held the job for three to six months, the agency, usually the department of vocational rehabilitation, will "close" the case. Thereafter, no further services are provided by the agency. Although such rehabilitation programs have achieved a certain amount of success, they have not addressed the issue of employment for persons with serious vocational handicaps, such as severe mental retardation, emotional disturbance, or multiple handicaps, who usually need lifelong vocational services.

Supported Employment

Research and demonstration projects (see, e.g., Berkell et al., 1986; Catapano & Kramer, 1986) have documented the employment potential of individuals with severe disabilities when appropriate support services have been provided.

Through such supported employment, persons with severe disabilities may receive the necessary services and assistance to learn specific job skills, develop interpersonal and other job-related skills, and even travel to and from their work setting. By providing both employment opportunities and ongoing support services, supported employment affords the benefits of working to persons with severe disabilities (Bellamy, Rhodes, & Albin, 1986) by offering an alternative that lies between competitive employment and sheltered employment or day treatment programs. Supported employment has three essential elements (Lagomarcino & Rusch, 1987): (1) wages paid, (2) work performed in an integrated setting, and (3) ongoing support services provided.

Job Coach Model

The new concept of supported work was designed to offer the assistance necessary to help clients succeed in nonsheltered work settings. Efforts to place individuals in competitive work settings usually use job coaches or instructors who accompany handicapped persons to their jobs on the first day of work. These instructors have already learned how to perform the jobs and now teach their clients all the specific job tasks and general work behaviors required for successful employment. The first few days or weeks may require instructors to be with employees continuously to provide one-to-one assistance and instruction. As time passes and employees gradually learn their jobs, job coaches fade from the work sites so that the employees spend more time working independently. As support is reduced, supervision is gradually turned over to one or more of the co-workers or job supervisors. After weeks or months, job coaches will have completely left the work settings. Subsequently, they will monitor the progress of workers through occasional follow-up visits or phone calls.

Work Crew Model

In a second type of supported work model, a group of handicapped persons perform work in a nonsheltered context. For example, a mobile work crew might travel around the community to perform landscaping or housecleaning tasks, or a small group of handicapped employees would work as a unit within a factory (Rhodes & Valenta, 1985). Crews and enclaves have a degree of isolation within an integrated context. The groups may vary in size from four to ten, and there is usually constant supervision from an instructor (with little fading). Persons in crews or enclaves tend to have more severe disabilities so that they require more intense supervision throughout their career. Yet crews and enclaves offer an integrated alternative to sheltered work.

Volunteer Work

Another nonsheltered work option, which has stirred a great deal of controversy, is the placement of persons with quite severe handicaps in actual work settings as volunteers. These individuals tend to produce at such a slow pace, for example, 1 percent of normal workers' rates, that most employers would never hire them as regular employees. Brown et al. (1984) defined the primary goal of nonsheltered work as a socialization experience where persons can have age-appropriate interactions with nonhandicapped peers. For Brown et al., payment for work is a secondary goal. Others, like Bellamy and colleagues (1984), have strong concerns about working without pay because of the long history of the peonage of persons with disabilities; if volunteer work were permitted, employers might take advantage of such volunteer arrangements and opt not to pay these workers.

Although the potential for abuse is present, Brown et al. (1984) assert that volunteer work offers a realistic work option for persons with the most severe disabilities; they believe that if nonsheltered employment entails minimum wage or substantial pay, many persons with severe disabilities will be excluded from such possibilities. If carefully monitored, an employment service system should be able to distinguish among regular pay, subminimum wage, and volunteer work.

Pumpian, West, and Shepard (1988) have developed a comprehensive adult education program for individuals with severe handicaps. Based at a local community college, the participants receive a comprehensive program of vocational, recreational, and community living instruction. These individuals are rotated through different work experiences as part of a vocational assessment process that can last as long as five years. When appropriate paid work positions are procured, these individuals are duly placed (at minimum or subminimum wage). Sometimes extended volunteer positions are obtained. The program is appealing because it coordinates employment with other programmatic domains like recreational activities, community living, and continuing education.

SUMMARY

The transition from school to work for persons with disabilities has received increasing attention in recent years. The main impetus for addressing transition issues emerged from concern about high unemployment rates among adults with disabilities and the fact that many individuals were not participating in any form of day program. The adult service delivery system differs from school programs, where all children receive an education and where there are many innovative vocational preparation programs.

The concept of transition has involved moving students from school programs to least restrictive adult programs. One form of transition merely makes appropriate referrals from school to adult services and ensures that individuals are followed up by an agency and not lost in the service system.

A second level of transition formalizes interagency working agreements between schools and adult service agencies. These administrative arrangements should go beyond lip service or paper agreements between agencies. In addition, clear demarcations of who will fund which key services should be made. For example, a school might provide an initial placement and training in a permanent job. An adult service agency might commit to provide extended, follow-up employment services. Such interagency linkages are critical to the provision of extended adult service delivery.

A third level of transition deals with actual program implementation. There are numerous components of transition programs, including instructional technology, counseling, family involvement, and administration. Although many impressive demonstrations have been made, we are still in a developmental phase of efforts to improve the efficacy of transition programs.

Transition programs serve students with a wide variety of disabilities. Certainly, the employment needs of mildly and severely handicapped youths will differ on many accounts. For example, employment services for severely handicapped workers might focus more on teaching specific job skills. Employment services for mildly handicapped youths might offer more counseling or attempt to remediate math or reading skills needed for job success.

Although transition has focused on employment processes, it should also address quality-of-life issues related to community living, recreation, and continuing education. A full-day adult program should not include only three hours of work, with the rest of the time spent at home. Although work is a key value and goal of transition programs, one should ensure that persons are not socially isolated at work or in other contexts and that transition plans assemble the pieces into a total program, which helps individuals have meaningful adult lives. Fortunately, a coalition of professionals and consumers has formed to support the development of transition programs, and of great importance, a substantial amount of funding has been allocated for transition (P.L. 98–199) and supported employment. Thus, the future appears promising for the successful transition of youths with disabilities if the current transition initiative can be successfully maintained and can evolve as future needs and changes emerge.

REFERENCES

Barraga, N. (1976). *Visual handicaps and learning: A developmental approach.* Belmont, CA: Wadsworth.

Bellamy, G. T., Rhodes, L. E., & Albin, J. M. (1986). Supported employment. In W. E. Kierman & J. A. Stark (eds)., *Pathways to employment for adults with developmental disabilities.* Baltimore: Paul H. Brookes.

Bellamy, G. T., Rhodes, L. E., Wilcox, B., Albin, J., Mank, D. M., Boles, S. M., Horner, R. H., Collings, M., & Turner, J. (1984). Quality and equality in employment services for adults with severe disabilities. *Journal of the Association for Persons with Severe Handicaps, 9,* 270–277.

Bellamy, G. T., & Wilcox, B. L. (1981, September). From school to what? Transition services for students with severe handicaps. Paper presented to the Wales Seminar on the Handicapped Adolescent. Cardiff, Wales.

Berkell, D. E., Tieman, P. E., Berry, P. J., Lapsley, D., Ufheil, J., Fichandler, C., & Walden, N. (1986). Community based vocational training for autistic students. In A. Gartner (Ed.), *Reflections on transition: Model programs for youth with disabilities.* New York: Center for Advanced Study in Education.

Brolin, D. E. (1982). *Vocational preparation of persons with handicaps* (2nd ed.). Columbus, OH: Charles E. Merrill.

Brown, L., Nietupski, J., & Hamre-Nietupski, S. (1978). The criterion of ultimate functioning. In L. Brown, N. Certo, & T. Crowner (Eds.), *Papers and programs related to public school services for secondary-age severely handicapped students* (Vol. 6, Part 1). Madison, WI: Madison Metropolitan School District.

Brown, L., Shiraga, B., York, J., Kessler, K., Strohm, B., Ragan, P., Sweet, M., Zanella, K., VanDeventer, L., & Loomis, R. (1984). Integrated work opportunities for adults with severe handicaps: The extended training option. *The Journal of the Association for Persons with Severe Handicaps, 9,* 262–269.

Caparosa, C. A. (1985). *Opportunities after high school for persons who are severely handicapped.* Washington, DC: Heath Resource Center.

Catapano, P. M., & Kramer, M. E. (1986). Nice work if you can get it: Project employment team. In A. Gartner & B. Flugman (Eds.), *Reflections on transition: Model programs for youths with disabilities.* New York: Center for Advanced Study in Education.

Clarizio, H. F., & McCoy, G. F. (1983). *Behavior disorders in children* (3rd ed.). New York: Harper & Row.

Elder, J. K., Conley, R. W., & Noble, J. H., Jr. (1986). The service system. In W. E. Kiernan & J. A. Stark (Eds.), *Pathways to employment for adults with developmental disabilities.* Baltimore: Paul H. Brookes.

Gaylord-Ross, R. (1987). Vocational integration for persons with mental handicaps: A cross-cultural perspective. *Research in Developmental Disabilities.*

Gollay, E. (1981). *Operational definition of developmental disabilities.* Sante Fe, NM: Gollay & Associates.

Grossman, H. J. (Eds.). (1983). *Manual on terminology and classification in mental retardation* (rev. ed.). Washington, DC: American Association on Mental Deficiency.

Halpern, A. S. (1985). Transition: A look at the foundations. *Exceptional Children, 51,* 479–486.

Hardman, M. L., Drew, C. J., & Egan, M. W. (1987). *Human exceptionality: Society, school, and family* (2nd ed.). Boston: Allyn & Bacon.

Hasazi, S., Gordon, L., & Roe, C. (1985). Factors associated with the employment status of handicapped youth exiting high school from 1979 to 1983. *Exceptional Children, 51,* 455–469.

Hasazi, S. B., Gordon, L. R., Roe, C. A., Hull, M., Finck, K., & Salembier, G. (1985). A statewide follow-up on post high school employment status of students labeled, "mentally retarded." *Education and Training of the Mentally Retarded, 20,* 222–234.

Heward, W. L., & Orlansky, M. D. (1980). *Exceptional children: An introductory survey to special education.* Columbus, OH: Charles E. Merrill.

Hill, M. L., Banks, P. D., Handrich, R. R., Wehman, P. H., Hill, J. W., & Shafer, M. S. (1987). Benefit-cost analysis of supported competitive employment for persons with mental retardation. *Research in Developmental Disabilities, 8,* 71–89.

Human Services Research Institute. (1985). *Summary of data on handicapped children and youth.* Washington, DC: U.S. Department of Education.

Ianacone, R. N., & Stodden, R. A. (1987). Overview: Transition issues and directions for individuals who are mentally retarded. In R. N. Ianacone & R. A. Stodden (Eds.), *Transition issues and directions.* Reston, VA: Council for Exceptional Children.

Kiernan, W. E., Smith, B. C., & Ostrowsky, M. B. (1986). Developmental disabilities: Definitional issues. In W. E. Kiernan & J. A. Stark (Eds.), *Pathways to employment for adults with developmental disabilities.* Baltimore: Paul H. Brookes.

Lagomarcino, T. R., & Rusch, F. R. (1987). Supported employment: Transition from school to work. *Interchange, 8*(1), 1–5.

Lerner, J. W. (1985). *Learning disabilities: Theories, diagnosis, and teaching strategies.* Boston: Houghton Mifflin.

McDonnell, J., Sheehan, M., & Wilcox, B. (1983). *Effective transition from school to work and adult services: A procedural handbook for parents and teachers.* Lane County, OR: Lane County Education Service District.

Meyen, E. L. (1982). *Exceptional children in today's schools: An alternative resource book.* Denver: Love Publishing.

Phelps, L. A., & Frasier, J. R. (1988). Legislative and policy aspects of vocational special education. In R. Gaylord-Ross (Ed.), *Vocational education for persons with handicaps.* Palo Alto, CA: Mayfield Publishing.

Powell, T. H., Rainforth, B., Hecimovic, A., Steere, D. E., Mayes, M. G., Zoback, M. S., & Singer, A. T. (1985). *Developing integrated public school programs for students with severe handicaps.* Storrs: University of Connecticut.

Pumpian, I., West, E., & Shepherd, H. (1988). Vocational education for persons with severe handicaps. In R. Gaylord-Ross (Ed.), *Vocational education for persons with handicaps.* Palo Alto, CA: Mayfield Publishing.

Rhodes, L., & Valenta, L. (1985). Industry-based supported employment: An enclave approach. *Journal of the Association for Persons with Severe Handicaps, 10,* 12–20.

Rusch, F. R. (Ed.). (1986). *Supported employment.* Baltimore, Paul H. Brookes.

Rusch, F. R., & Phelps, L. (1986). Secondary special education and transition from school to work. In J. Chadsey-Rusch, C. Hanley-Maxwell, L. A. Phelps, & F. R. Rusch (Eds.), *School to work transition issues and models.* Champaign, IL: Secondary Transition Intervention Effectiveness Institute.

Sailor, W., Halvorsen, A., Anderson, J., Goetz, L., Gee, K., Doering, K., & Hunt, P. (1985). Community intensive instruction. In R. Horner, L. Meyer, and H. D. Fredericks (Eds.), *Education of learners with severe handicaps: Exemplary service strategies.* Baltimore: Paul H. Brookes.

Schneider, K., Rusch, F., Henderson, R., & Geskey, T. (1982). Competitive employment for mentally retarded persons: Costs vs. benefits. *Interchange.* Champaign, IL: Office of Career Development for Special Populations.

Semmel, D. S., Cosden, M. A., & Konopak, B. (1985). *A comparative study of employment outcomes for special education students in a cooperative work placement program.* Santa Barbara: University of California.

Summers, J. (1981). The definition of developmental disabilities: A concept in transition. *Mental Retardation, 19*(6), 259–265.

Suran, B. G., & Rizzo, J. V. (1979). *Special children: An integrative approach.* Glenview, IL: Scott, Foresman.

Terkel, S. (1974). *People talk about what they do all day and how they feel about what they do.* New York: Pantheon.

U.S. Commission on Civil Rights. (1983). *Accommodating the spectrum of individual abilities.* Washington, DC: U.S. Government Printing Office.

U.S. Department of Education. (1977, December 19). Federal Register, Part III. *Education of handicapped children.* Washington, DC: U.S. Department of Health, Education, and Welfare.

Wehman, P. (1981). *Competitive employment.* Baltimore: Paul H. Brookes.

Wehman, P., & Kregel, J. (1985). A supported work approach to competitive employment of individuals with moderate and severe handicaps. *Journal of the Association for Persons with Severe Handicaps, 10*(3), 3–11.

Wehman, P. H., Kregel, J., Barcus, J. M., & Schalock, R. L. (1986). Vocational transition for students with developmental disabilities. In W. E. Kiernan & J. A. Stark (Eds.), *Pathways to employment for adults with developmental disabilities.* Baltimore: Paul H. Brookes.

Weicker, L. P. (1987). A look at policy and its effect on special education and vocational rehabilitation services. *Career Development for Exceptional Individuals, 10,* 6–9.

Will, M. (1984). *OSERS programming for the transition of youth with disabilities: Bridges from school to working life.* Washington, DC: Office of Special Education and Rehabilitative Services.

Wood, F. W., & Lakin, K. C. (1979). *Defining emotionally disturbed/behaviorally disordered populations for research purposes. Disturbing, disordered or disturbed? Perspectives on the definition of problem behavior in educational settings.* Minneapolis: Advanced Institute for Training of Teachers for Seriously Emotionally Disturbed Children and Youth.

CHAPTER 2

Lifelong Career Development

Donn E. Brolin and Bard Schatzman*

Life consists of a series of transitions. Young children must make the transition from home environments to school and then progress through the grades as they gradually become more competent and independent individuals. At the conclusion of high school, students are expected to find employment or seek further training so they may acquire the skills necessary for employment and community living. Other transitions typically associated with leaving the parental home are relocation, marriage, friendships, parenthood, and job changes.

Transitions occur throughout one's lifetime and include both paid work and the work roles of students, homemakers, family members, volunteers, and retirees, as well as productive recreational, avocational, and leisure activities. Many people encounter problems when making various transitions. Adults in transition, especially many of those with disabilities, sometimes become confused and need special assistance to help them solve their problems and make wise decisions. The "transition from school-to-work" concept is inextricably

---

*Donn E. Brolin is a professor of educational and counseling psychology at the University of Missouri in Columbia. He received his Ph.D. at the University of Wisconsin-Madison in Special Education and Rehabilitation Psychology. Dr. Brolin was the charter president of the Division on Career Development (DCD) of The Council for Exceptional Children. He has written several textbooks on the topic of career and vocational preparation of persons with handicaps.
Bard I. Schatzman is a doctoral candidate in the Department of Educational and Counseling Psychology at the University of Missouri in Columbia. He has worked as a vocational resource educator with handicapped and disadvantaged students and as a clinical psychologist.

related to the career development concept that has been theorized and implemented in various education and agency settings for many years.

This chapter will attempt to explain the concept, establish its importance for persons with disabilities, introduce the concept of a "work personality," present a life-centered career education approach to meet these needs, and conclude with a discussion of important factors associated with implementing the approach. The chapter will focus on those individuals who can best be described as having mild or moderate intellectual, behavioral and emotional, learning, sensory, and/or multiple handicaps that require special services from schools and community service providers.

THE CONCEPT OF CAREER DEVELOPMENT

The term *career* has different connotations to people. A typical conception is to equate it solely with occupations. Another view is to consider a career as all the productive work activity a person engages in—paid and unpaid. A third perspective defines one's career in terms of all the major roles one assumes during the course of a lifetime—in work or nonwork.

Super (1976) defined a career as "the sequence of major positions occupied by people throughout their preoccupational, occupational, and postoccupational lives including work-related roles such as those of student, employee, and pensioner, together with complementary avocational, familial, and civic roles" (p. 20). Hoyt (1975), former director of the U.S. Office of Career Education, defined a career as "the totality of work one does in his or her lifetime," *work* being defined as "conscious effort, other than that involved in activities whose primary purpose is either coping or relaxation, aimed at producing benefits for oneself and/or oneself and others" (p. 3).

As a Lifelong Process

In the opinion of many leading theorists (e.g., Gysbers & Moore, 1975, 1981; Herr & Cramer, 1979; Hoyt, 1984; Super et al., 1963) career development is a lifelong process that focuses on the human growth and development of the total person. Super (1984) identified five developmental periods that comprise the career-development process:

1. Growth (birth-age 14/15), characterized by the development of capacity, attitudes, interests, and needs associated with self-concept;
2. Exploratory (ages 15–24), characterized by a tentative phase in which choices are narrowed, but not finalized;
3. Establishment (ages 25–44), characterized by trial and stabilization through work experiences;
4. Maintenance (ages 45–64), characterized by a continual adjustment process to improve working position and situation; and

5. Decline (ages 65 +), characterized by preretirement considerations, work output, and eventual retirement. (p. 10)

Super (1984) noted that some prefer to call the last stage "disengagement" rather than decline. It is important to understand that the ages at which individuals make transitions from one stage to another are flexible and that each transition does not involve recycling through all stages. For example, high school graduates on their first jobs go through a period of growth in the new role and become established in it until they are ready to make another job change, when disengagement then occurs.

Super conceived of career development as involving the interaction of various life roles over one's life span. He called it the "life career rainbow." He emphasized that as people mature they normally play a variety of roles in many different settings. The roles are those of child, student, leisurite, citizen, worker, and homemaker, and one's "career" is the combination and sequence of all these roles that one plays during a lifetime and the pattern in which they fit together (Super, 1975; Super & Hall 1978).

Gysbers and Moore (1975, 1981) used the term "life career development" to expand career development thinking from an exclusively occupational perspective to a wholistic life perspective. They conceived of careers as encompassing individuals' total life styles, for example, occupation, education, personal and social behavior, learning how to learn, social responsibility, and leisure activities. Their "life career development" concept, which focuses on individuals' human growth and development, includes all the *roles* (parent, consumer, student, worker, citizen) and *settings* (home, school, work, community) that people engage in and the *events* (entry job, marriage, divorce, retirement) they experience over a lifetime.

Gysbers and Moore (1987) suggested that lifelong career development infuses cognitive processes; life career themes and learning styles; personality and character traits; environmental, family, and social influences; and all aspects of existence in the process of developing life careers and of becoming total people.

As the Development of a Work Personality

Another important conceptualization of career development is the one undertaken at the University of Minnesota by Dawis, Lofquist, and Weiss (1964, 1968). These researchers developed the Minnesota Theory of Work Adjustment (MTWA). The MTWA gives considerable attention to individuals' environments and early experiences, assuming they are important to the development of individuals' work personalities. In this theory, the work personality is "an individual's unique set of abilities and needs which form from birth based on the interaction of the person's unique set of response potentials with reinforcers in the environment." As one's experience builds, the individual develops a set of abilities and needs that eventually form a mature work personality.

A work personality comprises more than abilities and needs. It also includes those attitudes and behaviors that characterize the individual. When the needs of the individual are met and the individual meets the demands of the work environment, there is correspondence and, thus, job tenure. The level of correspondence between these two factors is a dynamic process that changes as the needs of the individual and job change.

It is our preference to conceive of career development as the broader context of productive work activity—paid or unpaid—including all important life roles that people engage in during their lifetimes. Although there are many other theories of career development, the ones discussed in this section seem to be most relevant to the approach we will present in this chapter.

THE NEED FOR A CAREER DEVELOPMENT APPROACH

It is important to avoid stereotyping persons with disabling conditions as all having special needs and problems. Many of these individuals have the ability to function better in their environments than so-called nondisabled persons. But there also are many who don't cope well, and it is these individuals for whom we should be concerned. People who are different are often shunned and ridiculed by others. They are made to feel different, especially when they have academic and/or social problems in school. Feelings of inferiority or estrangement result, often compounded by withdrawal and a poor self-concept.

It is widely known that the majority of former special education students either become unemployed or underemployed after they leave the education system. The fact that the employment success rate of these individuals has not improved significantly in the last 25 years should be of utmost concern to the education and human services fields since an army of professionals has emerged over the past decade. Although it has been found that over time many former students gain in functional skills and develop informal support systems (Browder, 1987), it is very clear from most recent follow-up studies (e.g., Edgar, 1987; Levine, 1985) and recently released publications (Brolin, 1987; Chadsey-Rusch et al., 1986; Clark & Knowlton, 1987; Ianacone & Stodden, 1987; Phelps, 1986) that much still remains to be done if students who receive special education and rehabilitative services are to lead satisfying and productive adult lives.

The White House Conference

It has been more than ten years since over 100,000 persons with disabilities and their advocates participated in local, state, and national White House

Conferences on the Handicapped to present to Congress and the president their views and recommendations on how this country's human services system could better meet their needs. The delegates to the national conference presented 815 major recommendations (from an original list of 22,000) and pleaded for equality of opportunity and equal access to all aspects of society and to their equal rights as guaranteed by the Constitution of the United States. One major recommendation made by the delegates was for a better organized and coordinated human services delivery system (White House Conference on Handicapped Individuals, 1977).

Congress responded to many of the needs of individuals with disabilities, which were identified by White House conference participants. Several important pieces of legislation were passed before and since the 1977 conference in Washington to pressure professionals to offer education and adult services that address these needs.

Important Legislation

Important special education, vocational education, rehabilitation, developmental disabilities, and labor legislation that relate to the lifelong career development needs of persons with disabilities have demonstrated this nation's concern for this area. Major legislation that readers should be familiar with is presented briefly below.

Public Law 93–112, Rehabilitation Act of 1973
This act prohibits discrimination in programs receiving federal funds. Section 503 of the act is directed toward recruiting, hiring, training, and promoting individuals with disabilities. Employers are encouraged to use local education agencies to train persons with disabilities to develop vocational skills. Section 504 of the act prohibits discrimination (e.g., employment and program accessibility) on the basis of handicap in any private or public program or activity receiving federal financial assistance. This landmark legislation has sometimes been called The Bill of Rights for the Handicapped.

Public Law 93–203, Comprehensive Employment and Training Act of 1973 (CETA)
This legislation was based on the philosophy that solutions to local labor problems are best solved at the local level. CETA was created to provide job training and employment opportunities for economically disadvantaged, unemployed, and underemployed persons. It was administered by the U.S. Department of Labor and combined the resources and services of the Economic Opportunity Act (Neighborhood Youth Corps, e.g.) and the Manpower Development and Training Act. This act required the active coordination of

services with other employment and training-related programs, that is, Employment (Job) Service, Vocational Education, and Vocational Rehabilitation.

Public Law 94–142, The Education for All Handicapped Children Act of 1975
The act requires that a written Individualized Education Plan (IEP) be developed for each student for purposes of developing important skills including those needed for securing employment. Besides special education, this act addresses related services, regular education, and specially designed vocational education if needed. Vocational education is defined as " . . . organized educational programs which are directly related to the preparation of individuals for paid or unpaid employment." This legislation seeks to expand the opportunities for all individuals with disabilities to function in their own communities to the best of their ability in the least restrictive environment. The act requires cooperation between educational and other service agencies such as vocational education.

Public Law 94–482, Vocational Education Act of 1976
This act mandates a federal commitment to handicapped individuals who had not previously had adequate access to publicly supported vocational education programs. It sets aside 10 percent of vocational education funds to pay for the additional costs of educating individuals with disabilities and offers support for placing them in employment settings. This law also encourages educational experiences to take place with nonhandicapped students whenever possible. Public Law 94–482 has been a boon to vocational training opportunities for students with disabilities and has funded many new types of personnel to carry out such services.

Public Law 95–207, Career Education Incentive Act of 1977
When this act was passed Congress declared that "A major purpose of education is to prepare every individual for a career suitable to that individual's preference." The act provided federal incentive funds to states and local school districts willing to make career education a sustaining initiative for all students (including special education students) after federal funds were exhausted. This "sunset" type of legislation expired at the end of fiscal 1983. It was assumed that during the period of its enactment both state education agencies and local school districts would have sufficient time to decide for themselves whether they wanted to use their own funds to make career education part of their educational offering (Hoyt, 1982).

Public Law 95–524, CETA Amendments of 1978
These amendments direct CETA prime sponsors to assist persons with disabilities by requiring the prime sponsors to include descriptions of employment

and training services to these individuals in their master and annual plans. The annual plan had to include an affirmative action program for outreach, training, placement, and advancement of persons with disabilities. The act established planning, state employment, and training councils and required representatives with disabilities to be included in their membership. The act prohibited discrimination on the basis of handicap and permitted part-time, flex-time, and other work arrangements for individuals unable because of age, disabilities, or other factors to work fulltime.

Public Law 95–602, Rehabilitation, Comprehensive Services, and Development Disabilities Act of 1978

This act promotes transition to independent living through vocational rehabilitation services by offering (1) intake counseling to assess the needs of severely disabled persons, (2) advocacy to ensure that clients receive services to which they are entitled, (3) help in locating accessible housing and transportation, and (4) other services that help clients become independent.

Public Law 97–330, Job Training Partnership Act of 1982 (JTPA)

This act replaced CETA and shifted its administrative responsibilities from the federal level to the governor's office and private industry councils. JTPA's purpose is to promote programs that prepare youths and unskilled adults for employment and to train those clients who have special needs in relation to vocational preparation programs. Persons with disabilities can benefit from many services and activities funded by JTPA. For example, career development for individuals with disabilities is greatly enhanced by funding for job training (i.e., remedial education, classroom instruction, vocational counseling, temporary work experience, on-the-job training, job upgrading and retraining, job search assistance, and job placement), support services, administration, and statewide coordination.

Public Law 98–199, Education Handicapped Act Amendments of 1983

This act authorizes funding for research, training, and demonstration pertinent to the transition process. Included in the law is the mandated collection of data regarding students who leave the education system and a requirement to conduct follow-up studies about their educational lives. The law addresses strategies and services in the following areas: (1) development of transition strategies and techniques that may lead to independent living; (2) establishment of demonstration models emphasizing vocational, transition, and job placement services; (3) provision of demographic studies on numbers and types of disabling characteristics of students and related services required; (4) initiation of collaborative models between education agencies and adult community service agencies; and (5) development of procedures for evaluation of programs in the area of transition. A very significant result of this legislation was the creation of a Secondary Transition Intervention Effectiveness Institute, which is now located at the University of Illinois, to study the issues and problems related to secondary education and transitional services for persons with disabilities (Rusch & Phelps, 1986).

Public Law 98–524, The Carl Perkins Vocational and Technical Education Act

This act promotes the development of quality vocational education programs and expands existing ones. Assurances that disadvantaged persons and individuals with disabilities will have access to quality vocational programs are supported by the allocation of special funds within this act. Vocational assessments of students' interests, abilities, and special needs relative to vocational education and services are also mandated by this legislation. The range of special services offered varies from adaptation of curriculum, instruction, and facilities to career opportunities and employment programs. This act mandates equal access in recruitment, enrollment, and placement activities compared to individuals without disabilities. Information about opportunities in vocational education programs and eligibility for enrollment in these programs should be provided to students and parents before students enter these secondary programs.

Public Law 98–537, Developmental Disabilities Act of 1984

This act focuses on (1) planning, coordinating, and demonstrating specialized services to persons with developmental disabilities; (2) providing interdisciplinary training for personnel; and (3) protecting the legal and human rights of all persons with developmental disabilities. The act advocates that persons with developmental disabilities should receive the care, treatment, and other services necessary to enable them to achieve their maximum potential in terms of increased independence, productivity, and integration into the community. The act also places a high priority on preparation for employment and minimizes the strong emphasis on social development services.

Public Law 99–506, Rehabilitation Act Amendments of 1986

This act redefines employability and severe handicaps. The amendments revise the requirements for Individualized Written Rehabilitation Plans (IWRP) and create a permanent section for supported employment programs. The amendments define supported employment as paid work experience in business, industry, and government, supported by those services necessary to maintain indiviudals' involvement and productivity in that work environment (Parker,

1987). The act also requires cooperative transition planning between state vocational rehabilitation agencies and education agencies.

Public Law 99–457, Education Handicapped Act Amendments of 1986

These amendments reauthorize the transition program and specify that funded activities may serve students who have left secondary school programs as well as those still in school. The amendments expand Public Law 94–142 to include encouraging the improvement of vocational and life skills and conducting studies of dropouts with disabilities. Grants for demonstration projects and technical assistance in the transition area are also permitted.

A concerted attempt through federal legislation has occurred to respond to the career development needs of persons with disabilities. Unfortunately, society is sometimes slow and resists responding to the intent of legislation. In our opinion, Congress has laid the foundation for meeting the career development needs of people with disabilities. It is now up to persons in the field to carry out effective and responsive services and efforts.

DEVELOPING A WORK PERSONALITY

The previous sections of this chapter have focused on establishing a rationale for changing our educational practices to meet the career development needs of persons with disabilities. The unacceptably low levels of employment and community adjustment that have been maintained over the past 25 years should not continue to plague our society and the lives of these individuals and their families.

Transition services should begin early and continue as needed throughout the client's lifetime. Ianacone and Stodden (1987) described the transition process as " . . . movement through life phases, or the methodology associated with the life development process of persons as they move from the structure of one social institution to that of another . . . independent living, employment, and other productive life situations" (p. 3).

As Browder (1987) pointed out, "The life domains of work, home and family, leisure, and community are interrelated such that the inability to transition successfully in one domain has spillover effects to other domains" (p. 84). She also noted other important dimensions to successful transition: (1) Transition is characterized by instability and uncertainty; (2) transition requires mastery of the skills needed by workers, spouses, parents, and home caretakers; (3) transition requires participation in normative activities and interaction with nondisabled persons; and (4) positive social relationships are important to successful adult adjustment.

Earlier we introduced the concept of a work personality that consists of an individual's unique set of abilities, including work habits, values, interests, and other important employability-oriented skills. An appropriate work personality is an important component to successful career development and adult success. Weisenstein and Elrod (1987) illustrated this concept by asking what criteria are generally used to judge the success of adults? Most would suggest the following indicators of success: a good job, high-income level, happiness, respect from persons in the community, and a good family life. The following success indicators would probably not be included: reading at a sixth-grade level or completing long-division problems with 80 percent accuracy (even though they are important skills for realizing some successes). However, these factors are not in themselves measures of successful adult living.

General Employability and Adaptability Skills

An important dimension of career development is the existence of a good work personality and the opportunity to develop a set of general employability and adaptability skills in school, community, and adult agency settings. A myriad of skills have been identified by many experts and researchers that fall into this category. The employability skills formulated in 1981 by the U.S. Department of Education's Division of Career Education are particularly relevant for this discussion since they deal with skills needed by *all* students for adult success. Those skills are in the following areas:

1. The basic academic skills of mathematics and of oral/written communication.
2. Using and practicing good work habits.
3. Developing and employing personally meaningful sets of work values that motivate individuals to want to work.
4. Gaining a basic understanding of the American system of private enterprise—including organized labor as part of that system.
5. Self-understanding and understanding of available educational/occupational opportunities.
6. Career decision-making processes.
7. Job-seeking/finding/getting/holding.
8. Making productive use of leisure time through unpaid work—including volunteerism and work performed within the home/family structure.
9. Overcoming bias and stereotyping as they tend to deter full freedom of career choice for all persons.
10. Humanizing the workplace for oneself. (Hoyt, 1981)

The next section will present a comprehensive transitional lifelong career development approach that requires a systematic focus on such employability and life skills and the collaboration of educators, parents, employers, and representatives from many agencies that should be contributing to the preparation of individuals for adulthood.

A LIFELONG CAREER DEVELOPMENT APPROACH

We propose a lifelong career development approach, called the Life-Centered Career Education (LCCE) Transitional Model, based on the competency-based LCCE curriculum published by the Council for Exceptional Children (Brolin, 1978, 1983, 1988).

The ten employability skills mentioned earlier relate very closely to those skills contained in the LCCE curriculum developed at the University of Missouri–Columbia. The curriculum has 22 competencies and 97 subcompetencies that fall into three major categories: (1) daily living, (2) personal-social, and (3) occupational skills (see Table 2.1). These categories were identified through a series of projects and research efforts over a 15-year period. The latest revi-

TABLE 2.1 LIFE-CENTERED CAREER EDUCATION COMPETENCIES

Daily Living Skills

1. Managing Personal Finances
2. Selecting and Managing a Household
3. Caring for Personal Needs
4. Raising Children and Meeting Marriage Responsibilities
5. Buying, Preparing, and Consuming Food
6. Buying and Caring for Clothing
7. Exhibiting Responsible Citizenship
8. Utilizing Recreational Facilities and Engaging in Leisure
9. Getting Around the Community

Personal-Social Skills

10. Achieving Self-Awareness
11. Acquiring Self-Confidence
12. Achieving Socially Responsible Behavior
13. Maintaining Good Interpersonal Skills
14. Achieving Independence
15. Making Adequate Decisions
16. Communicating with Others

Occupational Guidance and Preparation

17. Knowing and Exploring Occupational Possibilities
18. Selecting and Planning Occupational Choices
19. Exhibiting Appropriate Work Habits and Behavior
20. Seeking, Securing, and Maintaining Employment
21. Exhibiting Sufficient Physical-Manual Skills
22. Obtaining Specific Occupational Skills

sion has resulted in further refinement and updating of the competencies and their previously identified 102 (now 97) subcompetencies.

The LCCE Transitional Model is a conceptualization of the lifelong efforts of persons to meet their career-development needs, including those persons with disabilities.

The Propositions

The LCCE model is based on 12 important propositions that are the result of previous research and experience on the process of career development, education, and preparation of individuals with disabilities. The model, illustrated in Figure 2.1, contains a kindergarten to adult services scope and sequence that focus on the students' acquisition of the 22 major competencies and their 97 subcompetencies.

1. The development of *a work personality* (i.e., an individual's own unique set of abilities and needs) *begins shortly after birth* and matures sufficiently only if provided with early and adequate reinforcers in one's environ-

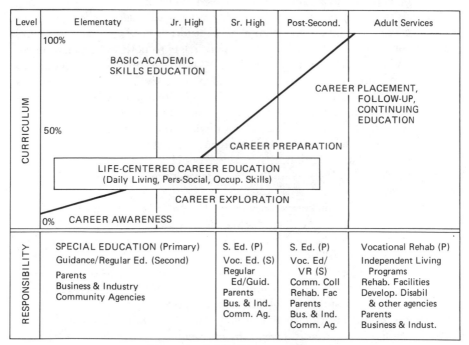

Figure 2.1 LCCE Transition Model

ment. Thus, it is critical that schools and parents provide (early in the students' schooling) the experiences and reinforcements that are necessary for appropriate career development and maturity to occur.

2. *A career is more than occupation.* Careers include the important unpaid work and other life roles that persons engage in at home and in various community functions. Thus, besides employment, careers also include the productive activity that is done at home, in avocational and leisure pursuits, and in the community. This is particularly important for many individuals with disabilities because although they may be unemployed at times, their need to work and engage in productive activities can still be realized.

3. There are *four sequential stages of career development* that should be addressed if individuals are to acquire the necessary skills commensurate with their potential and needs and attain career satisfaction. *Career and self-awareness* activities should begin almost immediately in elementary school curricula and should continue into adult life. The three other stages of career development begin later (as depicted in Figure 2.1), and the level of need varies with each individual. Sufficient career awareness and career exploration are essential for later admission to and success in vocational education courses.

4. *Four major domains of instruction* are necessary for successful career development and living skills to be achieved: (a) *academic skills,* (b) *daily living skills,* (c) *personal-social skills,* and (d) *occupational skills. Academic skills* include those basic fundamental skills students need to read, write, and compute adequately. *Daily living skills* relate to both independent living and occupational functioning (e.g., being able to manage finances, maintain a home, care for personal needs, prepare food) and also future occupational possibilities. *Personal-social skills* relate to knowing oneself, interpersonal relationships, problemsolving, independent functioning, and other qualities that are necessary for living and working. The final important domain, *occupational skills* preparation, should begin early and be given greater attention by school personnel so that vocational interests, needs, aptitudes, and abilities are identified and developed during the formative years.

5. Career education competency *instruction should be infused into most subject areas.* As indicated earlier, the four domains are inextricably interrelated and can often be taught concurrently (e.g., important math skills can be taught in relation to an LCCE competency and to a stage of career development). Career education programs should not be viewed as separate courses but rather the infusion of career-enhancing concepts into the lesson plans of regular subject matter courses.

6. Successful career development and transition efforts require *active partnerships among schools, parents, business and industry, and community agen-*

cies, which are organized to provide various health, social, psychological, and vocational services for individuals with disabilities. Although these relationships are generally developed as the need occurs, in practice these joint working relationships have been difficult to achieve. In the LCCE model, these relationships are inherent throughout the school years and beyond, not just at the high school level. Education should take place in more places than just within the walls of school buildings.

7. *Hands-on experiential learning* is an important instructional approach in the LCCE curriculum. Many students are more able to respond to learning activities that are motivating, relevant, and familiar in the real world and its vocational, social, and daily living requirements. Educators should incorporate as many of these experiences as they can into their curricula.

8. *Mainstreaming* through the *principle of normalization* is critical to successful career development and transition efforts. Persons with disabilities should learn to live and work in the community if they are to survive as meaningful adults. Administrators and special educators are key to accomplishment of this goal. General education teachers and counselors should be taught methods of integrating mainstreamed students appropriately into their programs and should be given the time and consideration they need to carry out such efforts.

9. *Cooperative learning environments* represent a factor that can be used to help learners with disabilities acquire higher self-esteem levels, interact more, feel accepted by teachers and nondisabled students, achieve more, and behave more appropriately in regular classrooms. Cooperative learning environments (as opposed to competitive and individualistic approaches) can build positive relationships between students with disabilities and nondisabled learners (Johnson & Johnson, 1983).

10. *Informal and formal career and vocational assessment* also play an integral role in successful career development and transitional planning programs. These efforts should begin during the elementary years and evolve by late junior high or early senior high years into more highly organized, formal assessments by trained vocational evaluators using a broad array of reliable and valid measures—including specialized or standardized interest and aptitude tests, work samples, job analysis techniques, and job-site evaluations.

11. *Transitional Resource Coordinators* are necessary to assume responsibility for monitoring and carrying out programs. They should have a local team of persons to execute programs as noted in the study by Harold Russell Associates (1984). The most logical persons to assume this role are special educators and vocational rehabilitation counselors.

12. Appropriate *interagency agreements* and *cross-agency in-service training* are important to secure so that everyone involved agrees on and understands

transition programs' goals; roles and responsibilities; and the allocation of resources, facilities, and money. Written guidelines should be developed after in-service discussions and agreements.

The Process

The LCCE model requires transition to begin in the elementary years and extend indefinitely into postsecondary and adult services as they are needed throughout clients' lives. The model assumes a broad view of the term *work* which is conceived of as including both paid and unpaid productive activity such as that involved in family living, avocations, and volunteer work in the community. Factors relating to an indivdual's residential environment (living and recreational) and the adequacy of social and interpersonal networks (family support, friendships, intimate relationships) should also be included, and transitional programs should be directed specifically toward each of these dimensions.

The LCCE Transitional Model requires careful sequencing of career development experiences almost immediately after students enter school. If basic personality structures are formed primarily during the first years of life, it seems logical that the same applies to the work personality. Thus, the *elementary years* are very critical to career development processes and should provide the necessary career and self-awareness activities for many of the LCCE skills and student needs. Parents and community resources can help students learn more about the community, work that people do, and some emerging interests that may eventually lead to meaningful careers.

During the *middle school and junior high school* years it is important that a planned sequence of career awareness experiences and career exploration opportunities be included within school curricula, with generous use of home and community assignments. Althoug'1 academic skills continue to be important, greater amounts of time should be devoted to career development and the LCCE competencies. Educators can incorporate a variety of prevocational activities, work samples, in-school work experiences, meaningful industrial arts and home economics projects, and work assignments in the home. Other important roles, such as avocational, homemaking, and volunteer activities, can also be emphasized during this time.

During the *high school* years, career awareness, career exploration, and more specific preparational activities should form the major part of students' education programs. Academics should be deemphasized except as they help students to acquire the major career development competencies. Most students should be able to make appropriate choices and benefit from vocational education programs and work experience because they have had better preparation for the skills those programs require. Some may need a thirteenth year or postsecondary training that will better prepare them in the more technical vocational skill areas.

Postsecondary and adult services should become more available to persons with disabilities. The need for training in daily living, personal and social, occupational, and academic skills does not stop automatically upon completion of a secondary program. Some students will immediately need more education and/or rehabilitation services; others will need them later on. Thus, a continuing education component is as critical for these individuals as for everyone else. Community colleges, vocational-technical institutions, adult education programs, and rehabilitation facilities (for some) are major sources of continuing education. Browder (1987) proposed the formation of neighborhood-based transition service activity centers, which provide social and recreational services to attract young adults to the centers and where interaction with nondisabled peers is possible. Such centers could offer a variety of transition services such as adult education, individual and group counseling, advocacy and referral to other community services, and outreach services.

A lifelong continuum of career development services is critical for ensuring the adult adjustment of people with disabling conditions. School districts and human services agencies should organize their programs if the needs of persons with disabilities are to be adequately addressed. Factors associated with this need are discussed in the next section.

IMPLEMENTATION CONSIDERATIONS

How can a comprehensive lifelong career develpment approach become a reality for students with disabilities? Ianacone and Stodden (1987) pointed out, "One needs only to visit a secondary level resource room to find an overwhelming emphasis on remedial academics, talk with teachers and other school system personnel to find that they do not view their role as being directly focused on preparation for employment, view a service delivery structure that yields a tremendous variety or paucity of career related activities, and/or survey school-based service providers to find that they have little awareness of what options are available beyond secondary school" (p. 3).

Schools should make commitments to transition and career development from kindergarten through high school. As stated by Weisenstein and Elrod (1987), "teaching transition skills involves the same systematic approach to education that has been characteristic of special education programs" (p. 39). Teachers should identify essential skills that students need, assess students' skill levels, determine appropriate teaching strategies, identify appropriate instructional settings, involve personnel in other disciplines and agencies, and devise an evaluation plan to measure results. This should be done on a district-wide basis as well. Weisenstein and Elrod suggested the LCCE curriculum as an established transition curriculum that provides a framework for initiating such an approach.

The Barriers

We noted earlier that considerable federal legislation has attempted to respond to the career development needs of persons with disabilities. Since the late 1970s, memorandums of understanding have been promulgated by the federal agencies representing special education, developmental disabilities, labor, vocational education, and vocational rehabilitation. These documents have pledged coordinated and collaborative services. Yet over the years, little has changed in the philosophies and practices of many schools and agencies. The question of why the obvious has not been instituted in the schools and agencies is not easy to answer.

People become comfortable in what they do and how they do it. Unless there is a crisis most people are not really interested in changing—it takes extra work and effort. Most professionals feel they are already overworked and underpaid and little appreciated. If teachers are not taught career development techniques in their teacher training programs, many will resist using such approaches later in their work. Some other barriers to change are professional rivalries, "turfmanship," theoretical differences, administrative barriers within agencies, too many students or clients to serve and limited time, lack of knowledge and training to collaborate, past failures with collaborative efforts, fear of appearing less than competent, unwillingness to share, and fear that others will expect the impossible.

Nadolsky (1985) noted that a major problem is that the field of special education still believes its role is helping children to become children rather than adults. Also, in his opinion, vocational rehabilitation has not really made the necessary commitment to help special education students to become productive adults.

Cooperative Efforts

If comprehensive and lifelong career development services are to be implemented sufficiently, professionals should collaborate and work together for a unified human services delivery system. Organizers of change should also take into account that to gain cooperation, professionals should recognize the need to collaborate; participate only if they freely decide to do so; have the time and authority to participate meaningfully and have the support of their superiors; believe they will be listened to by others; believe others will also be committed; believe the effort will amount to something; receive credit and recognition for their efforts; get sufficient communication from others; share the cost, time, and credit; and have clear roles and responsibilities.

Implementing a lifelong career development approach will require the active support and participation of appropriate school personnel, parents, agencies, and employers in the community. People in groups should be committed to building a continuum of experiences and services that will result in successful transitions from school to work and will provide the extra support system (e.g., career and personal guidance and counseling, retraining, adult education, independent living) that some of these individuals will need during their lifetime.

Rehabilitation counselors are a key resource to help individuals with disabilities to adjust to their environments and to aid personnel in those environments to recognize and accommodate the needs of individuals (Szymanski, 1985). Together, both special educators and rehabilitation counselors should be able to assess students and to provide specific skill instruction needed for transition from school to work. The two disciplines should begin to merge their goals and organizational structures if students with disabilities are to become adequately prepared for adulthood.

A Community Interagency Transition Committee should be established to assume responsibility for transition—something that has been missing in most communities to this point. A Community Interagency Transitional Committee operated by the two major agencies responsible for the career development of persons with disabilities—special education and vocational rehabilitation—is recommended to implement a lifelong career development approach. This committee would provide overall leadership to transitional efforts by promoting appropriate services in the schools and agencies utilizing parents, employers, and other community resources. The committee could serve as a clearinghouse and fixed point of referral to appropriate agencies and services and manage a registry for lifelong services for persons with disabilities.

Madeleine Will (1984) stated in her opening address to the General Session of the Council for Exceptional Children (CEC) Annual Convention, "The major challenge we face is not primarily one of limited resources. It is, rather, a question of will and character" (p. 12). The major obstacle facing persons attempting to meet successfully the career development needs of persons with disabilities lies in ourselves. Let us refocus our efforts to meet this final challenge successfully.

REFERENCES

Brolin, D. (Ed.). (1978, 1983, 1988). *Life-centered career education: A competency based approach* (1st, 2nd, 3rd eds.). Reston, VA: The Council for Exceptional Children.

Brolin, D. (Ed). (1987). Exceptional individuals [Special issue]. *Journal of Career Development*, 13(4).

Browder, P. M. (1987). Transition services for early adult age individuals with mild mental retardation. In R. N. Ianacone & R. A. Stodden (Eds.), *Transition Issues and Directions* (pp. 77–90). Reston, VA: The Council for Exceptional Children.

Chadsey-Rusch, J., Hanley-Maxwell, C., Phelps, L. A., & Rusch, F. (1986). *School-to-work transition issues and models.* Champaign, IL: U.S. Department of Education.

Clark, G. M., & Knowlton, H. E. (1987). Transition from school to adult life. *Exceptional Children, 53*(6), 1–96.

Dawis, R. V., Lofquist, L., & Weiss, D. (1964, 1968). *Minnesota studies in vocational rehabilitation: XXIII, A theory of work adjustment* (rev. ed.). Minneapolis: Industrial Relations Center, Work Adjustment Project, University of Minnesota.

Edgar, E. (1987). Secondary programs in special education: Are many of them justifiable? *Exceptional Children, 53*(6), 555–561.

Gysbers, N. C., & Moore, E. J. (1975). Beyond career development—Life career development. *Personnel and Guidance Journal, 53,* 647–652.

Gysbers, N. C., & Moore, E. J. (1981). Selecting and using a developmental guidance program model. In V. C. Neri (Ed.), *Improving Guidance Programs* (pp. 53–102). Englewood Cliffs, NJ: Prentice-Hall.

Gysbers, N. C., & Moore, E. J. (1987). *Career counseling skills and techniques for practitioners.* Englewood Cliffs, NJ: Prentice-Hall.

Hasazi, S., Gordon, L., & Roe, C. (1985). Factors associated with the employment status of handicapped youth exiting high school from 1979–1983. *Exceptional Children, 51*(6), 455–469.

Herr, E. L., & Cramer, S. H. (1979). *Career guidance through the life span: Systematic approaches.* Boston: Little, Brown.

Hoyt, K. (1975). *An introduction to career education: A policy paper of the U.S. Office of Education.* Washington, DC: U.S. Office of Education.

Hoyt, K. (1981). *Career education: Where it is and where it is going.* Salt Lake City: Olympus Publishing Company.

Hoyt, K. (1982). Federal and state participation in career education: Past, present and future. *Journal of Career Development, 9*(1), 5–15.

Hoyt, K. (1984). Career education and career guidance. *Journal of Career Education, 10*(3), 148–157.

Ianacone, R. N., & Stodden, R. A. (1987). Overview: Transition issues and directions for individuals who are mentally retarded. In R. N. Ianacone & R. A. Stodden (Eds.), *Transition Issues and Directions* (pp. 1–7). Reston, VA: The Council for Exceptional Children.

Johnson, R. T., & Johnson, D. W., 1983. Effects of cooperative, competitive, and individualistic learning experiences on social development. *Exceptional Children, 49,* 323–329.

Levine, D. (1985). Follow-up and follow-along studies. Unpublished paper. Networking and Evaluation Team, Child Development and Mental Retardation Center, University of Washington, Seattle.

Mithaug, D., Horiuchi, C., & Fanning, P. (1985). A report of the Colorado statewide follow-up survey of special education students. *Exceptional Children, 51*(5), 397–407.

Nadolsky, J. (1985). Achieving unity in special education and rehabilitation. *Journal of Rehabilitation, 51*(1), 22–23.

Parker, R. (1987, March-April). ARCA's statement on the Rehabilitation Act Amendments of 1986. P.L. 99–506. *American Rehabilitation Counseling Association, 14*(3–4), 3.

Phelps, L. A., (1986). Transition from school-to-work: The education and training enterprise. In L. A. Phelps (Ed.), *School-to-work transition for handicapped youth: Perspectives on education and training* (pp. 1–18). Champaign: Illinois Office of Special Education and Rehabilitative Services, Department of Education.

Rusch, F., & Phelps, L. A. (1986). Secondary special education and transition from school to work: A national priority. In J. Chadsey-Rusch, C. Hanley-Maxwell, L. A. Phelps, & F. Rusch (Eds.), *School-to-work transition issues and models* (pp. 1–14). Champaign, IL: U.S. Department of Education.

Super, D. E. (1975). Vocational guidance: Emergent decision-making in a changing society. *Bulletin—International Association of Educational and Vocational Guidance, 29,* 16–23.

Super, D. E. (1976). Career education and the meanings of work. *Monographs on Career Education* (DHEW). Washington, DC: U.S. Office of Education.

Super, D. E. (1984). Career and Life Development. In D. Brown, & L. Brooks (Eds.), *Career Choice and Development.* San Francisco: Jossey-Bass.

Super, D. E., & Hall, D. T. (1978). Career development: Exploration and planning. *Annual Review of Psychology, 84,* 333–372.

Super, D. E., Starishesky, R., Matlin, N., & Jordaan, J. P. (1963). *Career development: Self concept theory.* New York: College Entrance Examination Board.

Szymanski, E. M. (1985). Rehabilitation counseling: A profession with a vision, an identity, and a future. *Rehabilitation Counseling Bulletin, 29*(1), 2–5.

Weisenstein, G. R., & Elrod, G. F. (1987). Transition services for adolescent age individuals with mild mental retardation. In R. N. Ianacone & R. A. Stodden (Eds.), *Transition Issues and Directions* (pp. 38–48). Reston, VA: The Council for Exceptional Children.

White House Conference on Handicapped Individuals. (1977). *Summary: Final report* (DHEW). Washington, DC: Office for Handicapped Individuals.

Will, M. (1984). OSERS programming for the transition of youth with disabilities: Bridges from school to working life. In J. Chadsey-Rusch, & C. Hanley-Maxwell (Eds.)., *Enhancing transition from school to the workplace for handicapped youth: Personnel preparation implications* (pp. 9–25). Urbana-Champaign, IL: National Network for Professional Development in Vocational Special Education.

CHAPTER 3

Economics of Transition

David L. Passmore*

Economic aspects of the transition of people with disabilities between school and work are examined in this chapter. These sources of public policy and program planning for people with disabilities often are overlooked because most people explore the field of economics no further than its description by the late British economist John Maynard Keynes as "the dismal science." Yet economics deals with human issues that are far from dismal and that strongly influence the well-being of people with disabilities.

As defined by Samuelson (1961), economics is the study of how individuals and society "*choose,* with or without the use of money, to employ *scarce* productive resources to produce various commodities over time and distribute them for consumption, now and in the future, among various people and groups in society" (p. 6). The term *commodities* in Samuelson's definition connotes more than merely consumer goods such as radios, cars, or spinach. Rather, concepts and methods of economics are applied to understand human choices of many kinds that are made to allocate scarce resources to achieve

---

*David L. Passmore is professor of vocational education and adult education in the College of Education and professor of mineral engineering management in the College of Earth and Mineral Sciences at Pennsylvania State University. He is also university director of the Office for the Protection of Human Subjects and faculty associate in the Institute for the Study of Adult Literacy at Penn State. He received his Ph.D. from the University of Minnesota. He served on faculties of the University of Massachusetts–Amherst, the National Technical Institute for the Deaf, and the University of Northern Iowa and has edited the *Journal of Industrial Teacher Education* and the Computer Applications Section of *Accident Analysis and Prevention.* His current research interests are in the study of youth employment problems and the epidemiology of occupational accidents.

desired ends. Becker (1964), Schultz (1962), and Thurow (1970) have extended economic theory to consider investments in *human capital*. These extensions have aided in the analysis of such diverse social phenomena as income distribution, labor market discrimination, migration, health care, job search, fertility decisions, and industrial training.

Thurow (1970, ch. 2) defined human capital as individuals' capacities to produce goods and services. Individuals, firms, and society invest in human capital to enhance and maintain these capacities. As with all investments, human capital investments are made to yield returns to investors in the form of current or future benefits. Benefits derived can be tangibles, such as lifetime earnings or productivity, or intangibles, such as feelings of pride in work or loyalty to employers.

Some people dislike the notion that labor should be considered a good to be bought or sold like bushels of corn or pounds of haddock. However, theorists conceptualize human capital as a commodity only in an allegorical, analogical, and metaphorical sense, not with the intention of treating human beings as commodities (cf., e.g., the distinction made by Chamberlain, 1969, pp. 230, 233). In practice, labor markets are very different from commodity markets and from markets for other factors of production. Employment involves a continuing personal relationship between an employer and an employee, whereas transactions in most other markets are brief and impersonal. Although most commodities are homogeneous, even people in the same occupation differ in their attitudes, motivations, and technical skills.

A primary means for enhancing and maintaining human capacities (some of which are innate, some of which can be developed) is through education, which, if defined broadly, includes more than formal schooling. Returns on investments in education are often sought by individuals and society through participation in the labor force. It is in this sense that the transition from school to work can be viewed through the lens of economics.

The remainder of this chapter is organized around two major topics that influence the economics of transition of people with disabilities from school to work. First, I consider the social and economic context for transition from school to work. Second, I analyze the supply and demand structures of labor markets, which might improve the transition of people with disabilities from school to work. This essay is not a *tour d'horizon* of diverse literature related to disability and employment. Rather, I have integrated and synthesized my previous research and studies with the needs I perceive of people with disabilies making the transition from school to work.

CONTEXT

In modern societies, the transition from school to work is an important and, for some people, a perilous developmental task. This is especially true for people with disabilities. Current means for development of human capital among people with disabilities—or for that matter, any group, such as former inmates or disadvantaged youths, who are already marginal to the labor force—tend to be relatively costly. The few opportunities for development of human capital by people with disabilities that are supported by public funds must be effective the first time offered because they do not recur as often as for people without disabilities. As a consequence, the transition of people with disabilities from school to work is a risky enterprise.

In this section, I describe (1) the motivations for successful career development of people with disabilities that drive the economic imperatives for their transition from school to work; (2) the common risks surrounding youth employment in modern, industrialized society; and (3) the specific risks to people with disabilities trying to make a successful transition from school to work.

Importance of Work

Notions of the importance of work fluctuate. At times, it is fashionable to promise a future filled with leisure based on beliefs that human labor will be replaced by automated labor. Theobold (1966), for example, argued, during a period when automation was a prominent public issue, that a time was rapidly approaching when a minimum income could be guaranteed for all people because machines could produce enough for all. He even went so far as to assert that money itself will become an anachronism in a cybernated era. Theobold's hopes are more modern expressions of Aristotle's ideal that "the goal of war is peace, of business, leisure."

The theme that the desire to toil is a pathological feature of human nature also recurs. Stephens (1869) wrote,

> Mr. Creech, it is said, wrote on the margin of the Lucretius which he was trans-
> lating, "Mem.—When I have finished my book, I must kill myself." And he
> carried out his resolution. Life . . . is a dreary vista of monotonous toil, at the
> end of which there is nothing but death, natural if it so happen, but if not,
> voluntary, without even a preliminary interval of idleness. To live without work
> is not supposed to enter into our conceptions. (p. 10)

Yet if life and work within it are so dreary, what causes most of us, for instance, to admire virtue over crime, to seek harmony over discord, to hope for the triumph of order over chaos and destruction—in short, to choose life over death? Just what is the point of work? The answer, for me at least, lies in the inseparability of work with our being.

Career development may be the most important life task that people face as they move between school and work in modern societies. This is hard for adults to recall because they have changed so much since they made the transition. Take a few minutes to examine your own high school yearbook picture.

Think. Could anyone have convinced this young person that eating stir-fried vegetables would be enjoyable later in life?

Remember? Perhaps you can recall that under the acne, through the agony of "relationships," and over all of your body's glandular surprises, you began to wonder what you would do. Not merely what you would do on your vacation, but what you would do with your life. Not merely where you would find work to obtain money (although that certainly was, and remains, important), but what you would do that could apply an enormous energy and developing faith to allow you to be admired and loved by others.

What will I do? This is the central question for career development. Finding an answer has enormous significance, as was described by American social philosopher John Dewey (1916):

> A vocation means nothing but such a direction of life activities as renders them perceptibly significant to a person and also useful to his associates because of the consequences they accomplish. An occupation is the only thing which balances the distinctive capacity of an individual with his social service. To find out what one is fitted to do and to secure an opportunity to do it is happiness. The opposite of a career is neither leisure or culture, but aimlessness, capriciousness, absence of cumulative achievement in experience, idleness, and parasitic dependence on others. (pp 358–359)

Work, then, is something that we do to *become* someone. Seen in this way, work provides opportunities to be purposeful, creative, responsible, useful, and compassionate—that is, to be the best that is human. To say that you do not have work, or that you do not know what you will do, is to say plenty. If you have not successfully made the transition from school to work, you are a long way from maturity, responsibility, and admission to the citizenry. Career development, then, is an important developmental task for all young people, including, of course, people with disabilities.

To be sure, a person can be working but not employed for pay under Dewey's definition of a career. Unfortunately, few opportunities for fulfilling work are available outside the wage and labor system in modern, industrialized societies. Therefore, the economic aspects of work are highly interrelated with realization of our humanity through work. This is why the economics of the transition from school to work are important aspects of the lives of people with disabilities.

Youth Employment Patterns

Young people and especially, as I shall detail in the next section of this chapter, young people with disabilities are at risk for employment problems. Young people, and particular demographic groups among young people, experience these problems more acutely than adults. Unfortunately for policy makers, little is known about the causes of these problems, but these problems are known to have long-term consequences for youths as well as for society. In addition, fundamental difficulties pervade attempts to measure youth labor force behavior. (Passmore, 1981a, as well as Passmore & Risher (1987) review the major measurement problems.)

Nature

People are classified as unemployed in official government statistics if they are not working, are able to work, and are actively seeking work. In recent years, 50 percent of the unemployed in the United States have been less than 25 years old, with 16- through 19-year-olds accounting for approximately one-half of this youth unemployment. During the previous 30 years, unemployment rates among 16- through 19-year-olds have been between 1.5 and 9 times as high as general unemployment rates, depending on whether race and school completion are considered. The rates of unemployment for nonwhite youths have been twice as high as those for whites.

High school dropouts—who have been more frequently black and Hispanic than white—have had two times the unemployment rates of high school graduates and three times the rates of college graduates. Nonwhite youths often have unemployment rates that are two to three times as high as those of white youths. I have elsewhere published a summary of youth labor market activity that may help interested readers to gain a better understanding of the nature of youth employment correlates and trends (cf. Passmore, 1981b).

Causes

The causes of youth employment problems are diverse and not understood well, even though this topic has been a hotbed for policy research and public debate for many years. Explanations of the causes of high youth joblessness rates vary, often in confusing ways, according to the ideologies and methods guiding the analysts providing the explanations (see Passmore, 1982, for a review of over 100 research studies). For example, some demographers see youth population trends dominating youth employment trends. Some educators point to attitudinal, technical, and basic skills deficits as the roots of youth employability problems. Some economists resort to explanations based on market failures or imbalances such as restrictive minimum wages or imperfect information about labor among youths and employers. Legal approaches to understanding youth employment problems often focus on discrimination or restrictive legal barriers to youth employment. Geographers have asserted that youths face a mismatch between their residences and the locations of jobs.

The difficulty faced by policy makers is that, although none of these explanations is the sole or major cause of youth joblessness, all of them probably interact to some degree to produce youth employment problems. As a consequence, effects of monetary and fiscal policy, public budget allocation, trade policy, and level and kind of effort by public education for youth employment levels are uncertain. For example, would control of the prime interest rate charged by the Federal Reserve Bank system be a more effective tool against youth employment problems than increases in public funds for vocational education? How would a change in the tax affect youth employment? How would a shift in the federal budget from social to defense programs influence the number and kind of jobs for people making the transition from school to work? These questions cannot be answered clearly because we have not established the causes of youth employment problems.

Consequences

Although the causes of youth employment problems remain unclear, the consequences of these problems are well documented (see Passmore, 1983, for a review of over 160 studies of the social and private costs of youth joblessness). For instance, a 1 percent increase in the unemployment rate has accounted for 64 percent of increases in annual federal outlays. Also, a positive relationship generally exists between crime and unemployment. Evidence also is emerging that lack of work is a strong determinant of stress-induced illness.

Perhaps most important is that joblessness while young is related to less frequent employment and lower earnings as an adult. Becker and Hills (1980) contend that economic theory points to

> the potential long-run consequences of inability to take advantage of on-the-job training opportunities. Diminished training levels, in turn, would contribute to lower future earnings and fewer weeks worked. The latter would be an expected consequence of the tendency of turnover costs to decline with skill level. (pp. 356–357)

Moreover, relatively sporadic work records for youths may signal potentially low productivity levels and job commitments to prospective employers. Seen in this light, lack of work while young creates lasting employment scars for young people. As shown in the next section, disabilities further depress youth employment prospects. Therefore, the propensity for negative consequences from youth employment problems is heightened for disabled youth.

Disability and Youth Employment

The school-to-work transition needs of people with disabilities have received considerable attention from policy makers in the United States, especially during the 1960s and 1970s. For example, the Education Amendments of 1976 earmarked 10 percent of the allotment of federal money to pay for 50 percent of the costs of training handicapped students. Affirmative action in employment of people with handicaps and disabilities was emphasized in the Rehabilitation Act of 1973. Amendments to the 1973 act provided incentives for employers to train and hire people with disabilities. President Kennedy established the President's Committee on Employment of the Handicapped in 1962, extending presidential efforts since the mid-1940s to highlight employment needs of handicapped and disabled Americans.

Although much of this legislative and political attention centered on education and employment of handicapped and disabled young people, few systematic and comprehensive estimates of the influence of health conditions on the employment of young people have been available to guide policy making and legislation (cf. studies of adults by Berkowitz, Johnson, & Murphy, 1976; Levitan & Taggart, 1977; and Wolfe, 1980). Moreover, data that address health and employment simultaneously are scarce (Rones, 1981, note 2).

In response to this lack of information, some of my students and I studied the relationships between employment and the incidence and duration of health conditions that limit the amount or kind of work young people can perform (Passmore, Ay, Rockel, Wade, & Wise, 1983). We examined data from a 1979 interview with 11,412 members of the Youth Cohort of the National Longitudinal Surveys of Labor Market Experience (described in Borus et al., 1980). The Youth Cohort was selected to represent civilian noninstitutionalized youths in the continental United States who were 16 to 21 years old in January 1979. Approximately 7 percent of youths in the United States reported during 1979 that their health limited the amount or kind of work they could do.

Definitions of health limitations applied in our study were similar to the U.S. Social Security Administration's definition of *secondary work limitations*. According to the Social Security Administration, people with secondary work limitations are able to work full time, regularly, and at the same work, but with limitations in the kind or amount of work they can perform. Loss or reduction in the ability to work following onset of illness or other conditions is a common element in virtually all definitions of disability (Haber, 1973). Slater (1974) described the problems faced by social scientists in defining and measuring disability through self-reports in social surveys rather than through direct medical evaluation and assessment of functional capacity. Our work, I am sure, suffered from these definitional and measurement problems, yet our analyses have produced the only population-based estimates of which I am aware of the employment correlates of health problems among young people.

In brief, we found that the employment of youths with health limits to amount or kind of work is influenced by the same factors that affect the employability of all young people—sex, race, age, marital status, high school completion status, rural or urban location of residence, and the robustness of the local labor market. In addition to these factors, however, youths with health limitations participated in the labor force about 16 percent less frequently than other young people, and their unemployment rate was 7.5 percent higher. Youths with health limitations did not differ, on the average, in their hourly wages, job satisfaction, and occupational prestige from other employed youths. Because the typical employed youth who reported health limitations worked about 14 fewer hours per week than a youth not reporting health limitations, the gross annual income from wages and salaries of a youth with health limitations was depressed.

We found that the longer youths had experienced the health conditions that limited their employment, the more likely they were to be employed during 1979 (see also tabulations from the entire U.S. population presented in U.S. Bureau of the Census, 1973, pp. 47–53). For instance, a youth with a health limitation that was acquired within several months of the 1979 interview was 19 percent less likely to be employed than a youth who reported a lifelong health limitation. Of course, many hypotheses could be generated to account for this relationship, but one interpretation is that this difference reflects work adjustment to the health limitation.

The depressed employment possibilities we observed for young people with health limitations obviously can be changed. This hope is realized, in fact, in the data we analyzed: When youths with health limitations became employed they enjoyed the same returns from work as other youths.

LABOR MARKETS

I established in the previous section of this chapter that the transition from school to work is an important developmental task for people with disabilities and that the difficulties they face while completing this task are even more severe than those experienced by young people in general. The current section examines three economic aspects of labor markets that can affect employment of people with disabilities and, as a consequence, can be the focus of productive attention by policy makers and program planners. First, I describe the somewhat elusive structure of labor markets compared with commodity markets to demonstrate the practical limits to an economic analysis of the transition problem. The market, a kernel concept in economics, is where buyers and sellers meet to exchange goods and services. Second, economic factors affecting the supply of labor are delineated. And third, I detail the economic determinants of the demand for labor. The supply and demand for labor are analyzed from macro- as well as microeconomic perspectives—that is, from perspectives from the entire economy as well as from the individual worker. Along the way, some economic jargon is defined and used to provide readers with some of the vocabulary necessary to discuss the transition from school to work in economic terms.

In a modern capitalistic economy, jobs do not come from the tooth fairy. The economic facts of life are that, in general, the level of employment in an economy is determined by the intersection of aggregate supply and aggregate demand. Aggregate demand represents desired total spending (i.e., consumption, investment, and government purchases), and aggregate supply embodies the total value of output of goods and services in an economy. Within this framework, the availability of jobs depends not only on the number of workers required to sustain a certain level of output but also on the number of people working or seeking jobs. The competition for employment in an occupation depends on the quantity and quality of labor demanded by individual industries, but it is also affected by the quantity and quality of labor supplied at a given wage rate.

People with disabilities obviously are affected by these economic facts of life. The general robustness of the economy will influence the employability of people with disabilities, who compete with other workers for available jobs. Therefore, a clear understanding of the features of occupational supply and demand yields a better understanding of the prospects for employment of people with disabilities and of the policy and programming options available to improve their employment prospects.

Interestingly, several added benefits accrue from probing the features of labor markets for people with disabilities that have been observed in studies of other populations marginal to the labor force. First, problems in the functioning of labor markets in modern, capitalistic, industrialized economies are more visible at the margins of the labor force. Second, not only do solutions to these problems help those at the margins of the labor force, but also knowledge and methods developed to make labor markets function more smoothly benefit all labor force participants. These benefits to the general population can emerge, of course, from solution of any problem faced by a special population, as has been well demonstrated with work on the problems of economically and academically disadvantaged youths.

Structure

A "perfect" market for a commodity has a number of features. The commodity bought or sold in the market is defined clearly. The number of buyers and sellers is too large to permit collusion to limit supply or demand of the commodity or to fix its price. The equilibrium price of a commodity is the amount of money for each unit of the commodity necessary to clear the market of the commodity. Shortages and surpluses of the commodity are eliminated quickly through rapid changes in price. Information about the quantities of the commodity available at a specified price is exchanged perfectly and instantaneously among buyers and sellers. Sellers are motivated to maximize their profits, buyers to minimize their costs. Perhaps the closest conformance to the features of the perfect market is the securities market.

Markets for labor, however, are far from perfect. Neither jobs nor workers are clearly defined commodities. Not all firms are alike, for example, in working conditions or attractiveness of location, nor are all workers in the same occupation alike in attitude, motivation, knowledge, and of course, skill. Depending on the mobility of firms and workers, geoeconomic boundaries of labor markets for the same occupation may be local, regional, national, or international.

Because there are more workers than employers, firms often collude to affect employment practices (e.g., "antipirating" agreements between employers not to try to hire each others' employees). Collective bargaining agreements often limit the hiring flexibility of firms. Some analysts assert that minimum wage laws set the price of labor higher than would be the case if firms were allowed a freer hand in bidding for labor in an open market.

In a perfect labor market all workers performing the same occupation would receive the same wage corresponding to their contribution to production. Yet wages differ within the same occupation, even within the same geographic area. All these factors work together to make the wage an employee receives an elusive measure of the balance between the supply and demand for labor.

Perfect and instantaneous exchange of information is the sine qua non of the perfect market. However, contrary to the premise of a perfect labor market model,

> surveys indicate that most workers have only the haziest ideas about alternative employment opportunities, even in their local community; they know even less about the wages, working conditions, and possibilities of promotion in job openings elsewhere; and even those workers who do state wage rates in other establishments are often grossly wrong in their estimates. . . . Efforts to improve labor-market information . . . [are] one investment in human beings which may have a higher rate of return than many other kinds of investment that have received considerably greater publicity. (Kreps, Somers, & Perlman, 1974, p. 27)

Much of the remainder of this chapter deals with prescriptions for policies and practices designed to improve information about the supply and demand for labor for policy makers and planners of programs for people with disabilities as well as for people with disabilities themselves.

In practice, all markets, even for well-defined commodities, are imperfect. Nevertheless, the conceptual and methodological apparatus of the classic perfect market often proves useful in the analysis of practical problems from an economic viewpoint. Therefore, consideration of occupational supply and demand data could aid vocational planning for people with disabilities.

Supply

The total supply of labor in an economy is the number of people willing to work at prevailing wages (cf. Perlman, 1969, ch. 9; Rees, 1973, p. 3). From the macroeconomic perspective, the supply of labor to occupations is described by a stock and flow model borrowed from economic demography. Then, from the microeconomic perspective, the decision to work or to seek work is analyzed as an economic choice made to maximize the well-being or, as economists describe it, the utility of the individual or family unit.

Macro Level
Attempts to estimate the supply of labor for occupations are made especially difficult by the character of American labor markets. The U.S. labor force is

highly flexible, with most workers capable of filling any of a large number of occupations. Similarly, hiring requirements for most occupations are flexible within a reasonably wide range. In this open system, people move, if not freely, at least with relative frequency from one occupation to another. The geographic and occupational mobility of the U.S. labor force is important in moderating and eliminating imbalances in occupational supply and demand, but it makes the forecasting of job openings a very difficult job, indeed. Moreover, the high attrition levels from the educational system and the tendency to emphasize "general" education programs result in large numbers of new labor force entrants lacking specific occupational preparation, a fact that complicates forecasting their probable occupational attachment.

The U.S. Bureau of Labor Statistics (BLS) defined occupational supply as the number of persons seeking work in an occupation as well as entries into and separations from an occupation (Sommers, 1974, p. 3). Current supply— the number employed in an occupation at a given time—positively contributes to occupational supply, as does the number of entrants into the occupation. Separation from the occupation negatively affects net occupational supply. The BLS model accounts for stocks (current supply) and flows (entries and separations) in a manner similar to demographic models of migration.

The BLS model is represented in Figure 3.1. Occupational supply compo-

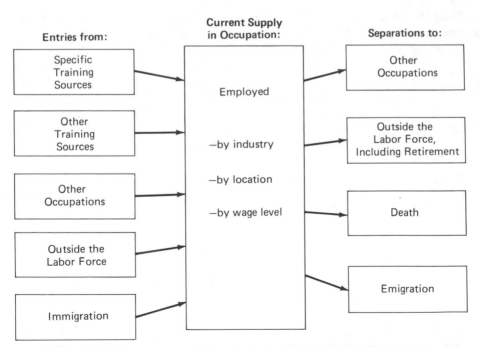

Figure 3.1. U.S. Department of Labor Statistics Model of Occupational Supply Structure

nents—current supply, entries, separation—are segmented further in Figure 3.1 into an exhaustive set of categories that are mutually exclusive. Information concerning the supply of workers to an occupation from each of these categories is useful in planning and policy deliberations about employment of people with disabilities.

Rosenthal (1966) provided an example of the use of the BLS model to forecast the supply of scientific personnel. Several colleagues and I have used this model to plan postsecondary training in bookkeeping and medical record technology for people with hearing impairments (Passmore, 1979a; Passmore et al., 1979; Passmore, Marron, Norton, & Mohamed, 1983; Passmore & Martin, 1977). The methodological details concerning application of the model are presented by Marron and Passmore (1979).

The BLS model of occupational supply could be helpful for career planning and policy making for people with disabilities in a number of ways. A case is made to enhance this point. The National Technical Institute for the Deaf (NTID) at the Rochester Institute of Technology was interested in determining whether it should continue to offer training for bookkeeping occupations. The NTID provides postsecondary technical training and education for hearing-impaired young people from throughout the United States. With a clientele that hoped to find work at a variety of geographic locations throughout the United States, the NTID was interested in determining the expected national employment outlook for bookkeepers. Estimation of occupational supply was one aspect of this planning effort.

The NTID analysis (documented in Passmore & Martin, 1977, and Passmore, 1979a) revealed that the current supply of workers to bookkeeping occupations was almost exclusively female. Many females reentering the labor force through bookkeeping were in the 35- to 45-year-old age range, which coincides with general age patterns of female labor force participation that include lower participation levels during prime childbearing years. Moreover, many entrants into bookkeeping occupations came from other clerical occupations.

Reviews of sex distributions of separations from bookkeeping occupations revealed that males were more likely to transfer out of bookkeeping occupations than females and that males were more likely to be upwardly mobile than females in these transfers. Females predominantly transferred to other clerical occupations. In addition, wages of bookkeepers were uniformly low, similar to many other clerical occupations—so low, in fact, that many bookkeepers' wages would leave them below poverty level even though employed full time.

Analysis of the occupational supply structure for bookkeeping occupations yielded many important items for the NTID planners. First, entry into bookkeeping did not seem to require heavy training investments, which was indicated by relative ease of reentry into the labor force through bookkeeping and the relative ease of transfer into bookkeeping from other occupations.

Second, most bookkeepers could not expect to follow a career ladder of upward mobility from bookkeeping. And third, wages offered to bookkeepers showed that employers find people with bookkeeping skills available, even when they offer low wage rates. The NTID planners cautioned that NTID graduates could expect keen competition for bookkeeping positions from even untrained people and that investments in bookkeeping training could have a long pay-back period.

Similar analyses of occupational supply could be completed for local or regional labor markets. Most of the data necessary for estimating occupational supply are available from state and local employment agencies (Sommers, 1974, lists data sources), with the exception of interoccupational mobility estimates (see, however, Sommers & Eck, 1977). Such analyses would be especially fruitful in occupations requiring relatively low skill levels for successful job performance. As shown by North (1974), Priore (1979), Wachter (1978), and Wool (1976), applicants for jobs in occupations requiring low skill levels are often in direct competition with recent immigrants. However, North and Wool also observed, using the BLS occupational supply model, that a chronic undersupply of workers in low-skill occupations is expected for some time. Grant and Hammermesh (1980) provided evidence that young people making the transition from school to work compete directly for jobs in the manufacturing sector with adult white women reentering the labor force and black males. Occupational supply analyses could yield information about with whom people with disabilities will compete in their quest for jobs.

Prospective analysts of occupational supply are cautioned that before components of the BLS model can be estimated, the occupation under analysis must be specified precisely. The expected employment outcomes of education and training programs are often stated in school literature as job names with which the school faculty or guidance personnel are familiar rather than as occupations extracted from some widely used occupational classification scheme. For instance, when the XYZ Business Institute advertises that it prepares "bookkeepers," are these the same as the "bookkeepers" prepared by the Smithtown Vocational School? Is the "bookkeeper" trained by these schools equivalent to the "bookkeeper" hired by General Motors? There is room for equivocation when occupational titles are not anchored to some more general occupational classification scheme, and results of occupational analyses might be unrelated to the information needs of various decision makers. Passmore and Marron (1978, 1982) presented case studies of the link of public occupational data to the expected employment outcomes of a training institute.

Micro Level

The supply of labor by an individual or by members of a household is the result of a decision by an individual or household members to participate in the labor force for a certain number of hours a week, with a particular level of effort, at prevailing wage rates (Rees, 1973, ch. 1, esp. pp. 3–4). At the most abstract level, individuals or households can choose to allocate their available time to labor or leisure. Time allocation decisions reflect total resources of individuals or households. Under the assumption that people prefer leisure over labor, an increase in resources (say, e.g., winning a lottery) should reduce labor supply. Or an increase in wages relative to other wages and prices could increase labor supply by inducing people to enter the labor force (say, for instance, a rise in schoolteachers' salaries, which draws former teachers back to teaching jobs).

People with disabilities often receive income support through social insurance programs and public assistance such as the U.S. Social Security Administration's Supplementary Security Income (SSI) program. Income support programs are directed at people who cannot achieve substantial gainful employment or whose income is at poverty levels. Income support is designed to maintain or improve factors such as health, nutrition, and housing of individuals and families. Economists define income support for an individual or household as a *transfer payment* because income is transferred from public funds without receiving a good or service in return.

Transfer payments affect the labor supplied by people with disabilities and can strongly affect motivations to make the transition between school and work. Income support could reduce the labor supply of people with disabilities by making work for pay less attractive and less profitable than participation in an income support program. Several studies (summarized in Berkowitz, Johnson, & Murphy, 1975) have shown that income support programs for people with disabilities act as disincentives to work. These studies observed that, as the amount of and scope of eligibility for benefits increased over the years, so did participation in income support programs by people with disabilities. In one study, each 10 percent increase in the ratio of benefits to average monthly wage at the last job was associated with a 2.4 percent increase in applications for benefits.

Untangling the web of causation in the studies summarized by Berkowitz, Johnson, and Murphy (1975) is difficult. Increases in participation in income support programs could be the result of increasing dependency of people with disabilities on transfer payments. Or more people with disabilities may have sought transfer payments because of declining job opportunities. The studies did not focus specifically on work disincentives caused by income support to people with disabilities making the transition from school to work. However, the role of transfer payments as work disincentives is quite common. During my three years as a researcher at the NTID I observed many graduates weighing placement in gainful employment against loss of SSI benefits.

Efforts by professionals trying to increase the economic responsibility and independence of people by improving school-to-work transitions can be hamstrung by the disincentive effects of income support programs on labor supply. Some economists have suggested a solution to this dilemma that creates uneasiness among people who educate or are advocates for people with disabilities. For example, Levitan and Taggart (1977) argue that careful choices in allocation of resources to people with disabilities must be made between rehabilitation and income support programs. Given that emphasis on education of people with severe disabilities for work has increased since 1973, they note that

> Benefit/cost estimates . . . have suggested that the payoff is higher for the less severely disabled. . . . The emphasis on the severely disabled should be reexamined. This is a complex issue that involves value judgments. . . . In the face of the limited employment potential of the most severely handicapped and the considerable resources investment needed to prepare them for gainful employment, consideration might be given to whether they might be better served with income support, so that scarce rehabilitation resources can be focused on others who might be helped more in the labor market. (pp. 116–118)

Of course, with no limitations on resources, both income support and rehabilitation could be provided for all people with disabilities. Nothing is clearer, however, in this era of budget deficits, trade deficits, high rates of consumer debt, and social program cuts than the fact that resources are scarce, indeed. Choices must be made.

Choices that influence the labor supply of people with disabilities raise some fundamental questions about how to use public resources for the well-being of people with disabilities. What does it mean to work in our society? What comprises dignity through work? What are the limits to social responsibility for economic welfare of all citizens, including citizens with disabilities? What are the most cost-beneficial means for reaching these ends?

Demand

The demand for labor in an economy is the number of workers needed to produce a desired amount and kind of goods and services for distribution and consumption (Rees, 1973, ch. 4). From the macroeconomic perspective, I use an interindustry model of the economy to describe the economic processes that generate jobs, and I link this model to the planning and policy making needed to smooth the transition from school to work for people with disabilities. Then, from the microeconomic perspective, I analyze selected economic and social factors that influence employers' demands for labor.

Macro Level
Money flows. The dollar paid to the baker for cake is spent, in turn, for sugar, whipped cream, and flour. The mill from which the baker buys the flour uses the baker's money to buy grain. The farmer who grew the grain purchases seed, fertilizer, and fuel from suppliers. The baker's cake sets up a complex flow of money through the economy. Banks, insurers, and health-care professionals, among others, have a piece of the action also.

Ultimately, many industries and workers are affected by the ripple made by even the most modest transaction. Add ripple to ripple, and you have a wave. These economic "waves" did not go unnoticed by economists. Based on the work of eighteenth- and nineteenth-century economists, Wassily Leontief (1936) developed a table during the 1930s that showed transactions among industries in the U.S. economy. Important descriptive, explanatory, and predictive information can be derived from a transaction table that could be useful in program planning and policy making to improve the employability of people with disabilities.

Leontief's method is called interindustry analysis because it portrays dependencies among industries. Sometimes it is called input-output analysis because it shows the inputs from various industries necessary to produce a unit of output in any industry. Leontief's ideas won him the Nobel Prize in economics.

I outline the mathematical details and general applicability of Leontief's model to human resource planning elsewhere (Passmore, 1979b, 1987). Brief, nontechnical descriptions of interindustry models were presented by Elliott-Jones (1971) and Miernyk (1957, 1965). Simply stated, though, Leontief's model divides the economy into sectors or industries. The basic notion is that each industry combines a set of inputs—land, capital, labor—in fixed proportions to produce its output, which, in turn, it sells to other industries to meet their input requirements.

Production of industries is driven by the material needs of society for goods and services through personal consumption expenditures, investments, imports, exports, and government expenditures. These material needs are expressed and measured by economists as components of the gross national product (GNP). Formally, the GNP is the value of goods and services produced, usually over one year. Another way to think about the GNP is that it is something like an order filed by society for its material needs to be filled by industries. In the U.S. economic system the components of the GNP are determined to some extent by government policy, but in most cases by the workings of product and resource markets. In countries like the Soviet Union, target levels and distributions of the GNP are almost entirely the result of national planning efforts.

Various industries are orchestrated to produce the desired GNP. To create its output, each industry requires various goods and services from other industries, as was shown in the cake-baking example. Each industry manages factors of production—land, capital, labor—to produce its output. An industry's demand for labor, then, is generated through a complex web of production requirements. Because outputs differ by industry, the amount and kind of labor required will differ by industry.

Leontief expressed these complex relationships among industries in a simple two-way table. Consider a hypothetical economy that has only two industries, agriculture and textiles. Figure 3.2 shows the input-output table for this

	Input			
	Agriculture	Textiles	Final Demand	Total Output
Agriculture	$20	$15	$65	$100
Textiles	$14	$6	$40	$60

Figure 3.2. Input-Output Table for Hypothetical Economy with Two Industries

economy—that is, it shows the amount of input in dollars needed from each industry to meet requirements of the economy for textile and manufacturing products. Some output from each industry is sold to the other industry. For example, $15 of agricultural goods and services are required by the textiles industry. However, some industrial output goes directly to satisfy final demand for the product. The final demand is the amount that is sold directly to consumers. Notice that industries use some of their own output as an input, as in the case of the textiles industry, which consumes $6 of its output so that it can produce textiles to meet final demand for textile goods and services. The total output of an industry is the sum of the industry's output. Gross national product is the sum of all industry output that is sold to other industries or goes to meet final demand.

A certain amount of labor is required to produce each dollar's worth of textiles or manufactured goods. The amount and kind of labor required differs between the two industries because they use very different technologies in the production process. Suppose in our two-industry economy that only two occupations exist, laborer and manager. If it takes 0.2 laborers to produce a dollar's worth of agricultural output, 20 laborers will be required to produce the level of agricultural output desired in the hypothetical economy. Leontief's model helps us describe how jobs are generated in an economy.

Now come the "what if" questions. What would happen to the need for laborers in the agricultural industry if fewer agricultural products were needed? If the textile sector increased its demand for agricultural output? If high technology were introduced to lower the labor requirement to 0.1 laborers per each dollar output? Input-output analysis is particularly helpful in exploring questions about the demand for labor in an economy. This form of analysis has been used to consider the probable effects of such diverse questions as whether the priorities indicated in a president's state of the union message could be met with existing human resources (Bullard & Pilati, 1976) or whether shifts in federal government expenditures (the classic "guns vs. butter" trade-off) would affect civilian employment (Bezdek, 1973). What seem to be simple, straightforward schemes for solving economic problems often are revealed through interindustry analysis to have unanticipated and negative effects.

Leontief's model is used by the BLS to project U.S. employment requirements in 201 industries for 421 occupations. The projections are used extensively in employment counseling and in industrial decision making. However, the widest attention received by these projections is through the BLS publication, *Occupational Outlook Handbook,* that is used by many school guidance counselors with their clients and is summarized frequently in the popular press. For this reason alone, the BLS interindustry model probably is the most influential source of occupational information available in the United States. Leontief's model also has been applied successfully to local and regional economies (see studies cited in Bourque and Hansen, 1967, and Giarrantani, 1976).

Some readers may be wondering whether it would just be simpler to collect employers' hiring plans through mail or telephone surveys. At least three problems occur with the validity of employers' surveys of human resource requirements (Passmore, 1979b). First, data about human resources plans for firms are often treated as proprietary information. Second, employers have difficulty basing their estimates on consistent economic, social, and political frameworks. Third, employers' estimates are subject to uncertainties, such as changes in economic growth rates or worker migration, that are not often considered in surveys of employers.

Leontief's model could help improve the transition from school to work in several ways for people with disabilities. First, already-existing industry and occupation employment projections could be analyzed one step further. The *Dictionary of Occupational Titles* (DOT) (U.S. Department of Labor, 1978) and its supplements contain information about physical and mental requirements for successful performance. Occupations with favorable employment growth patterns could be cross classified by DOT information to determine the set of occupations that represent feasible employment goals for people with various kinds of disabilities (Employment Development Department, 1976). Of course, we all know people with disabilities who are gainfully employed in occupations that many people would have believed impossible for them to master. Perhaps another way to use interindustry results combined with DOT information is to identify occupations that are ripe for careful analysis to determine whether they can be redesigned to accommodate various disabilities.

As asserted in the beginning of this chapter, people with disabilities must make effective training investments because these investments are perceived to be costly and, therefore, cannot be expected to be made frequently over the disabled person's career cycle. Another use for results of interindustry studies is to help people with disabilities select occupations for training investment that are relatively insensitive to fluctuations in the economy. For example, the demand for coal miners is quite sensitive to the relative price of various energy sources. When oil prices rise, extraction of coal becomes more profitable; declining oil prices depress the demand for coal. As a result, coal mining has a risky employment outlook. On the other hand, an occupation such as book-keeping is relatively insensitive to fluctuations in the pattern of demand for goods and services in the economy because bookkeepers are needed in virtually every industry. Therefore, training for bookkeeping is a less risky investment (considering occupational demand information only) than coal mining.

Micro Level

Many aspects of the demand for labor by individual employers with applicability to people with disabilities could be probed in this chapter. I will consider two: employment discrimination and employer incentives.

Many people, not merely employers, hold many stereotypes about the productive abilities and capacities of people with disabilities. Many times these stereotypes do not adequately represent the true capabilities of disabled individuals. Many people believe that some employers unfairly discriminate against people with disabilities in hiring and promotion decisions. Seminal work on the economics of discrimination by Becker (1971, 1976, ch. 2) clarifies the losses to individuals and firms because of discrimination.

Becker has shown that when one group discriminates against the other (say, employers against people with disabilities) by not buying otherwise useful goods and services from a seller with whom the buyer does not want to consort, the discriminator is not better off economically. In fact, the discriminator's income is reduced. In addition, boycotts of the discriminating employer in retaliation for discrimination also reduce the well-being of the person discriminated against. Seen in the light of economic theory, employment discrimination against people with disabilities hurts the employer, and retaliation against the employer reduces the welfare of people with disabilities. The conclusion I draw is that reduction of stereotypes about the work potential of people with disabilities is in the economic interests of everyone.

Another micro-level aspect of the demand for labor includes consideration of incentives for employers to hire people with disabilities. Incentives can take the form of such instruments as lower than legal minimum wages for employees with disabilities or tax credits for employers who hire people with disabilities. The rationale for providing incentives is to transfer some portion of the presumably higher costs of employing people with disabilities from firms to the public. The actual effectiveness of incentive plans is keyed to comparison of their benefits versus their costs. For example, targeted tax credits seemed to provide a real incentive for employers to hire people with disabilities. However, many employers failed to use the tax credit program or to cash in their credits because of the costs of the paperwork involved. As the old maxim goes, "Everything has its price," and employer incentives to hire are no exception.

SUMMARY

This chapter was designed to demonstrate the economic approach to the problem of improving the transition from school to work for people with disabilities. The success of this transition is central to the expression of the humanity of people with disabilities. However, research data show that people with disabilities make this transition with difficulty. Techniques in the analyses of labor markets that are designed to improve the supply and demand for labor to the economy were reviewed. Application of these techniques to the problem of transition from school to work is likely to improve the well-being and social contribution of people with disabilities.

REFERENCES

Becker, B. E., & Hills, S. M. (1980). Teenage unemployment: Some evidence of the long-run effects on wages. *Journal of Human Resources, 15(3),* 354–372.

Becker, G. S. (1964). *Human capital: A theoretical and empirical analysis, with special reference to education.* New York: National Bureau of Economic Research.

Becker, G. S. (1971). *The economics of discrimination* (2nd ed.). Chicago: University of Chicago Press.

Becker, G. S. (1976). *The economic approach to human behavior.* Chicago: University of Chicago Press.

Berkowitz, M., Johnson, W. G., & Murphy E. H. (1975). *Policy and the determinants of disability.* Princeton, NJ: Rutgers University Press.

Berkowitz, M., Johnson, W. G., & Murphy, E. H. (1976). *Public policy toward disability.* New York: Praeger.

Bezdek, R. H. (1973). Manpower impacts of changes in federal budget priorities. *Economics of Planning, 13(3),* 211–223.

Borque, P. V., & Hansen, G. (1967). *An inventory of regional input-output studies in the United States* (Occasional Paper No. 17). Pullman: University of Washington, Graduate School of Business Administration.

Borus, M. F., Crowley, J. E., Rumberger, R. W., Santos, R., & Shapiro, D. (1980). *Pathways to the future: A longitudinal study of young Americans* (Preliminary report: Youth and the labor market 1979). Columbus: Ohio State University, Center for Human Resources Research. (ERIC Document Reproduction Service No. ED 195 796.)

Bullard, C. W., & Pilati, D. A. (1976). Direct and indirect requirements for a project independence scenario. *Energy, 1,* 123–131.

Chamberlain, N. W. (1969). Some further thoughts on the concept of human capital. In G. G. Somers & W. D. Wood (Eds.), *Cost-benefit analysis of manpower policies.* Madison: University of Wisconsin, Center for Studies in Vocational and Technical Education.

Dewey, J. (1916). *Democracy and education.* New York: Macmillan.

Elliott-Jones, M. F. (1971). *Input-output analysis: A nontechnical description.* New York: The Conference Board.

Employment Development Department. (1976). *USOE/DOT-Census cross-reference.* Los Angeles: State of California.

Giarrantani, F. (1976). *Regional and interregional input-output analysis: An annotated bibliography.* Morgantown: West Virginia University.

Grant, J. H., & Hammermesh, D. (1980). *Labor market competition among youth, white women, and others* (Working Paper No. 519). Cambridge, MA: National Bureau of Economic Research.

Haber, L. D. (1983, Summer). Some parameters for social policy in disability: A cross-national comparison. *Milbank Memorial Fund Quarterly,* pp. 319–340.

Kreps, J. M., Somers, G. G., & Perlman, R. (1974). *Contemporary labor economics: Issues, analysis, and policies.* Belmont, CA: Wadsworth.

Leontief, W. (1936). Quantitative input-output relations in the economic system of the United States. *The Review of Economics and Statistics, 43,* 105–125.

Levitan, S. A., & Taggart, R. (1977). *Jobs for the disabled* (Policy Studies in Employment and Welfare No. 28). Baltimore: Johns Hopkins University Press.

Marron, M., & Passmore, D. L. (1979). Occupational supply information for planning education for work. *Journal of Industrial Teacher Education, 17(1),* 39–56.

Miernyk, W. H. (1957). *A primer of input-output economics.* Boston: Northeastern University, Bureau of Business and Economic Research.

Miernyk, W. H. (1965). *The elements of input-output analysis.* New York: Random House.

North, D. S. (1974). *Immigrants and the American labor market.* Washington, DC: U.S. Department of Labor.

Passmore, D. L. (1979a). The bookkeeping occupation: What does the future hold? *Journal of Studies in Technical Careers, 1(2),* 162–171.

Passmore, D. L. (1979b). Use of interindustry analysis to plan education for work. *Journal of Industrial Teacher Education, 17(1),* 7–24.

Passmore, D. L. (1981a). Measuring youth joblessness: Concepts, tools, and issues. *Journal of Studies in Technical Careers, 3(2),* 109–125.

Passmore, D. L. (1981b). Youth joblessness and career education. *The Journal of Epsilon Pi Tau, 7(1),* 8–20.

Passmore, D. L. (1982). Barriers to youth employment. *The Journal of Epsilon Pi Tau, 8(1),* 25–38.

Passmore, D. L. (1983). Social and private costs of youth joblessness. *The Journal of Epsilon Pi Tau, 9(1),* 11–29.

Passmore, D. L. (1987). Theory: Adapting human resources to organizational change. In R. A. Swanson & D. Gradous (Eds.), *Human resources and organizational change.* Alexandria, VA: American Society for Training and Development.

Passmore, D. L., Ay, U., Rockel, S., Wade, B., & Wise, J. (1983). Health and youth employment. *Applied Economics, 15,* 715–729.

Passmore, D. L., & Marron, M. (1978). *Expected employment outcomes from educational programs of the National Technical Institute for the Deaf* (Division of Management Services Report No. 20). Rochester, NY: Rochester Institute of Technology, National Technical Institute for the Deaf.

Passmore, D. L., & Marron, M. (1982) Stating expected employment outcomes of occupational programs: A case study. *Journal of Studies in Technical Careers, 4(1),* 13–26.

Passmore, D. L., Marron, M., Hamil, F., & Fowler, M. (1979). *National employment outlook for medical record technicians* (Division of Management Services Report No. 29). Rochester, NY: Rochester Institute of Technology, National Technical Institute for the Deaf.

Passmore, D. L., Marron, M., Norton, W. P., & Mohamed, D. (1983). National employment outlook for medical record technicians. *Journal of Studies in Technical Careers, 5(1)*, 27–34.

Passmore, D. L., & Martin, K. M. (1977). *National employment outlook in bookkeeping occupations* (Division of Management Services Report No. 6). Rochester, NY: Rochester Institute of Technology, National Technical Institute for the Deaf.

Passmore, D. L., & Risher, G. (1987). Labor force attachment of youth. *Journal of Technical and Vocational Education, 4*, 44–60.

Perlman, R. (1969). *Labor theory.* New York: Wiley.

Priore, M. J. (1979). *Birds of passage: Long distance migrants in industrial society.* New York: Cambridge University Press.

Rees, A. (1973). *The economics of work and pay.* New York: Harper & Row.

Rones, P. (1981). Can the Current Population Survey be used to identify the disabled? *Monthly Labor Review, 104*, 37–38.

Rosenthal, N. (1966). Projection of manpower supply in a specific occupation. *Monthly Labor Review, 89*, 1262–1266.

Samuelson, P. (1961). *Economics.* New York: McGraw-Hill.

Schultz, T. (1962). Investment in human beings. *The Journal of Political Economy, 70* (5, Supplement, all of part 2).

Slater, (1974). The definition and measurement of disability. *Social Science and Medicine, 8*, 305–308.

Sommers, D. (1974). *Occupational supply: Concepts and sources of data for manpower analysis* (Bureau of Labor Statistics Bulletin 1816). Washington, DC: U.S. Government Printing Office.

Sommers, D., & Eck, A. (1977). Occupational mobility in the American labor force. *Monthly Labor Review, 100*, 3–19.

Stephens, L. (1869). Vacations. *Cornhill Magazine, 20*, 10–22.

Theobold, R. (1966). *The guaranteed income: Next step in economic revolution.* New York: Doubleday.

Thurow, L. (1970). *Investment in human capital.* Belmont, CA: Wadsworth.

U.S. Bureau of the Census. (1973). *Persons with work disability* [PC(2)-6C]. Washington, DC: U.S. Government Printing Office.

U.S. Department of Labor, Employment and Training Administration. (1978). *Dictionary of occupational titles* (4th ed.). Washington, DC: U.S. Government Printing Office.

Wachter, M. L. (1978, May 22). Second thoughts about illegal immigrants. *Fortune*, pp. 80ff.

Wolfe, B. L. (1980). How the disabled fare in the labor market. *Monthly Labor Review, 103*, 48–52.

Wool, H. (1976). *The labor supply for lower level occupations.* Washington, DC: U.S. Government Printing Office.

CHAPTER 4

Identification, Assessment, and Placement of Persons Needing Transition Assistance

James P. Greenan*

INTRODUCTION

The provision of school-to-work transition assistance for persons with disabilities should include appropriate identification, assessment, and placement services. These services may be provided through vocational education, special education, rehabilitation, or other related programs or agencies whose goals include employment education and training for disabled persons. The settings for these services may be in schools, rehabilitation centers, or work environments. The target populations for identification, assessment, and placement services include mildly, moderately, and severely disabled persons. Disabled persons who are served by transition providers typically possess one or more of the following disabilities: (1) mental retardation, (2) learning disabilities, (3) physical disabilities, (4) speech impairments, (5) visual impairments, (6) hearing impairments, (7) emotional or behavioral disabilities, or (8) health impairments. Multihandicapped persons also are in need of transition services. The nature, type, and extent of services will differ depending on the severity of the disability and the person's individual needs.

This chapter focuses on identification, assessment, and placement services for persons with disabilities needing transition assistance. The roles of various service providers, assessment strategies, interagency collaboration procedures,

*James P. Greenan is associate professor and chairperson of vocational education at Purdue University. Dr. Greenan received his Ph.D. in vocational education from the University of Minnesota. He has published extensively in the areas of vocational and special education. His research interests include generalizable skills instruction and special populations.

emerging models, and placement alternatives are presented and discussed. The information presented should be useful to practitioners in transition-related programs and agencies and to leadership development professionals responsible for preparing transition service providers.

IDENTIFICATION

The identification section discusses strategies and procedures for identifying persons requiring transition services. The roles of various transition agencies that do provide or could provide identification services are discussed. The need for interagency collaboration in the identification process is also discussed.

Role of Special Education

The field of special education has traditionally maintained the responsibility of identifying persons needing special instruction and support services in education programs, particularly in vocational programs. It is, however, common for students to have been identified for special services in the primary elementary grades (kindergarten through third) in advance of receiving vocational programming services.

Special education has several major roles and responsibilities or levels of involvement in the identification process: (1) referral, (2) parent/guardian awareness, (3) learner evaluation, (4) evaluation review, (5) placement recommendation, (6) parent/guardian alternatives, and (7) appeal process (Brolin, 1982; Meers, 1987; Sarkees and Scott, 1985). Public Law 94–142 (Education for All Handicapped Children Act of 1975) has mandated this procedural process to ensure the right of due process for parents or guardians and their children (Federal Register, 1977). Due process is designed to eliminate the negative effects of labeling. Labeling may affect access and equity regarding instruction and services in employment-related programs. Due process procedures attempt to prohibit dysfunctional placements; eliminate culturally biased tests, especially those used to identify minority students for special education; and ensure parental or guardian awareness and involvement in identification, assessment, and placement processes. Perhaps most important, a single test can no longer be used for identifying a disabled person for special education programming.

Public Law 94–142 has required state education agencies (SEA's) (i.e., state departments or boards of education) to develop policies, guidelines, and procedures to ensure due process and for the referral, identification, evaluation, and placement of persons with disabilities into special education and regular education programs. Local education agencies (LEA) (local school districts or corporations) must use the policies, guidelines, and procedures developed and required by the SEA for referral, identification, evaluation, and placement of students with disabilities into education programs. Students usually remain in their original program or programs in which they were referred until due process and evaluation procedures are completed and final placement decisions are made. The general identification process that most SEAs and LEAs use is illustrated in Figure 4.1.

Referral

Students are commonly referred initially for evaluation from regular education programs or classes by content teachers, coordinators or supervisors, administrators, guidance counselors, social workers, medical personnel, parents or guardians, or other personnel. Referrals are typically based on low achievement, behavior problems, or social difficulties as observed or measured by regular educators. Problems or difficulties may be caused by one or more particular mental, physical, behavioral, emotional, health, or communication disabilities.

The major purpose of the referral process is to identify or diagnose functional problems and assess the need to prescribe an appropriate educational plan for delivering the necessary instructional and support services for individual students. The referring person should provide written descriptions of the events and situations leading to the referral. For example, the student's measured and observed functional program-related learning strengths and problems should be described. The referring person should give an unbiased description of his or her relationship with the referred student, a report of the

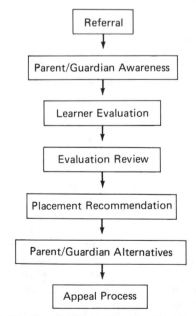

Figure 4.1 The Special Education Identification Process

discrepancy between behaviors and program or class expectations, and the extent to which behaviors demonstrated by the student impede the teaching-learning processes. The learning environment in which the behaviors have occurred should be made clear. The nature, type, extent, frequency, and duration of both positive and negative behaviors should be well documented and described.

Parent or Guardian Awareness

School personnel should provide to the parents or guardians of the referred student, in writing, the purpose of the referral; an explanation of the evaluation process; and a description of the parents' or guardians' right to access, review, and input regarding all school records and information pertaining to their child. School officials should encourage parents to contact appropriate personnel with questions or clarification regarding the referral process. The written notification also should solicit informed consent and release (in writing) from the parents or guardians allowing school personnel to assess and evaluate their child. School personnel are required to inform parents of their rights to participate fully in the referral process (e.g., attend evaluation activities, review evaluation results, serve on review committees, agree with or appeal committees' recommendations). Parents must receive notice of referral activities within predetermined time periods.

Parents or guardians may or may not grant persmission to the school to evaluate their child. If permission is granted, a comprehensive evaluation is conducted. If permission is not granted, an appeal may be made followed by evaluation. Parent or guardian participation is, therefore, necessary in identification and eventual placement of a student in a special education program. Confidentiality with respect to all files and information should be ensured by school personnel.

Learner Evaluation

The purpose of learner evaluation is to conduct a comprehensive assessment or evaluation to diagnose the educational (cognitive), psychological, psychomotor, medical, and social (affective skills) strengths or problems a student had or has currently. Personal or demographic information also may be collected. Educational information may include ability tests (e.g., intelligence tests), achievement tests, aptitude tests, school records, teachers' reports, observations, referral forms, mathematics skills, writing skills, reading skills, verbal skills, and listening skills. Psychomotor skills could include manual dexterity, eye-hand coordination, mobility, endurance, and gross motor dexterity. Medical information may be gathered from medical history reviews, physical examinations, and vision or hearing tests. Social or affective information may be collected from social workers regarding family history and through observations regarding interests, likes, and dislikes.

The identification and eventual placement of a student into special education programs should be based on a synthesis of this type of information and not on one single source or test. Reliable and valid instruments and procedures are necessary to yield meaningful information to make important programmatic decisions for individual students. Evaluation instruments and procedures must be modified or adapted for some students, such as learning disabled students or minority students and students with limited English proficiency for whom instruments and procedures may be biased in culture or language. Student evaluation also could be conducted by a "third party" (i.e., outside of school) if the services are requested and obtained by the parents or guardians. Students should also be evaluated formatively (i.e., periodically) to verify that appropriate identification and placement decisions have been made.

Evaluation Review
Personnel including regular education teachers, administrators, coordinators and supervisors, medical personnel, psychologists, special educators, guidance counselors, social workers, vocational evaluators, psychometrists, parents or guardians, and other appropriate persons may participate as committee members to review the results of the comprehensive evaluation. The committee reviews all pertinent information, referrals, tests, records, observations, and reports. Again, it is especially important for parents or guardians to be contacted and informed and encouraged to participate on the committee.

Placement Recommendations
After reviewing all relevant diagnostic evaluation and assessment information and results, the committee makes a placement recommendation. The parents or guardians must be informed in writing of the committee's placement recommendations and must be given a description of the program, instruction, and support services to be provided in the proposed placement. The parents or guardians may agree with or refuse the placement recommendation. School officials should make the parents or guardians aware of their rights to review all evaluation information, records, and results and inform them of the appeal procedure if they disagree with the recommended placement. The student's parents or guardians also may furnish additional information or request a community agency to conduct a separate evaluation for further committee review, which could affect placement.

Parents' or Guardians' Alternatives
Upon reviewing placement recommendations, parents or guardians may agree with and provide their written permission for placement, or they may disagree with the identification and placement decision. If they agree with the recommended placement, the student is placed in an appropriate special education program and by law will receive an individualized education program (IEP), be placed in the least restrictive environment, and receive the necessary instructional and support services within 30 days of placement. If the parents or

guardians disagree with the committee's recommendations, they may request an independent evaluation followed by committee review of the evaluation results and discuss appropriate placement based on the results. The parents or guardians may accept or refuse the recommended placement and make further appeals.

Appeal Process

The appeal process requires an additional review by a different committee or, possibly, by litigation (court of law). The recommendation or decision made in an appeal is binding on both the school and the parents or guardians. In either case, students with disabilities should be evaluated formatively to determine appropriate identification, assessment, and eventual placement and to verify that students are receiving the necessary instruction and support services to succeed in their educational programs (Sarkees & Scott, 1985).

Role of Vocational Education

Public Law 98-524 (Carl D. Perkins Vocational Education Act of 1984) and its rules and regulations for implementation have adopted the definitions and guidelines of Public Law 94-142 for identifying students with disabilities. Frequently, these students have been identified in the primary elementary grades and, therefore, are mainstreamed into vocational education (e.g., grades 9 through 12) already identified as having a handicapping condition. However, sometimes vocational teachers are unaware of the presence of handicapped learners in their programs. This is especially true in the case of students with mild disabilities (e.g., educable mentally handicapped and learning disabled students). Sometimes teachers become aware of disabilities only after students experience functional learning problems in their vocational programs.

The identification process in vocational education commonly begins with a referral to special education by a vocational teacher of a student suspected of having special needs in his or her vocational program. Prior to referral, vocational teachers should carefully observe and document learner characteristics, specific behaviors, achievement, and other factors useful to persons responsible (e.g., special educator or guidance counselor) for making referrals in the evaluation process. This information should be recorded on the official referral forms used by schools. Parents or guardians are then informed of the referral and should provide their written consent for their child to be evaluated. If parents or guardians give their permission to evaluate the learner, a committee (typically including the referring vocational teacher) is organized to collect and review pertinent information, such as observations, reports, test results, medical information, and any other appropriate information that will be used to determine appropriate placement, instruction, and support services needed by the student. Upon completing all evaluation activities, the committee reviews all pertinent information. The referring vocational teachers' participation in this review is very important. They should convey to committees the nature of the referral and discuss all critical observed characteristics, behaviors, and other relevant information. Decisions regarding placement, instruction, and services, if agreed on by all personnel, may recommend that a student remain in the vocational class or program with specified support services. At this point an IEP (including an individualized vocational education plan) should be updated or developed. The content of the IEP should assist vocational and special educators to work collaboratively in delivering the required instructional and support services to serve the learner with disabilities.

Role of Rehabilitation

The identification of disabled persons needing transition assistance in rehabilitation usually is initiated by a referral from special education, vocational education, or another employment-related agency. The identification process begins by determining client eligibility. Public Law 93–112 (Rehabilitation Act of 1975) defines a disabled or handicapped person as "any person who has a physical or mental impairment which substantially limits one or more major life activities, has record of such impairment, or is regarded as having such an impairment." The regulations governing Section 504 of the act state that the term *handicapped* includes those persons who have impairments or disabling conditions such as "speech, hearing, visual, and orthopedic impairments, cerebral palsy, epilepsy, muscular dystrophy, multiple sclerosis, cancer, diabetes, heart disease, mental retardation, emotional illness, and specific learning disabilities." The act also considers alcohol and drug addicted persons as disabled. When reviews of available testing, observations, reports, medical and other types of information, and additional evaluation by rehabilitation or other service providers suggest that an individual meets the eligibility criteria, he or she is nominated to receive rehabilitation services. This definition and these criteria are functional and relate directly to individuals' skills and abilities and the requirements of work environments.

Upon referral a client is interviewed by an intake person, who also reviews existing information and determines the need for additional testing or information to determine eligibility for rehabilitation services. Comprehensive vocational evaluation follows eligibility determination to identify further occupational interests, abilities, and aptitudes and to determine the need for specific rehabilitation services for qualified clients. Services may incude providing adaptive equipment, vocational guidance, wheelchairs, reader services for the blind, and interpreters for the deaf. Based on the results of comprehensive vocational evaluation efforts, an individualized work rehabilitation plan (IWRP) is developed that specifies the type(s) of vocational education or training to be received, such as vocational exploration, on-the-job training, work adjustment, or work evaluation. Clients are evaluated on an ongoing basis throughout their programs. When clients are ready, they may be placed into the competitive world of work.

Role of Employment and Training Programs

Employment and training programs such as the Job Training Partnership Act (JTPA) (P.L. 97–300) also contribute to the identification of persons with disabilities who require transition assistance. The act defines disability and related services eligibility as "any individual who has a physical or mental disability which for such an individual constitutes or results in a substantial handicap to employment." Disabled or handicapped persons, by this definition, may be identified and eligible for JTPA services according to the definition of economically disadvantaged if they meet the income requirements. Income requirements are based on individual rather than family income and, therefore, promote independence for disabled persons. Clients with disabilities are typically referred to JTPA personnel by vocational education, special education, rehabilitation, or other related agency personnel; referral is followed by an intake interview. If a potential client meets these criteria and is identified as having a disability, JTPA personnel review existing evaluation information and/or conduct a comprehensive vocational evaluation to assess the person's needs, interests, abilities, and aptitudes. After a committee reviews the comprehensive evaluation results, appropriate placement, instruction, and support services are recommended. Services such as on-the-job training, work adjustment, and remedial reading may be recommended. The person with the disability and the services provided are evaluated regularly. Clients are placed in competitive employment immediately with the required support services or when they are ready for the transition.

Role of General Education

General educators (teachers in content areas such as mathematics, English, physical education, art, music, and history) also can refer students in their classes who may have special needs. The referral, evaluation, and identification processes are similar to those described for vocational education. In addition, general educators may provide valuable input to special educators and vocational educators with respect to students' employment-related education needs. For example, mathematics and reading teachers may assist in providing suggestions when teaching and evaluating mathematics and reading skills necessary for success in vocational programs for identified disabled students.

Role of Social Service Agencies

People with disabilities are often referred to social service agencies for transition assistance by education and rehabilitation agencies. Organizations such as the Lions Club, Easter Seals, Goodwill Industries, and the United Way offer numerous services for disabled persons. Some agencies provide broad-based services whereas others serve persons with specific disabilities. Public or private, nonprofit social service agencies may provide services such as modified or adaptive equipment and materials, prosthetic devices, interpreters, job training programs, guidance and counseling, and assessment services. Social service agencies may have formal or informal working agreements with vocational education, special education, and rehabilitation in some states or locales.

ASSESSMENT

This section focuses on types of data and information that are necessary in conducting assessments for persons with disabilities who require transition assistance. Assessment strategies and procedures also are presented. Ability, achievement, aptitude, work behaviors, attitudes, interpersonal skills, and interest tests and inventories are described relative to their purposes, reliabilities, validities, uses, strengths, and limitations for diagnostic and prescriptive applications. Interagency collaboration and uses of assessment data and information are discussed relative to vocational programs. Emerging assessment strategies and procedures also are described and several models are presented.

Purpose

Vocational assessment, also known as vocational evaluation, has been defined and its purposes described from various perspectives. For example, the Vocational Assessment Committee of the National Association of Vocational Education Special Needs Personnel (Peterson, Madden, & Ley-Siemer, 1981) defined and identified the purposes of vocational assessment:

1. Help students change behaviors, improve their self-concept, and enhance their personal career development;
2. Provide information for use in developing individual career and vocational education plans; and
3. To provide recommendations concerning: (a) vocational training; (b) prevocational and independent life skills training; (c) job readiness and placement; (d) support services and related agency services; (e) student learning needs, teaching techniques, and curriculum modifications; and (f) academic course selection. (pp. 2–3)

The Division on Career Development of the Council for Exceptional Children (Sitlington et al., 1985) defined vocational (career) assessment as

a developmental process beginning at the elementary school level and continuing through adulthood. Career assessment is a broad term that includes "vocational assessment" or "vocational evaluation," much as career education encompasses vocational education. The career assessment process should be integrally related to all aspects of career education, including not only preparation for employment, but also preparation for the roles of productive family member, citizen, and participant in leisure, recreational, and avocational activities that are of benefit to oneself or others. (p. 3)

The Vocational Evaluation and Work Adjustment Association (1975) defined vocational assessment (evaluation) as

a comprehensive process that systematically utilizes work, real or simulated, as the focal point of assessment and vocational exploration, the purpose of which is to assist individuals in vocational development. Vocational evaluation incorporates medical, psychological, social, vocational, educational, cultural, and economic data in the attainment of the goals of the evaluation process. (p. 86)

Vocational assessment also has been defined as "a holistic approach which considers an individual's total career development . . . [whose purpose] is to collect and provide objective career information for parents, educators, the student, and others to use in planning appropriate educational experiences to enhance the student's employability" (Peterson & Hill, 1982, p. 1).

Vocational assessment (Dahl, Appleby, & Lipe, 1978) may be perceived as

a comprehensive process conducted over a period of time, involving a multidisciplinary team approach, with the purpose of identifying individual characteristics, and education, training, and placement needs, which provides the educators the basis for planning an individual's program and which provides the individual with insight into his or her vocational potential. (p. 103)

The vocational assessment process also has been described as having five chronological phases or functions that utilize various procedures and instrumentation appropriate to the assessment of learners with disabilities: (1) screening, (2) program placement, (3) program planning, (4) monitoring of individual progress, and (5) individual student program evaluation. These purposes or functions focus on identifying appropriate vocational curriculum, specifying support services, identifying necessary program modifications and adaptations, prescribing changes in support services; and evaluating instructional and support services (Cobb, 1983, 1985; Cobb & Larkin, 1985; Salvia & Ysseldyke, 1978).

The major purpose of assessment is, therefore, to identify the vocational potential, needs, functional abilities, aptitudes, achievements, interests, skills, and knowledge of persons relative to the functional skills and knowledge required in vocational programs and occupations. The vocational assessment process generally involves identification of students, referral, interview, behavioral observations (orientation, work samples, psychometric testing, situational assessment, feedback conferences, and other methods), reports, conferences, implementation of recommendations, and follow-up (Leconte, 1985). Reliable, valid, and pertinent assessment data and information can be very useful in helping to identify individual students' personal needs, learning styles and characteristics, education and training needs, career aspirations, need for support services, and appropriate placement alternatives. Vocational assessment results should facilitate individualized education planning; suggest program modifications and adaptations; assist in guidance and counseling; and provide a base on which vocational education, special education, and related agencies can work collaboratively to educate learners with disabilities in vocational programs. In addition, vocational assessment enhances efforts to improve persons' self-concept and self-confidence and provides suggestions for teaching methods (Leconte, 1985).

Vocational assessment, therefore, is an ongoing process of collecting information regarding persons' functional learning strengths and limitations and using the information to suggest prescriptions and interventions with respect to the functional learning requirements of vocational programs and the world of work (Mori, 1982; Peterson, 1985; Roberts et al., 1983; Sitlington & Wimmer, 1978). Hence, vocational assessment should not be viewed as a screening device for vocational programs. Assessment should begin before and continue after placement into a vocational program.

Types of Assessment Data and Information

An important part of the vocational assessment process is the development of learner profiles, which are charts or lists that describe the skills and attributes of learners with individual special needs. These profiles should contain data and information in the following areas: (1) academic, (2) psychological, (3) psychomotor, (4) medical, (5) social, and (6) vocational. Information in these areas may be gleaned from several sources:

1. Referrals and reports (e.g., by teacher, counselor, and social service agency; anecdotal; home visitation)
2. Records (e.g., attendance, achievement, student profiles, academic, and medical)
3. Observations (e.g., by teacher, counselor, supervisor, employer, and psychologist)
4. Communications (e.g., from parent, teacher, employer, and supervisor)
5. Evaluations (e.g., professional, vocational, skill performance, diagnostic assessment, learning prescriptions)
6. Interviews
7. Conferences

All relevant existing information and data should be included in learner profiles and be used during vocational assessment processes. Information obtained during vocational assessment also should be added to these profiles.

Academic

The academic component of a learner profile includes skills in areas such as mathematics, communications (e.g., grammar, reading, writing, spelling, listening, and speaking), reasoning (e.g., problem solving, planning, and verbal skills), perceptual skills, and cognitive skills. The common indexes are achievement measures that yield test scores, ratings, and observations. Transcripts, reports, and records may provide useful information to help determine the need for additional vocational assessment and support services, program modifications and adaptations, and appropriate placements. Academic information can be especially helpful if it relates to the vocational curriculum and is drawn from assessment procedures designed to identify the functional learning strengths and problems of learners with disabilities.

Medical

The medical component of learner profiles is useful for determining the person's general health, especially as it relates to vocational programming or work environments. Medical information contained in these profiles may be obtained from general medical examinations, medical tests, medical history reports, or vision and hearing tests. Tactile (touch) and olfactory (smell) sensory tests also may be needed. Medical information is helpful in determining the need for making adjustments in programs or jobs for persons with medical problems. For example, teachers and employers need to know if a person is taking prescribed medication and its possible effects on the person's job performance, interpersonal relations, and emotional stability. These considerations are especially important when clients are working around potentially dangerous facilities, equipment, and materials.

Psychological

The psychological component of learner profiles may contain information regarding the abilities, aptitudes, or behaviors of students. Psychological information and data may be obtained from intelligence tests, aptitude tests, or adaptive behavior measures. Psychological tests are usually administered by specialists such as psychologists, psychometrists, or counselors and often yield information that group students into discrete categories and suggest potential special needs. They may, however, have limited usefulness for functional diagnostic prescriptive purposes in vocational and employment settings.

Psychomotor

The psychomotor component of learner profiles relates to the physical attributes of persons relative to the physical requirements of various vocational programs and occupations. Physical attributes or skills may include mobility, endurance, strength, fine motor skills (e.g., manual and finger dexterity and eye-hand coordination), and gross motor skills (e.g., lifting, reaching, climbing, standing, twisting, jumping, kneeling, bending, stooping, pushing, and pulling). Physical attributes may be measured by standardized tests or observations. Psychomotor information indicates physical strengths and physical disabilities. The information can be useful in planning for and prescribing program placements or occupational modifications or adaptations necessary for persons to perform successfully.

Social
The social component of learner profiles involves interpersonal relations skills that are important in society as well as those that are important in vocational programs and occupations. Social skills include those skills that relate to work behaviors, habits, and attitudes; social interaction; safety; cooperation; relationships with others (e.g., peers and authority figures); coping skills; independence; maturity; loyalty; motivation; self-control; responsibility; personal hygiene; conformity; and sensitivity. Social information is typically obtained through observations, reports, interviews, and ratings.

Vocational
The vocational component of learner profiles focuses on vocational awareness, orientation, exploration, preparation, and employment experiences. It also includes prevocational (e.g., work adjustment) experiences and vocational interest information. Information may be available or obtained from vocational aptitude tests, work samples, job tryouts, laboratory work projects, situational assessments, interest surveys, interviews, work experiences, previous vocational classes or programs, knowledge tests, student self-reports, and teachers' reports. Vocational information should be helpful in assisting clients to make career-oriented decisions.

Assessment Strategies and Procedures

Several kinds of assessment strategies and procedures may be used to collect data and information in the vocational assessment process. Psychometric tests, work samples, curriculum-based assessments, computer-assisted assessments, and community-based assessments represent sources that typically use tests, ratings, inventories, critical incidents, interviews, and hands-on methods to collect appropriate assessment information. Assessment strategies and procedures are commonly used to measure and identify the abilities, achievements, aptitudes, and interests of persons with disabilities who need transition assistance. Similar information can be helpful in determining appropriate vocational placements and needed support services for individual persons.

Psychometric Tests
Psychometric procedures and strategies have been used traditionally for testing small or large groups of persons on a particular trait or series of traits. Many

of the available instruments are norm- rather than criterion-referenced and have been developed in the field of psychology. Psychometric tests have been used to measure or assess ability, achievement, aptitude, interest, personality, and social traits. Tests typically include objective, closed-type items (e.g., correct-incorrect answers) but may also include subjective, open-ended items, depending on the traits being measured.

Psychometric assessment methods have several clear strengths or advantages in comparison to other assessment methods. For example, because psychometric tests are quantitative, it is usually easier to estimate their reliability and validity with respect to the trait(s) to be measured. In addition, administrative procedures are typically standardized, which permits data collection from large groups in a short time and increases precision of measurement and reduces the possibility of measurement error. Although psychometric tests are commonly administered by trained specialists (e.g., psychologists) and are administered easily and interpreted efficiently, they are relatively expensive and time consuming. Assuming sufficient reliability and validity, psychometric tests are objective measures and can be used to make decisions regarding some programmatic recommendations. Psychometric measures, however, should not be used as the only source of information for making programmatic decisions for individuals.

Psychometric tests have several disadvantages or limitations regarding their use in vocational programs. For example, they tend to focus on large groups and students' relative position in a "normal" population rather than on individual functional learning problems and strengths. Individual psychometric tests may have questionable reliability and validity with respect to the purpose for which the results will be interpreted and used. In addition, psychometric tests often have limited functional diagnostic usefulness because of low content validity and limited prescriptive value. The results and information obtained from psychometric tests, therefore, may have limited utility in instructional planning, implementation, and evaluation. Table 4.1 presents several types of psychometric tests.

Work Samples
Work samples are vocational assessment strategies that simulate actual jobs or tasks and focus on practical hands-on performance skills. They use the tools, equipment, and materials utilized in the job. Work sample strategies can yield helpful assessment information because actual work behaviors may be observed objectively. Vocational potential and functional strengths and limitations such as psychomotor skills, work behaviors and attitudes, interpersonal relations, and communications skills can be identified and diagnosed. Vocational or occupational goals and objectives and alternative program placements can be identified by using work samples. Work samples also may help promote a person's self-esteem, motivation, attitudes, and interests regarding careers and occupations. In addition, the information provided by work sam-

TABLE 4.1. TYPES OF PSYCHOMETRIC TESTS

Ability	Achievement	Aptitude	Interest	Personality	Social
Culture Fair Tests	Adult Basic Learning Examination (ABLE)	Adaptability Test	California Picture Interest Inventory	California Psychological Inventory	AAMD Adaptive Behavior Scales
Gates MacGintie Reading Test	Basic Skills in Arithmetic Test	Appraisal of Occupational Aptitudes	Career Assessment Inventory (CAI)	California Test of Personality	Adjustment Inventory
Haptic Intelligence Scale for Adult Blind	Brigance Diagnostic Inventory of Essential Skills	Bennett Hand Tool Dexterity Test (Bennett)	Career Awareness Laboratory	Career Maturity Inventory	Money Problem Checklist
MacQuarie Test for Mechanical Ability	California Achievement Test (CAT)	Bennett Mechancial Comprehension Test (BMCT)	Career Occupational Preference Interest Inventory (COPS)	Edwards Personal Preference Schedule	Social and Prevocational Information Battery (SPIB)
Otis Lennon Mental Ability Test Advanced Level (Otis-Lennon)	Key Math Test Metropolitan Achievement Test (MAT)	Career Ability Placement Survey (CAPS)	Geist Picture Interest Inventory–Revised (GPII–R)	Minnesota Multiphasic Personality Inventory (MMPI)	Vineland Social Maturity Scale
Otis-Quick Scoring Mental Ability Test	Nelson-Denny Reading Test	Computer Operator Aptitude Battery (COAB)	Gordon Occupational Checklist	Rotter Incomplete Sentence Blank	
Peabody Picture Vocabulary Test (PPVT)	Peabody Individual Achievement Test (PIAT)	Computer Programmer Aptitude Battery (CPAB)	Interest Checklist (ICL)	Sixteen Personality Test	
Raven's Standard Progressive Matrices (SPM)	Test of Adult Basic Education	Crawford Small Parts Dexterity Test (Crawford)	Kuder General Interest Survey (Form DD)		
Revised Beta Examination, 2nd Ed. (BETA)	Wide Range Achievement Test–Revised (WRAT–R)	Differential Aptitude Test (DAT)	Kuder Preference Record		
Slosson Intelligence Test (SIT)	Woodock Reading Mastery Tests (Woodcock)	Flannigan Aptitude Clarification Tests (FACT)	Minnesota Importance Questionnaire (MIQ)		
			Minnesota Vocational Interest Inventory (MVII)		

Stanford-Binet Intelligence Test (SIT)

Wechsler Adult Intelligence Scale–Revised (WAIS–R)

Wechsler Intelligence Scale for Children–Revised (WISC–R)

General Aptitude Test Battery (GATB)

General Clerical Test

Lincoln-Oseretsky Motor Development

McDonald Vocational Capacity Scale

Minnesota Rate of Manipulation Tests (MRMT)

Minnesota Spatial Relations Test

Nonreading Aptitude Test Battery (NATB)

O'Connor Finger and Tweezer Dexterity Tests

Office Skills Test

Pennsylvania Bimanual Work Sample

Personnel Test for Industry-Oral Directions Test (PTI-ODT)

Occupational Interest Inventory (OII)

Ohio Vocational Interest Survey

Picture Interest Exploratory Survey (PIES)

Picture Interest Inventory (PII)

Program for Assessing Youth Employability Skills (PAYES)

Reading-Free Vocational Interest Inventory–Revised (RFVII)

Self-Directed Search (SDS)

Singer/Graflex Pictorial Interest Screening

Strong Campbell Interest Inventory (SCII)

Strong Vocational Interest Blank (SVIB)

Vocational Interest

TABLE 4.1. TYPES OF PSYCHOMETRIC TESTS

Ability	Achievement	Aptitude	Interest	Personality	Social
		Purdue Pegboard	Inventory (VII)		
		Purdue Perceptual Motor Dexterity	Vocational Interest and Sophistication Assessment Survey		
		Revised Minnesota Paper Form Board Test (R–MPFB)	Wide Range Interest Opinion Test (WRIOT)		
		San Francisco Vocational Competency Scale			
		Short Employment Test (SET)			
		Short Tests of Clerical Ability			
		SRA Clerical Aptitudes			
		SRA Pictorial Reasoning Test (PRT)			
		SRA Test of Mechanical Concepts			
		Stromberg Dexterity Test			
		Typing Test for Business			

ples is helpful when providing career guidance and counseling, writing occupational objectives, identifying appropriate placements, prescribing necessary program modifications and adaptations, and specifying essential support services. Successful use of commercial work samples depends on each student's readiness for assessment method and content, usability for teachers and other personnel, coordination of assessment goals among personnel, continuous coordinated instructional and counseling services, and information relevant for making cost-effective and cost-beneficial vocational exploration or transition preparation decisions (Botterbusch, 1982).

Although work samples have several advantages, they also have some potential disadvantages. For example, they require a considerable amount of time and specialists to administer; they may oversimplify complex tests so as to make them unrepresentative of the jobs sampled. Work samples usually require a considerable amount of training time to be effectively administered. They also may produce information of questionable or limited reliability and validity. The norms developed for work samples may be unrelated to the specific population being evaluated. For instance, norms may be available for learning disabled but not for physically disabled persons. In addition, work samples are relatively expensive.

Work samples should allow for differences in experience among persons and permit repeated trials for persons having difficulties. Persons using work samples should understand the directions and tasks to be completed. In addition, personnel reviewing work samples should evaluate them by using the following criteria and guidelines: (1) development, (2) organization, (3) physical aspects, (4) work evaluation process, (5) administration, (6) reliability and validity, (7) scoring and norms, (8) observation of clients, (9) reporting, (10) utility, (11) training in the system, (12) technical considerations, and (13) cost (Botterbusch, 1982).

Work samples may be project- or product-oriented. They may use audiovisuals to illustrate jobs, tools, equipment, and materials. Step-by-step procedures may be provided to help explain how to complete the activity or product. A client's performance is observed; recorded; and commonly evaluated for quality, accuracy, and speed. Self-report evaluations are also sometimes used.

In summary, work samples, whether formal (commercial) or informal (locally developed), should be selected or developed with respect to the philosophy, purpose, and conceptual framework of vocational assessment at the state and/or local level. Further, work samples should relate to the context and content of vocational programs and the needs of the local job market and be representative of the full range of jobs in the community. In addition, work samples should be practical, reliable, and valid for individual persons with disabilities. Users should ensure that work samples selected for use are appropriately adapted for persons with disabilities in regard to their assumptions about the attainment of basic (academic) skills, the assessment environment, and allowances for unexpected difficulties incurred during administration. Table 4.2 lists several types of commercial work samples.

Curriculum-Based Assessment

Curriculum-based vocational assessment, which takes place in vocational, special, and content-related education programs, may be more practical, less time consuming, and less expensive than other assessment methods (Cobb, 1983; Phelps & McCarty, 1984; Posey, 1982; Sitlington, 1979; Stodden, 1980, 1981). Procedures used in vocational samples and vocational exploration curriculum-based assessment activities may be used in place of, or in addition to, other types of vocational assessment methods.

Vocational Samples. Vocational samples are informal work samples developed and validated in local vocational programs. They closely resemble the content in local vocational programs and the requirements and expectatons of jobs in local labor markets. Vocational samples are typically developed collaboratively by vocational education, special education, and rehabilitation personnel. They are usually inexpensive to develop and administer and use the actual materials,

TABLE 4.2. TYPES OF WORK SAMPLES

APTICOM	Prep Work Samples	Valpar Component Work Sample Series (VALPAR)
Comprehensive Occupational Assessment and Training System (COATS)	Pre-Vocational Readiness Battery (Valpar 17)	Vocational Information and Evaluation Work Samples (VIEWS)
Hester Evaluation System (HES)	Singer/Graflex Vocational Evaluation System (Singer)	Vocational Interest, Temperament, and Aptitude System (VITAS)
Jewish Employment and Vocational Services (JEVS) Work Sample System	Systematic Approach to Vocational Education (SAVE)	Vocational Skills Assessment and Development Program (Brodhead-Garrett)
McCarron-Dial Work Evaluation System (McCarron-Dial or MDS)	System for Assessment and Group Evaluation (SAGE)	Wide-Range Employment Sample Test (WREST)
MESA	Talent Assessment Programs (TAP)	Work Skill Development Package (WSD)
Micro-TOWER	Test, Orientation, and Work Evaluation in Rehabilitation (TOWER)	
Occupational Assessment/Evaluation System (OAES)		

tools, equipment, and facilities used in local vocational programs. Vocational samples may include actual program activities, tasks, or projects; local job skills; and required skill proficiencies and performance.

Vocational education, special education, and rehabilitation personnel should work collaboratively in developing, implementing, and evaluating vocational samples. They need to identify their roles and responsibilities and assign activities to be completed. First, personnel need to conduct a survey and examination of local vocational program curricula and the local job market. Considering variables such as occupational supply and demand, resources, and occupational interests, personnel should decide which programs, courses, or classes will be chosen for developing vocational samples. Second, personnel should analyze the chosen programs regarding the tasks, skills, and knowledge from which vocational samples will be developed. Third, as personnel develop vocational samples they should consider the following: (1) purpose and objectives; (2) procedures; (3) prerequisite skills; (4) materials, tools, equipment, and facilities; (5) work conditions and environment; (6) administration and demonstration procedures; (7) evaluation criteria; and (8) scoring criteria (e.g., work habits, quality, quantity, and speed) (Sarkees & Scott, 1985). Vocational instructors should review the entire vocational sample and procedures before their initial use. The work sample can then be tested and subsequently revised as necessary. Vocational samples are advantageous since they allow for a range of career exploration experiences and permit clients to evaluate their interest, attitudes, and work behaviors and to identify functional abilities, aptitudes, and problems. Vocational samples are inherently motivational because they are practical and relate directly to the skills and abilities required in vocational programs and occupations. Vocational samples may also be administered formatively or summatively in vocational programs.

Vocational Exploration. Vocational exploration assessment provides opportunities to try out components of different vocational programs. Evaluations may include observations and performance checklists. Vocational exploration placements are usually determined from existing assessment information from interest surveys, tests, and classes. Vocational exploration experiences are helpful for determining ultimate vocational placements. Vocational education, special education, and/or rehabilitation personnel should work cooperatively in planning, implementing, and evaluating exploration experiences. Vocational teachers work directly with the student being assessed in regular class or program activities. Vocational exploration as an assessment strategy has several benefits. For example, the assessment environment is essentially the same as the program environment. Therefore, the person's motivation, interest, expectations, and self-esteem may be enhanced. Also, instructional planning, communication, and assessment among the student, vocational teacher, and other personnel can be initiated.

Situational Assessment

Situational assessment attempts to evaluate general work skills rather than job-specific skills and occurs in education, rehabilitation, or employment and training environments. Assessment activities may involve real or simulated jobs or work tasks in simulated or actual job environments. In some local settings there may be a limited number of jobs available. In such cases, situational assessment can involve work experiences in groups rather than individual evaluations in various work settings. Skill performance levels are evaluated by using behavioral observations in areas such as work behaviors, interpersonal relations, and communications skills. When testing is conducted in groups, administrators should ensure that peers do not affect negatively a person's performance levels.

Observational assessment methods are especially appropriate measurement techniques to identify instructional goals and objectives, determine behavior baselines, compare workers, and identify appropriate placements (Glasecoe & Levy, 1985). Observations, however, tend to be subjective, and their reliability and validity depend on well-trained personnel who observe, record, and interpret work behaviors. Ratings and performance checklists are typically used to observe, record, and evaluate behaviors. Personnel from various agencies may be involved cooperatively in situational assessment. Situational assessment may occur in simulated education settings, rehabilitation workshops, institutional industries, and work activity centers.

Several benefits or advantages are associated with situational assessment. For example, meaningful work samples provide real or simulated work activities in natural work settings, which help promote interest and motivation. Jobs or tasks encountered, therefore, should include skilled jobs and provide a sufficient degree of challenge. Situational assessment allows multiple evaluations in a wide range of work settings, situations, behaviors, and conditions. Vocational and essential interpersonal relations, communications, and reasoning skills can be observed. Situational assessment activities often are more efficient (require less time), are easily administered, and cost less than other assessment strategies. Work adjustment, modifications, and adaptations can be made relatively easily when necessary. In addition, stress related to traditional testing techniques may be reduced or eliminated.

Community-Based Assessment

Labor Market Survey. The purpose of a labor market survey is to collect information regarding employment opportunities, the number of job vacancies, job skill requirements, working conditions, salaries, and education and training requirements. Labor market surveys are especially helpful in collecting job analysis information. Personnel may use mail or telephone surveys, observations, or personal interviews to collect data. The scope of a survey and the amount of time consumed will depend largely on the prevalence of businesses and industries in the community. Initially, personnel should locate existing businesses and industries by using local sources such as the telephone directory, chamber of commerce, civic organizations, business organizations, government agencies, advisory committees, economic development councils, and labor organizations.

Job Analysis. Job analysis is a practical community-based assessment method used in vocational programs. The purpose of job analysis is to analyze specific jobs in the local community in terms of (1) job requirements and expectations, (2) job procedures, (3) job environments, and (4) job purposes. The results of job analysis have several practical applications. For example, information can be used to develop instructional objectives, develop work samples, develop vocational curricula, identify community resources and sources of further information, and specify support services needed for individual persons. The same knowledge, skills, and standards identified in job analysis should be adopted in assessment activities in vocational programs. Following job analysis, personnel should develop appropriate assessment strategies for using job analysis information. Rating scales, observation forms, and performance checklists are possible assessment applications. Major advantages of job analysis are that it occurs in the local community, reflects the local labor market, identifies real skill requirements, and can be adapted for the range of persons with disabilities. Job analysis is a practical strategy used in community-based assessment for personnel in vocational education, special education, rehabilitation, employment and training, and other related agencies.

DICTIONARY OF OCCUPATIONAL TITLES   The *Dictionary of Occupational Titles* (DOT) is an index or inventory of occupations and jobs and is developed and published through the U.S. Department of Labor (1977). The DOT specifies the performance (knowledge, physical, and skill) requirements and environmental (working) conditions for specific jobs and the relationships among occupations and jobs. Information in the DOT was collected from more than 75,000 on-site job analyses.

The DOT contains information regarding job duties and related information for 20,000 occupations. Each title contains information regarding job purpose, job description, job requirements, job procedure, job environment, worker functions, job industry location, and alternative job titles. The DOT also contains a nine-digit classification system that includes the Occupational Group Arrangement Code and a Worker Trait Arrangement number. The first three digits indicate the field of work: (1) category (first digit), (2) division (second digit), and (3) group (third digit). The nine primary occupational categories are:

0/1 Professional, Technical, and Managerial Occupations
  2 Clerical and Sales Occupations
  3 Service Occupations

4 Agricultural, Farming, Fishery, Forestry, and Related Occupations
5 Processing Occupations
6 Machine Trades Occupations
7 Bench Work Occupations
8 Situational Work Occupations
9 Miscellaneous Occupations (pp. xvi-xvii)

The Worker Trait Arrangement, which is represented by the middle three digits of the code number, specify the extent to which a worker functions in relation to data (fourth digit), people (fifth digit), and things (sixth digit). The higher the number the less complex is a worker function in terms of responsibility and judgment. Similarly, the lower the number the more complex is a worker function. The last three digits indicate the order of titles within six-digit code groups and distinguish one occupation from all others. The nine digits, therefore, give each occupation a unique code. The DOT has several practical assessment applications. It can be used by vocational personnel in writing instructional and training objectives, developing education and work plans, developing work samples, and conducting a job analysis and interest assessment. In addition, the DOT may be used in job placement to assist in matching job requirements and workers' skills.

DICTIONARY OF WORKER TRAITS The *Dictionary of Worker Traits* (DWT) provides information regarding required characteristics of workers in various occupations (Kerns & Neeley, 1987). The worker characteristics in the two-volume DWT are called worker traits in the DOT and include (1) aptitude, (2) interests, (3) temperament, (4) physical demands, (5) environmental conditions, (6) general educational development (GED), and (7) specific vocational preparation (SVP). The DWT provides ratings of all occupations or jobs listed in the DOT and uses current occupational data from the Department of Labor. Occupational ratings are referenced by Worker Trait Groups, which cluster occupations with similar worker functions and activities as in the DOT.

Occupations are listed in Worker Trait Groups in ascending order of DOT codes in the Worker Traits arrangement of Titles and Codes. Each Worker Trait Group includes (1) description of occupations, (2) Qualifications Profile (frequencies and percentages of occupations in the group that are rated at each level of each Worker Trait), (3) frequencies and percentages of occupations in the groups with each worker function number, and (4) frequencies and percentages of Guide for Occupational Exploration work groups and subgroups represented by occupations in the Worker Trait Group (p. x). The DWT has several practical uses, such as job placement, curriculum development, vocational assessment, career guidance and counseling, and individualized educational planning.

ENCYCLOPEDIA OF CAREERS AND VOCATIONAL GUIDANCE The three-volume *Encyclopedia of Careers and Vocational Guidance* identifies occupations with a code number based on the DOT (Hopke, 1984). It contains occupational information pertaining to (1) career planning, (2) future world of work, (3) test results in career planning, (4) finding a job, (5) career opportunities, and (6) specific occupational information (nature of the work, education and special requirements, history, methods of entry, advancement, employment outlook, earnings, working conditions, social and psychological factors, and sources of further information). Over 900 occupations and related occupations are listed, defined, and described, each having a DOT number. Occupational data and information were obtained from personnel in government, education, business and industry, and specialized fields. The encyclopedia is especially appropriate in career guidance and vocational planning, as well as in curriculum and assessment activities.

GUIDE FOR OCCUPATIONAL EXPLORATION The purpose of the *Guide for Occupational Exploration* (GOE) is to provide information regarding the work activities, skills and abilities, physical demands, work settings, preparation, licenses or certificates, and sources of information about occupations (Harrington & O'Shea, 1984). The guide organizes the occupations listed in the DOT into 12 interest areas (artistic, scientific, plants and animals, protective, mechanical, industrial, business detail, selling, accommodating, humanitarian, leading-influencing, physical performing), 66 work groups, and 348 subgroups. This section of the GOE is called "Information About the World of Work." The GOE also lists for each work group work values, leisure and home activities, skills, abilities, and school subjects related to occupations; this section is entitled "Information About the Person Making Career Decisions." The GOE, therefore, provides information that permits a person to relate and compare his or her interests, skills, aptitudes, and values with the requirements of a job or occupation. The GOE is particularly useful in career guidance, vocational exploration, and job placement activities.

OCCUPATIONAL OUTLOOK HANDBOOK The Occupational Outlook Handbook (OOH) provides detailed information regarding 200 occupations, which represent three out of every five jobs; another 200 jobs are listed, which represent 20 percent of all jobs in the economy (U.S. Department of Labor, 1986). The Bureau of Labor Statistics in the U.S. Department of Labor collects occupational and employment data and information. Occupations are grouped or clustered according to the 1980 *Standard Occupational Classification Manual* and include

- Technicians and related occupations
- Professional specialty occupations
- Construction occupations
- Mechanics and repairers
- Transportation and material moving occupations

- Management support occupations
- Marketing and sales occupations
- Service occupations
- Administrative support occupations, including clerical
- Extractive occupations
- Agricultural, forestry, and fishery occupations
- Production occupations
- Managers and administrators
- Handlers, equipment cleaners, helpers, and laborers

The OOH contains the following information regarding each job:

- Nature of work
- Working conditions
- Employment
- Training, other qualifications, and advancement
- Job outlook
- Earnings
- Related occupations
- Source of additional information

Each occupation listed has a DOT code. The OOH can be useful for identifying career interests, curriculum development, and job placement activities.

V-TECS CURRICULUM A major source of vocational curriculum related to job requirements is the Vocational-Technical Education Consortium of States (V-TECS) catalogs. Over 140 V-TECS catalogs provide job descriptions and specify the technical or psychomotor requirements of more than 350 job titles listed in the DOT. The catalogs are practical and include more than 23,000 worker tasks gleaned from more than 16,000 workers on the job. Each catalog contains a table of contents, glossary, development process review, and performance objectives. Each performance objective contains the following information: (1) duty, (2) task, (3) standard of performance, (4) conditions for performance, (5) source for standard, (5) performance guide, and (6) appendixes. Further information regarding V-TECS may be obtained from Vocational-Technical Education Consortium of States, 795 Peachtree Street, N.E., Atlanta, Georgia 30365.

Emerging Assessment Strategies and Procedures

Vocational assessment has traditionally focused on diagnosis of specific abilities, aptitudes, and achievements for the purpose of determining placement into specific programs. Assessment results have often had limited prescriptive and instructional uses. However, increasingly, assessment strategies and procedures that identify the functional learning strengths and problems of persons are being utilized in vocational education, special education, rehabilitation, and employment and training programs. Functional assessment methods are practical because they are usually based on vocational curriculum and occupational requirements. Functional assessments provide diagnosis as well as prescriptions necessary for identifying the appropriate instructional interventions and support services for individuals. In addition, functional assessments provide information useful in developing individualized education plans and specifying needed program modifications and adaptations. A sample of emerging assessment strategies and procedures is presented later.

Generalizable Skills

Generalizable skills are cognitive, affective, or psychomotor skills that are basic to, necessary for success in, and transferable within and across vocational programs and occupations (Greenan, 1983a, 1983b). Generalizable skills are functional and important because they are common vocational curriculum components that facilitate learners' transition from vocational programs into the world of work or postsecondary education and training. Persons who possess generalizable skills should be able to adapt to changes in vocational programs, careers, occupations, or jobs, thereby enhancing their employability.

Generalizable skills curricula in vocational programs and occupations include the cognitive and affective learning domains. Mathematics, communications, interpersonal relations, and reasoning skills have been identified and validated as being generalizable in vocational programs and occupations (Greenan, 1983a). Table 4.3 presents the major skill areas of a generalizable

TABLE 4.3. GENERALIZABLE SKILLS CURRICULUM

Mathematics (28 skills)	Communications (27 skills)	Interpersonal Relations (20 skills)	Reasoning (40 skills)
Whole numbers (5 skills)	Words and meanings (9 skills)	Work behaviors (10 skills)	Verbal reasoning (16 skills)
Fractions (4 skills)	Reading (8 skills)	Instructional and supervisory conversations (6 skills)	Problem solving (10 skills)
Decimals (6 skills)	Writing (3 skills)		Planning (14 skills)
Percentages (2 skills)	Speaking (3 skills)	Social conversations (4 skills)	
Mixed operations (4 skills)	Listening (4 skills)		
Measurement and calculation (6 skills)			
Estimation (1 skill)			

skills curriculum. Psychomotor or technical skills tend to be occupationally specific.

Vocational education, special education, rehabilitation, and employment and training personnel should work collaboratively in examining and revising their vocational curricula to include generalizable skills instruction. Generalizable skills can be used in developing individualized education programs and vocational goals and objectives. Generalizable skills curricula should also be considered in activities related to vocational assessment, instructional planning, instructional resources, program modifications and adaptations and support services, and program evaluation.

Identifying a person's generalizable skills requires the use of functional assessment strategies and procedures. Assessment instruments should provide practical diagnostic information that allows personnel to develop learning prescriptions and identify necessary support services. Student self-ratings, teacher ratings, and performance measures have been developed, validated, and used to identify the generalizable skills of persons in vocational programs. Student self-ratings (SSR) and teacher ratings (TR) may use a combination of Likert-type scales and open-ended responses. Performance criterion measures may contain singular multiple formats such as closed (e.g., multiple-choice) items, open-ended items, and demonstrations.

Student self-ratings, TRs, and performance assessments tend to have a high degree of content and face validity. In addition, they possess a relatively high degree of reliability (internal consistency [$r > .82$], test-retest [$r > .60$], interrator) with respect to producing precise and stable measures. Standard errors of measurement for performance measures are usually low. Student self-ratings, TRs, and performance assessments are commonly reliable for males and females, different vocational programs, learners with different levels of achievement, and learners with various handicapping conditions. Also, they are capable of being adapted or modified for individuals' special needs. However, SSRs and TRs often do not correlate or agree with criterion measures. They may reflect an over- or underestimation of a learner's actual generalizable skills. Student self-ratings and TRs, therefore, may measure constructs other than the constructs they intend to measure. For example, SSRs may actually reflect learners' self-esteem, or TRs may be indicating teacher bias or some other variable(s). School personnel should be aware of this when using SSRs or TRs. Although these assessment strategies have potential for providing useful information, precaution should be taken for possible misinterpretations.

Student self-ratings, TRs, and performance assessments have several uses. For example, they may provide input into individualized education plans. Students and teachers can become more familiar with the skill requirements in vocational programs. In addition, these assessments can increase learners' and teachers' knowledge of students' functional learning strengths and problems. Further, SSRs assist students to become more actively involved in assessment processes and become more independent in their learning experiences. Student self-ratings, TRs, and performance assessments may be used throughout students' vocational programs: (1) upon entry, (2) formatively during the program, and (3) upon exiting the program. Assessment results of SSRs and TRs yield information that may be used in instructional planning, intervention, and evaluation activities. Several practical strategies, procedures, and resources are available to assist personnel in using SSRs and TRs for assessing the generalizable skills of students in vocational programs (Greenan & Jefferson, 1987; Greenan & McCabe, 1986, 1987; Greenan, Marton, & Powell, 1985; Greenan & Powell, 1984; Greenan, Powell, & Dunham, 1986; Greenan & Richard, 1985; Greenan, Winters, & Browning, 1987).

Minnesota Transition Model
The Minnesota Transition Model of Educational Adjustment is designed to enhance the transition of learners with special needs into, through, and out of (postsecondary) vocational programs and into the world of work (Brown, 1987) (see Figure 4.2). The focus of the model is on the identification of functional learning strengths and problems and the provision of the necessary in-

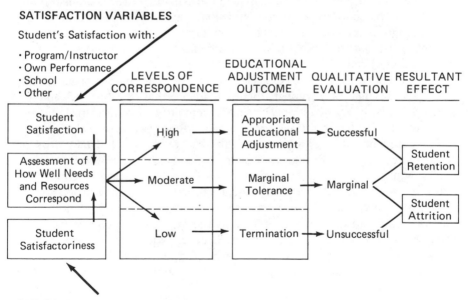

Figure 4.2 Model of Theory of Educational Adjustment

struction and support services for learners who need transition assistance to succeed in their vocational programs. The model suggests that regular assessment should occur to determine the degree of correspondence between the needs and resources of individual students and the resources and requirements of their vocational programs. Efforts to determine the extent to which learners and their vocational education environment correspond are based on the assumption that students and their programs interact to enhance or inhibit students' successes.

Accordingly, a set of instruments was developed and validated to assess the extent of students' vocational educational adjustment. The Student Satisfaction instrument is designed to measure students' degree of satisfaction with their vocational programs. Items contained in the instrument focus on attitudes regarding the students' instructors, education services provided by instructors, students' academic abilities, support services provided, students' interpersonal skills, and students' work behaviors and attitudes. The internal consistency reliability of the instrument is $\alpha = .92$. The Student Satisfactoriness instrument is intended to determine the degree of satisfactoriness of students in regard to the requirements of their vocational programs as measured by instructors' ratings. Items contained in the instrument focus on instructors' opinions or perceptions regarding students in areas of students' abilities to attain program-specific knowledge and skills, mathematics skills, communications skills, maturity, motivation, work behaviors, and attitudes. The internal consistency reliability of the instrument is $\alpha = .96$.

The theory of the model suggests that if each instrument produces high or positive ratings for a student, there is evidence that the student is likely to succeed in his or her vocational program. Similarly, if each instrument produces low or moderate ratings for a student, there is evidence that suggests that the student is likely to have difficulty succeeding in, and may drop out of his or her vocational program. Low ratings on either or both of the instruments require appropriate instructional and support services to "correct, circumvent, or compensate" for the student's functional learning problems. The relationship or correspondence between the Student Satisfaction and Student Satisfactoriness instruments, therefore, is the extent to which a student possesses vocational education adjustment. Learners with high degrees of vocational education adjustment are likely to succeed, and those students with low degrees of vocational education adjustment are unlikely to succeed in their vocational programs.

PLACEMENT

This section focuses on the placement of persons with disabilities needing transition assistance into educational programs. Career, as well as vocational development, is important in the transition through programs and services in vocational education, special education, rehabilitation, and employment and training programs. Career and vocational awareness, orientation, exploration, preparation, and placement experiences are essential for successful transition. The full array of programs, program delivery systems, and support services must be accessible to and equitable for persons with disabilities in least restrictive environments.

Career and Vocational Development

Career and vocational development includes five major phases: (1) awareness, (2) orientation, (3) exploration, (4) preparation, and (5) placement. Career and vocational development experiences assist the person with disabilities to relate what is learned to what is important in the world of work. For example, career and vocational development activities provide occupational information, guidance and counseling, job experiences, basic skills instruction, placement, and follow-up services. The fields of vocational education, special education, rehabilitation, and employment and training all deliver vocational program and support services along the career and vocational development continuum (see Figure 4.3).

Awareness
Career awareness occurs in the elementary grades. The major purpose of this phase is to provide learners with instruction and activities to enhance their awareness about occupations, jobs, and the roles people have in them. This phase also intends to provide opportunities for identifying career interests, self-awareness, and relationships to others. Learners may gain an understanding of the importance of work and development of a work ethic. Basic generalizable skills (e.g., reading, writing, and mathematics) as well as the interpersonal and social skills essential for transition are developed. In many instances, career and vocational development activities may be infused in the regular subject content areas (e.g., mathematics and reading). Activities also could occur in separate vocational classes taught by an industrial arts, agriculture, or other vocational teacher.

Orientation
Career orientation occurs in the junior high or middle school grades. The major purpose of this phase is to identify career interests further, try out the full range of occupations through hands-on experience, become familiar with work environments, and master the basic skills required in programs and occupations. Vocational orientation experiences (e.g., six-week laboratory in industrial arts or home economics) may be required for many students. For example, drafting, construction, manufacturing, and graphic arts may represent an industrial arts experience; and food preparation, textiles and clothing, child

		PROGRAM PHASES		Placement 13→
Awareness (K-6)	Orientation (7-9)	Exploration and Preparation (10-12)		World of Work or Continuing Education
General Education		General Education (Comprehensive High School)	Occupational Education (Area Vocational Center/ Comprehensive High School)	Prv/Pub Sect. Bus./Indus. Community Col.
Elementary	Junior High			

PROGRAM AREAS

Program Area	Awareness (K-6)	Orientation (7-9)	General Education (10-12)	Occupational Education (10-12)	World of Work
Agricultural Occupations	Infusion or Separate Class	Infusion, Gen. Labs, or Courses	Exploration • Horticulture • Conservation Co-op Education Work-Study Student Organizations	Skill Training • Production • Agricultural Mechanics Student Organizations	Employment • Veterinary Technology
Business and Marketing Occupations			Exploration • Typing • Business Law Co-op Education Work-Study Student Organizations	Skill Training • Secretarial • Accounting Student Organizations	Employment • Data Processing
Health Occupations			Exploration • Health Science • Human Anatomy Co-op Education Work-Study Student Organizations	Skill Training • Nurse Aide • Medical Records Student Organizations	Employment • Registered Nursing
Home Economics Occupation			Exploration • Family Living • Nutrition Co-op Education Work-Study Student Organizations	Skill Training • Food Preparation • Child Care Student Organizations	Employment • Child Development
Industrial Occupations		• Manufac- turing • Construction	Exploration • Electronics • Drafting Co-op Education Work-Study Student Organizations	Skill Training • Carpentry • Graphic Arts Student Organizations	Employment • Mechanical Technology

• Examples

Special Education
(Prevocational, Work Adjustment, Work Study)

Rehabilitation
(Training, Support Services)

Employment and Training
(Training, Support Services)

Figure 4.3 Career Vocational Program Areas and Phases

care, and nutrition may represent the content in a home economics experience. Career orientation activities also may take place in semester- or year-long classes or in regular content area programs. Career orientation experiences further develop the learner's interpersonal relations skills; self-concept; work experience; and economic, social, and personal values of work. They also provide the opportunity for acquiring positive work behaviors and knowledge about jobs and workers.

Career Exploration

Career exploration occurs in the high school grades. The major purpose of this phase is to provide learners with exploratory hands-on work experiences directly related to occupations and careers existing in the world of work. Exploration experiences allow the learner to exercise independence by making career choice decisions. Career exploration experiences assist students to define their career interests, goals, and work behaviors and values; relate learned skills to work requirements; and develop interpersonal relations skills. Students explore the use of the actual facilities, equipment, environment, materials, and requirements of specific occupations and jobs. The work situations may be real or simulated. Vocational guidance and counseling, prevocational and work adjustment, and vocational assessment services are appropriate in this phase. Learners should also develop self-reliance in their career planning. Occupational information, resources, and requirements regarding preparation programs and jobs are important. Industrial arts classes are an example of a general vocational career exploration program. Career exploration experiences are usually offered through vocational education classes in a comprehensive high school.

Career Preparation
Career preparation typically occurs in the high school grades. The major purpose of this phase is to provide the necessary instruction, support services, and work experiences in vocational programs for entry into the world of work or into postsecondary or adult education. Programs (e.g., carpentry, horticulture, foods and nutrition, secretarial, and nurse's aide) should provide instruction in cognitive (mathematics, communications, and reasoning), affective (interpersonal relations), and psychomotor (occupational or job-specific) skills. Career preparation permits students to practice their generalizable skills in contexts in which they are learning and in which they will apply them. Learners may confirm their occupational interests and assess their self-esteem in work situations. Instruction may occur in simulated environments or in actual work sites. Preparation experiences assist students to validate their values, occupational choices, and career goals and determine the need for additional occupational information. They also allow students to participate increasingly in career decision making and relate their occupational experiences to their personal life. Career and vocational preparation experiences are commonly offered in general high schools, comprehensive high schools, vocational high schools, and area vocational centers. Career preparation also may take place in special education, rehabilitation, and employment and training settings.

Placement
Career placement occurs at the end of high school and represents the first major transition from school to the world of work. The major purpose of this phase is to place students into the workforce or postsecondary or adult education. At this point students should have the necessary entry-level skills needed to acquire a job. Some on-the-job training or additional education may be necessary initially to obtain and maintain the job. Technical updating or

further education will probably be necessary to maintain and advance in the occupation or to change occupations or careers. Some students will not enter the world of work directly after high school graduation from vocational preparation programs. These experiences, however, will facilitate their entry into continuing education in settings such as community colleges, technical institutes, area vocational schools, or specialized vocational schools and will encourage them to seek vocational-technical certificates or two-year associate degrees. Other students may choose four-year university or college programs that are not "vocational" but for which vocational exploration and preparation were very appropriate. Systematic ongoing services such as follow-up and articulation are crucial for disabled persons to make the transition from school into the world of work.

Vocational Placement

Program Areas

Vocational education, special education, rehabilitation, and employment and training offer various program areas and program alternatives for persons with disabilities. The major vocational program areas are (1) agriculture, (2) business and marketing, (3) health occupations, (4) home economics, and (5) industry. These program areas contain numerous specific programs (see Table 4.4). Vocational programs may be delivered through comprehensive high schools, vocational high schools, area vocational or career centers, community colleges, technical institutes, specialized (public or private) vocational schools, rehabilitation centers, or business and industry. Vocational programs may prepare persons for careers within a broad array of occupations, a particular occupation, or job-specific training. Vocational instruction also may focus on task-specific training.

Methods of Service Delivery

Skill Training. Skill training vocational programs may occur during orientation, exploration, or preparation levels of instruction. They commonly focus on a specific occupational cluster or particular occupation. Skill training may involve a class (e.g., eight weeks or a semester) or a series of classes (e.g., one or two years), which make up a program. Skill training programs provide students with opportunities to acquire skills and knowledge relevant to the use of the equipment, tools, materials, processes, and facilities of specific occupations. Generalizable skills (e.g., interpersonal and reasoning skills) are also essential components of these programs. Students in orientation or exploration programs apply the skills and knowledge acquired to make decisions about entering preparation programs or for continuing education at the postsecondary level. Students in preparation programs acquire the entry-level skills and

TABLE 4.4. SAMPLE VOCATIONAL PROGRAM AREAS AND PROGRAMS

Agriculture	Business and Marketing	Health Occupations	Home Economics	Industrial
Business and Management	Accounting and Computing	Biomedical Equipment Technology	Chef/Cook	Aeronautical Technology
Forestry Conservation/Natural Resources	Advertising	Dental Assisting	Child Care	Aircraft Maintenance
Horticulture	Banking and Finance	Dental Hygiene	Child Development	Airline Piloting and Navigation
Mechanics	Business Administration and Management	Dental Lab Technology	Clothing/Textiles Management, Production, and Service	Appliance Repair
Processing	Business Computer and Console	Emergency Medical Technology	Consumer Education	Architecture Design
Production	Business Data Entry Equipment	Fire Control and Safety	Dietetic Assisting	Auto Body
Student Organizations	Business Data Peripheral Equipment	Health-Care Assisting	Family/Individual Health	Auto Mechanics
Future Farmers of America (FFA)	Business Data Processing Systems	Health Occupations	Family Living and Parenthood	Building Maintenance
	Clerical	Medical Assisting	Food Management, Production, and Service	Carpentry
	Computer Programming	Mental Health/Human Services	Food and Nutrition	Civil Technology
	Corrections/Criminal Justice	Medical Laboratory Technology	Home Management	Coal Mining Technology
	Entrepreneurship	Medical Records/Medical Records Technology	Hospitality (Travel and Travel Service)	Combine Metal Trades
	Executive Secretarial	Medical Secretarial	Hotel/Motel Management	Commercial Art
	Filing, Office Machines	Nurse Assisting	Housing, Home Furnishings, and Equipment	Commercial Photography
	General Merchandise (Sales)	Occupational Therapy Assisting	Institutional Management	Communications and Media Specialist
		Optometric Technology		Computer Technology
				Construction and Building Trades

TABLE 4.4. SAMPLE VOCATIONAL PROGRAM AREAS AND PROGRAMS

Agriculture	Business and Marketing	Health Occupations	Home Economics	Industrial
	General Office Clerking	Physical Therapy Assisting	Interior Decorating/Design	Cosmetology
	Keyboarding	Practical Nursing	Waiter/Waitress	Custodial Maintenance
	Law Enforcement	Respiratory Therapy	***Student Organizations***	Diesel Mechanic
	Legal Assisting	Surgical Technology	Future Homemakers of America (FHA)	Drafting
	Legal Secretarial	***Student Organizations***	Home Economics Related Occupations (HERO)	Electronics
	Office Supervision	Health Occupations Student Organization (HOSA)		Environmental Control Technology
	Personal Services (Sales)			Graphic Arts
	Secretarial			Heating, Air Conditioning, and Refrigeration
	Stenography			Home Remodeling and Renovation
	Supervisor			Industrial Electricity
	Word Processing			Industrial Maintenance
	Student Organizations			Industrial Technology
	Distributive Education Clubs of America (DECA)			Laser Electrooptic Technology
	Future Business Leaders of America (FBLA)			Machine Tool
	Future Data Processors (FDP)			Manufacturing Technology/Computer Integrated Manufacturing Technology
	Future Secretaries of America (FSA)			Masonry
	Office Education Association (OEA)			Millwork and Cabinet Making

Plastics Technology

Programmable Control

Quality Control Technology

Radio and TV Production Broadcasting

Radio/Television Repair

Small Engine Repair

Statistical Process Control

Tool and Die Making

Truck Driving

Warehousing

Welding

Student Organizations

American Industrial Arts Student Association (AIASA)

Vocational Industrial Clubs of America (VICA)

99

knowledge necessary for placement into the world of work or for continuing their education in postsecondary vocational-technical institutes, community colleges, or perhaps college or university programs.

Cooperative Work Education (CWE). Cooperative work education programs involve cooperative arrangements between schools and employers, usually community employers. Cooperative arrangements generally include part-time instruction in school and on-the-job training through part-time employment. Instruction involves a cooperative education class taught by a qualified (certified) vocational teacher and the classes required for high school graduation. The part-time job is intended to relate directly to what is learned in school and students' careers or occupational goals. The CWE program, therefore, can be an alternative or a complement to skill training programs as its goal is to prepare the student for gainful employment. Cooperative education may be program-specific (e.g., industrial cooperative education), or smaller schools may have a single instructor responsible for all vocational areas. The CWE teacher-coordinator provides advice, coordination, and appropriate training sites for individual students. The teacher-coordinator teaches a cooperative education class in the school that closely relates to the students' job experiences. The teacher-coordinator, along with the employer or supervisor, evaluates the student's learning and performance on the job. The teacher-coordinator also assists in placing students in jobs after program completion.

Work Study (WS). The major purpose of a work-study program is to encourage or motivate students to continue their high school education while concurrently maintaining part-time employment, commonly during the school day, with school approval and release. A major goal of the program, therefore, is to provide economic assistance to students so they may stay in and complete school and obtain their high school diploma. In general, there is no immediate or intended occupational goal since the student's job does not necessarily relate to his or her career objectives. Therefore, the student's work experiences and school instruction are not coordinated as they are in CWE programs. The student is expected to relate his or her job and instruction. A student, however, may be concurrently enrolled in a vocational course and have a job in the same occupational cluster. Work-study programs are commonly administered by vocational education, special education, vocational rehabilitation, and employment and training programs.

Youth Organizations. Youth organizations provide students opportunities to further their learning experiences in vocational programs. Organizations such as the Future Farmers of America (FFA), Future Homemakers of America (FHA), and Vocational Industrial Clubs of America (VICA) allow students to develop further their technical skills through activities such as contests, proficiency judging, and industry training. Moreover, youth organizations permit students to demonstrate and acquire the leadership, social, and interpersonal skills necessary for obtaining, maintaining, and advancing in careers and for their transition into the community. Vocational youth organizations exist in both secondary and postsecondary programs and include students who are enrolled in skill training, cooperative work education, and work-study programs. A vocational instructor serves as the advisor of a local chapter. Local youth organizations are usually affiliated with state and national organizations.

Support Services

Disabled persons often require specific support services relative to their identified needs to succeed in vocational programs. Sarkees and Scott (1985) have grouped support services into five categories:

1. **Coordination of auxiliary services**
   Housing
   Health services
   Child care
   Transportation
2. **Outreach services**
   Public relations that inform citizens about what vocational education is doing
   Recruitment services that actively seek students for programs
3. **Instructional support services**
   Basic skills assistance
   Job readiness training
   Work experience
   Information about laws and regulations governing specific occupations
4. **Guidance services**
   Counseling
   Information
   Provide relevant experiences
5. **Placement services**
   Job listings
   Resume preparation
   Interview skills
   Job follow-up (p. 93)

Sitlington (1986) identified needed support services in terms of who shall provide support services and what is the most effective method of attaining a match between learners' needs and available services. The continuum of support services includes (1) instruction by the regular vocational teacher with consultation, (2) instruction by the regular vocational teacher with in-class assistance by support personnel, (3) instruction by the regular vocational teacher with supplementary instruction from the resource room center, (4) vocational skill instruction in the regular program with a separate class in generalizable skills, and (5) a separate vocational program. Sitlington relates this concept to who provides instruction, environments in which instruction will occur, and the existing skills and attitudes of the student.

> Proponents of the first approach would argue that if special needs learners are to be taught . . . skills in regular vocational (education) programs, then existing curriculum and learning environments need to be modified while also working to modify the skills of the students. Advocates of the second approach would argue that regular vocational (education) programs are appropriate for teaching . . . as is, and that students should be changed to better fit the demands of vocational classrooms or other vocational programs. Programs following this rationale would concentrate on tutoring students in the needed skills, attempting to remediate learner deficiencies in . . . skills. Those who would argue for the third approach, "ignore the system" would state that . . . skills cannot be taught to learners in the current vocational (education) system. They would argue that a separate program should be designed solely for special needs learners, including instruction . . . in needed specific vocational skills.

Hartley and Lehman (1986) relate support services to instruction in terms of learning styles, instructional training methods, modifications, and adaptations potentially needed by persons with disabilities in vocational programs. Identifying individual learning styles and appropriate instructional methods involves the consideration of the visual, auditory, and kinesthetic learning modes relative to various instructional methods such as printed materials; verbal lecture materials; workbook sheets; audiovisual materials; and demonstrations using vocational tools, equipment, and concrete materials. A correspondence should exist, therefore, between a student's preferred learning style and selected instructional methods. In addition, the provision of support services should include modifications or adaptations that make instructional materials most effective for persons with disabilities. Modifications or adaptation may include (1) regular materials in braille; (2) large-print versions of regular material; (3) an interpreter for deaf students; (4) a note-taker; (5) a peer tutor; (6) outlines of class lectures; (7) oral tests and/or reports; (8) a person who serves as a reader; (9) self-instructional materials; (10) captioned films or television and overhead transparencies; (11) charts and other visual materials, and (12) modified facilities and equipment. Taped versions of written material and written versions of taped material (Alfest, Hartley, & Rocco, 1975) and language at appropriate reading level, using simplified versions of regular material (Phelps, 1977), also can be appropriate.

Additional modifications or adaptations could include (1) marginal gloss (questions, tasks, and/or statements are written in the right margin of the text and refer to the important concepts within the narrative); (2) highlighting (underlining important or key facts in the narrative with a colored marking pen), (3) boxing (drawing a box around directions or critical paragraphs); (4) grouping (grouping problems requiring the same functions); (5) sequence cards (developing sequence cards that identify the steps to be followed in completing a task); and (6) masking (placing a sheet of paper or cardboard cut to the width of the text to cover portions of the narrative) (Johnson, 1979). The availability and effective delivery of appropriate support services is essential for persons with disabilities to succeed in vocational programs and transition into the world of work.

SUMMARY

Several public, private, and community-based programs and agencies provide services for persons requiring transition assistance. Programs such as vocational education, special education, and rehabilitation have different procedures and varying services; however, they also have some common services. As increasing numbers of persons with disabilities are identified and/or request transition services, an increased need will occur for identifying existing or new agencies to respond to these demands. Personnel involved in providing transition services should continue to identify and expand the array of community agencies and resources that may potentially offer transition services. Future service providers may evolve from within business and industry or other areas of the private sector. It is important that personnel in vocational education, special education, rehabilitation, and employment and training seek new sources and help create an atmosphere for tapping these resources.

Increasingly, personnel in these programs and agencies should begin or continue to engage in formal and informal interagency cooperation and agreements. Available services and resources should be described. Roles and responsibilities should be defined and policies and procedures established to ensure effective service delivery. Duplicate services should be minimized and efficiency should be maximized.

The goal of assessment is to identify the individual abilities, aptitudes, achievements, interests, knowledge, skills, needs, and vocational potential of persons relative to the requirements of education programs and occupations. The provision of comprehensive vocational assessment services for persons with disabilities is essential for their successful transition into, through, and out of vocational programs and into the world of work. Academic, psychological, psychomotor, medical, social, and vocational assessment data and information are necessary in identifying appropriate instructional and support services for individual students.

A variety of assessment strategies and procedures such as psychometric tests, work samples, curriculum-based assessments, situational assessments, and community-based assessments are available to collect the necessary data and information for instructional planning, intervention, and program evaluation. In addition, several emerging assessment strategies and procedures emphasize identifying the functional learning strengths and problems of learners.

These strategies commonly are curriculum-based and use nontraditional assessment methods. Pancsofar (1986) states ten principles or guidelines that should be followed for vocational assessment, especially for moderately or severely disabled persons.

1. Collect and interpret data within an ecological framework.
2. Identify environmental cues to be associated with specific responses.
3. Follow a general case approach to selecting assessment examples that sample the range of placement opportunities in the community.
4. Include both quantitative (objective) and qualitative (subjective) measures.
5. Be aware of the externalities (politics) associated with the assessment process.
6. Give equal emphasis to baseline, formative, and summative phases of assessment.
7. Complete the Job Skill Inventories of requisite behaviors associated with community work opportunities.
8. De-emphasize reliance on developmentally sequenced assessments.
9. Focus assessment on work-related skills that influence longevity of work experience.
10. Increase the specificity of assessment as a worker advances through work experiences. (p. 93)

Effective and efficient assessment services provided to persons with disabilities depend, to a large extent, on the degree of collaboration among vocational education, special education, rehabilitation, employment and training, and other related service-providing agencies (Stodden, 1981). These agencies should develop informal and formal interagency cooperation and agreements with respect to defining roles, capabilities, and responsibilities for providing services. The variety and number of personnel involved in assessment depends on the type and quantity of data and information needed, availability of personnel, amount of financial resources, and amount of time allocated for assessment activities.

Assessment data and information should be used in developing individualized education programs, identifying appropriate prevocational or vocational exploration or preparation placements, specifying program modifications and adaptations, aiding career guidance and counseling, and evaluating and monitoring student progress in vocational programs. In addition, assessment information should assist in making recommendations for instructional strategies and interventions, support and remedial services, and career goals and instructional objectives in the individualized vocational education program. The full continuum of services should be available to ensure equitable, comprehensive vocational assessment and access to the array of vocational opportunities in vocational programs.

Numerous placement options exist for disabled persons requiring transition assistance. Career and vocational awareness, orientation, exploration, preparation, and placement opportunities are essential for effective transition from vocational programs into the world of work. There is a wide array of occupational programs for persons with disabilities. Skill training, cooperative work education, work-study, and vocational youth organization programs should be accessible to and equitable for persons with disabilities. In addition, such persons should have access to the support services necessary to succeed in vocational programs and to enter the world of work.

REFERENCES

Alfest, M., Hartley, N., & Rocco, R. (1975). *Vocational education for students with special needs: A teacher's handbook.* Fort Collins: Colorado State University, Department of Vocational Education.

Botterbusch, K. F. (1982). *A comparison of commercial vocational evaluation systems.* Menomonie, WI: Stout Vocational Rehabilitation Institute, Materials Development Center.

Brolin, D. E. (1982). *Vocational preparation of persons with handicaps.* Columbus, OH: Charles E. Merrill.

Brown, J. M. (1987). *Student satisfaction and satisfactoriness measures: Potential transition tools for students with disabilities in postsecondary vocational education programs.* St. Paul: University of Minnesota, Minnesota Research and Development Center for Vocational Education.

Cobb, R. B. (1983). A curriculum based vocational assessment. *Teaching Exceptional Children, 15*(4), 216–219.

Cobb, R. B. (1985, December). Vocational assessment of the special needs learner: A special education perspective. Paper presented at the American Vocational Association Convention, Atlanta, Georgia.

Cobb, R. B., & Larkin, D. (1985). Assessment and placement of handicapped pupils into secondary vocational and education programs. *Focus on Exceptional Children, 17*(7), 1–14.

Dahl, P. R., Appleby, J. A., & Lipe, D. (1978). *Mainstreaming guidebook for vocational educators.* Salt Lake City: Olympus Publishing.

Federal Register. (1977, August 23). *Education of handicapped children* (Vol. 42, No. 163). (Regulations for implementing P.L. 94–142.)

Glasecoe, F. P., & Levy, S. M. (1985). A multidimensional observational approach to vocational assessment and placement. *Career Development for Exceptional Individuals, 8*(2), 73–79.

Greenan, J. P. (1983a). Identification and validation of generalizable skills in vocational programs. *Journal of Vocational Education Research, 8*(3), 46–71.

Greenan, J. P. (1983b). *Identification of generalizable skills in secondary vocational programs: Executive summary.* Springfield: Illinois State Board of Education/Department of Adult, Vocational, and Technical Education.

Greenan, J. P., & Jefferson, D. (1987) *Generalizable reasoning skills assessment: Resource directory.* Springfield: Illinois State Board of Education/Department of Vocational and Technical Education.

Greenan, J. P., & McCabe, C. (1986). *Generalizable interpersonal relations skills assessment: Resource directory.* Springfield: Illinois State Board of Education/Department of Adult, Vocational, and Technical Education.

Greenan, J. P., & McCabe, C. (1987). Generalizable reasoning skills assessment: User manual. Springfield: Illinois State Board of Education/Department of Vocational and Technical Education.

Greenan, J. P., Marton, P., & Powell, J. (1985). *Generalizable communications skills assessment: Resource directory.* Springfield: Illinois State Board of Education/Department of Adult, Vocational, and Technical Education.

Greenan, J. P., & Powell, J. (1984). *Generalizable mathematics skills assessment: Resource directory.* Springfield: Illinois State Board of Education/Department of Adult, Vocational, and Technical Education.

Greenan, J. P., Powell, J., & Dunham, J. K. (1986). *Generalizable communications skills assessment* (2nd ed.). Springfield: Illinois State Board of Education/Department of Adult, Vocational, and Technical Education.

Greenan, J. P., & Richard, P. (1985). *Generalizable mathematics skills assessment: User manual* (2nd ed.). Champaign, IL: Office of Career Development for Special Populations.

Greenan, J. P., Winters, M, & Browning, D. A., (1987). *Generalizable interpersonal relations skills assessment: User manual* (2nd ed.). Springfield: Illinois State Board of Education/ Department of Adult, Vocational, and Technical Education.

Harrington, T. F., & O'Shea, A. J. (1984). *Guide for occupational exploration.* Circle Pines, MN: National Forum Foundation.

Hartley, N., & Lehman, J. P. (1986). Teaching generalizable skills. *The Journal for Vocational Special Needs Education, 9*(1), 29–33.

Hopke, W. E. (1984). *Encyclopedia of career and vocational guidance.* Chicago: Doubleday.

Johnson, C. J. (1979). *Expanding work options for exceptional children: A self-instructional manual.* Reston, VA: Council for Exceptional Children.

Kerns, A. F., & Neeley, R. E. (1987). *Dictionary of worker traits* (Vols. 1 and 2). Philadelphia: Vocational Research Institute.

Leconte, P. (1985). The uses of vocational evaluation. *VocEd, 60*(3), 41–43.

Meers, G. D. (1987). *Handbook of vocational special needs.* Rockville, MD: Aspen Publishers, Inc.

Mori, A. A. (1982). School-based career assessment programs: Where are we now and where are we going? *Exceptional Education Quarterly, 3*(3), 40–45.

Pancsofar, E. L. (1986). Assessing work behavior. In F. R. Rusch (Ed.), *Competitive employment issues and strategies.* Baltimore: Paul H. Brookes.

Peterson, M. (1985). Modes of vocational assessment of handicapped students. *Career Development for Exceptional Individuals, 8*(2), 110–118.

Peterson, M., & Hill, P. (1982). *Vocational assessment of students with special needs: An implementation manual.* Commerce: East Texas State University, Occupational Curriculum Laboratory.

Peterson, M., Madden, B., & Ley-Siemer, L. (1981, December). Issues and recommendations concerning vocational assessment of special needs students. Paper presented at the American Vocational Association Convention, Atlanta, Georgia.

Phelps, L. A. (1977). *Career exploration and preparation for the special needs learner.* Boston: Allyn & Bacon.

Phelps, L. A., & McCarty, T. (1984). Student assessment practices. *Career Development for Exceptional Individuals, 7,* 30–38.

Posey, V. (Ed.). (1982). *Arizona model for vocational assessment: A procedural guide.* Tucson: University of Arizona.

Roberts, S., Doty, D., Santleban, S., & Tang, T. (1983). A model for vocational assessment of handicapped students. *Career Development for Exceptional Individuals, 6*(2), 100–110.

Salvia, J., & Ysseldyke, J. E. (1978). *Assessment in special and remedial education.* Boston: Houghton Mifflin.

Sarkees, M. D., & Scott, J. L. (1985). *Vocational special needs.* Alsip, IL: American Technical Publishers.

Sitlington, P. L. (1979). Vocational assessment and training of the handicapped. *Focus on Exceptional Children, 12*(4), 1–11.

Sitlington, P. L. (1986). Support services related to generalizable skills instruction. *The Journal for Vocational Special Needs Education, 9*(1), 16–19.

Sitlington, P. L., Brolin, D., Clark, G., & Vacanti, J. (1985). Career/vocational assessment in the public school setting: The position of the Division on Career Development. *Career Development for Exceptional Individuals, 8*(1), 3–6.

Sitlington, P. L., & Wimmer, S. (1978). Vocational assessment techniques for the handicapped adolescent. *Career Development for Exceptional Individuals, 1*(2), 74–87.

Stodden, R. A. (1980). Vocational assessment for special needs individuals. Workshop report to participants at State Invitational Model Building Workshop, Framington, MA.

Stodden, R. A. (1981). Planning vocational assessment activities within education settings: An interdisciplinary focus with handicapped students. *Vocational Assessment: Policy Paper Series Document 6.* Urbana-Champaign: University of Illinois, Leadership Training Institute.

U.S. Department of Labor. (1977). *Dictionary of occupational titles.* Washington, DC: U.S. Government Printing Office.

U.S. Department of Labor. (1986). *Occupational outlook handbook.* Washington, DC: U.S. Government Printing Office.

Vocational Evaluation and Work Adjustment Association. (1975). *Vocational evaluation project: Final report.* Menomonie, WI: Stout Vocational Rehabilitation Institute, Materials Development Center.

CHAPTER 5

Educators' Roles in the Transition Process

Paul M. Retish*

Transition is a word that brings to mind many images. The pregnant mother having her child, the child leaving the safety of the house for the first time, the child entering school, the parents watching the child go to school, the child becoming an adolescent, the parents raising an adolescent, adolescents preparing to find their own way outside of school, and the parents' return to where they started in the relationship—all these events can be viewed as transitions. They mark points in peoples' lives and relationships where events have mandated change. The inevitable changes that occur in peoples' lives affect all parts of the societal systems involved, including the support systems related to the transitional process.

One of these support systems that affects and is affected by transition processes is the educational system. This chapter will discuss the comprehensive relationships between the various stages of transition and the education system and the educators involved in educating persons with disabilities.

There will be consistent themes throughout this chapter, such as transition and the community, transition and the curriculum, transition and the school, transition and the teacher, transition and the parents or guardian, and transition and the student. Readers will get a comprehensive view of transition as it affects all the school years and the personnel involved. Direct application to the curriculum will be explored with suggestions for strategies to meet the ever-

*Paul M. Retish is professor of special education at the University of Iowa. He received his Ed.D. from Indiana University in special education with a minor in business. He has served as the editor of *Career Development for Exceptional Individuals* and has published extensively on transition, career development, and stress.

changing economic, employment, and leisure roles available once schooling is ended.

It should be understood that there is no single time of transition, but rather it is an ongoing, minute-by-minute process. Transition, as it is reflected in preparation for out-of-school activities, will be emphasized, but readers are cautioned that this is not the only transition process that is occurring in individuals' or groups' lives; many changes are occurring that can be considered transition.

SCHOOLS

Schools of the twentieth century are not homogeneous in their entirety or within a community. To understand and change schools, individuals should learn the dynamics of each school. Students, teachers, principals, and neighborhoods are just some of the factors affecting each school. Yet there are commonalities among schools that we can compare and use for analytical purposes.

For the most part, elementary through middle schools are neighborhood schools. The student populations attending these schools *usually* reflect the neighborhoods in which the schools are located. In rare instances, usually related to desegregation actions imposed by the federal or state government, these populations are very diverse because of busing and crossing school boundary lines.

Jencks (1972) noted the differences between schools in his conclusions about public education:

> First, different individuals and groups get unequal shares of the nation's educational resources. Our second conclusion is that access to low-cost educational services is more equal than access to high-cost services. Our third conclusion is that making all of education free would not suffice to equalize people's actual use of either schools or colleges. (pp. 22–23)

Therefore, caution is needed when we discuss schools. Reports, such as those of the Carnegie commission (1986) and the Holmes groups (1986), have discussed in detail the status of the schools, occurrences in teacher training programs, test results, and many other areas. One might say that school bashing is in. But more important, there is a general consensus that schools, teachers, teacher training programs, taxpayers, and other interested groups need to recognize that schools are in transition, and this transition will cause unevenness in education programming, in-fighting, creativity, and excitement. When you speak or write about transition, you are discussing not only what is happening to people but also what is occurring to the systems.

Elementary Schools

The basic introduction most children get to school is when they enter kindergarten or first grade. They are entering a new part of their lives that is outside of their family, friends, and in some cases, neighborhoods. Elementary schools (kindergarten through fifth or sixth grade, sometimes through eighth grade) represent many children's introduction to human beings who are dissimilar and to a place where needs are focused not only on themselves but also on the needs of a group.

One of the most far-reaching laws affecting the education of children was the 1965 Elementary and Secondary Education Act (P.L. 89-10), which was designed to provide compensatory education for educationally disadvantaged children. This law recognized that elementary and secondary schools had a responsibility to provide all children with a broad education that would assist them in functioning outside of their home and school. Prior to this law's passage, only a select few of the disadvantaged population were being educated, and many who were in school were being ignored.

Another factor that impinged on educators' roles was the consolidation of school districts to save money and to offer higher-quality education programs. Unfortunately, this is yet to be proven (cf., Iowa legislative minutes, 1986–1987). The bringing together of small school districts into larger groups took young children further away from home and caused a larger, but not necessarily detrimental, step to occur. In some states, specific organizations were developed to deliver special education (e.g., Iowa Code 196, New York Code 196, and Colorado Code 196). These organizations were designed to give high-quality special education almost exclusively to elementary schools' special needs students.

Tied in with this reorganization was the research of Rosenthal and Jacobsen (1968), Beez (1968), and Retish (1968), which indicated that the labeling process may hurt the children being placed in special education classes. Such classes took recognition of deficiencies, lower expectations, and teaching strategies based on inaccurate premises.

The elementary school transitions for special needs children were ripe for dangerous conclusions, which could, and did, keep many of these children in inappropriate classrooms and probably had a negative influence on their future earning power as adults (Bellamy, Horner, & Inman, 1979; Brown et al., 1971; Gold, 1975).

Yet much was accomplished for special needs children. Many teachers recognized that there were large numbers of students who had unique learning needs, and many teachers sought to develop skills and programs that would enable them to help these students more effectively. Programs were modified to stop shielding these children from the world, and special needs students were taken into communities and taught how to use local systems, to demand their rights, and to open up vast new areas not thought appropriate for them (e.g., Special Olympics, and Arts for the Handicapped).

The reorganization of schools, the recognition that schools serve all people, and that we are living in an ever-expanding world has led educators and counselors to discuss transition and to begin career education in the elementary schools (Clark, 1979; Hoyt, 1973; Marland, 1971). There now is general agreement that transition is an on-going procedure occurring at all ages. To many people, one has to discuss transition only when students move from high school to post-high school settings. It is the author's contention that transition occurs from birth until death.

In elementary schools, especially in elementary public schools, children encounter new peers and adults of different sizes, beliefs, colors, preferences, and needs. All these cause individuals to build new repertoires of behavior. Curricula are designed to stimulate expansion, new knowledge, and changes necessary to deal with all these new stimuli. Transition is occurring whether the teachers or any other adults do or do not refer to it with this particular terminology.

For those who have chosen to recognize this process, specific actions, when appropriate, are occurring. Students are exposed to new parts of neighborhoods and communities and even larger areas through field trips, magazines, books, tapes, movies, radios, records, and most commonly, television. Under the guidance of educators, children take in more of the world in which they live and start to identify and assimilate many of the differences and opportunities that are possible.

Unfortunately, there is a relationship between the breadth of these experiences and the economics of the schools involved (U.S. Commission on Civil Rights, 1967). Economics and race are primary factors in determining if education programs are to expand or develop. For transition programs, this means many students will get only limited exposure to new opportunities and, therefore, will stay in the same frame of mind as they were before entering their programs.

Elementary school is very important to students in transition process. Many of these students drop out at 16 or younger and never get the exploratory opportunity to understand what they will face or what variety of opportunities are available.

Further transition experiences can occur as students are exposed to the multiple experiences of work and leisure. Speakers, tapes, movies, and television are just a few of the ways that elementary children start to understand the possibility of choices they have for work or leisure.

These processes are further enhanced by the openness of the elementary system as opposed to the junior high and secondary systems. Students spend long periods of time with each other and seem to be at an age when they are less inhibited about sharing times, experiences, and impressions (R. Eigenbrood, personal communication, March 13, 1987; D. Rosenthal, personal communication, May 6, 1986), and these students can benefit from exposure to new ideas and can accept startling new developments in their lives. This evidence supports the conclusion that not only are elementary school students experiencing new things but also they are more open to such exposures and are more willing to alter their own systems. Therefore, transition-enhancement activities should occur at this level since it may be the time at which the impact of being exposed to new ideas is greatest and when the willingness to learn new ideas is most intense.

Elementary school marks the beginning of transition—a time of setting the stage for future experiences of self-understanding and of moving through one stage to the appropriate next stage. However, the importance of selecting the correct time is lessened at the elementary school level by a lack of commitment to the concepts of transition. Along with the push for basic skills, students also need to be aware of the many new experiences and programs they will face and how to cope with these experiences. It then follows that teachers and administrators should be prepared to teach these concepts and to understand them in the light of the world that is emerging.

To quote from the Holmes Report (1986);

As we try to improve teaching and teacher education, then we cannot avoid trying to improve the profession in which teachers will practice. Here we find a curious situation. While the intellectual and social demands on teachers have escalated at an astonishing rate since this century began, the nature and organization of teachers' work has changed only a little since the middle of the nineteenth century. We now live in an age when many elementary school students have their own microcomputers. These students can put some of the most amazing achievements of modern science and technology to work in support of their learning. Yet their teachers are still working with the same job description that teachers had in the mid-1800s, when *McGuffey Readers* and spelling slates were the leading educational technology.

It is a painful contrast, one that embarrasses us as educators and as Americans. Consider these points. Many teachers still instruct whole classes of students in all subjects, as there is little or no academic specialization until high school. They still teach classes all day long, with little or no time for preparation, analysis, or evaluation of their work. They still spend all of their professional time alone with students, leaving little or no time for work with other adult professionals to improve their knowledge and skills. Nor are they thought worthy of such endeavors or capable of developing that requisite expertise. But teachers have a lengthening list of responsibilities. They must teach children with many special needs and disabilities—children who were rarely in school until recently. They must supervise extensive testing and evaluation programs for their students and try to make sense of the results. They must cope with a variety of state and federal programs and requirements and mandates. The list goes on.

Middle Schools

Many school districts have developed school programs based on the transition period between elementary and senior high school. These middle schools have been developed to assist students in this transitional period. Many of the children are starting to see and feel changes in their bodies and attitudes as they enter the middle school years. Without explanation, many of the students get lost and are ill at ease in the world in which they live at this age. These middle schools are designed to have teaching staff and support personnel who are aware and ready to assist these students.

The content of middle school programs has also been designed for change. At this level, a curriculum becomes increasingly related to the real experiences of the children who attend such schools. More attention is paid to the interaction of the children as they try to identify themselves in relation to each other.

For the special needs children in middle schools, careful attention should be paid to each emerging pattern of behavior and, most important, to how individuals recognize and cope with being labeled as different, as indicated earlier (Beez, 1968; Retish, 1968). The manner in which special needs individuals see themselves is important to how well they will cope with transitions in their lives.

Personal considerations with which schools should be concerned are focused on students' academic needs and their development of skills. In the area of academic needs, many special needs children should have continuous practice with the basic skills necessary to live independently as adults. These skills should be taught in such a manner that they are generalized to a variety of settings when possible by special needs students.

Education should also focus on teaching individuals how to survive as independently as possible. These teaching practices might take the form of enabling students to make their needs known, helping them to communicate effectively, shopping for items they want or need, and teaching students to carry on conversations with their peers.

At the social level, curricula should focus on assisting individuals to function as social human beings. In many ways, this means understanding rules of social interaction, taking on responsibilities, and beginning to make decisions that have positive or negative consequences.

This transition period again becomes important because it is the phase during which the groundwork is established for developing the skills necessary for young adults in and out of junior and senior high schools. Basic considerations should be given to assuring that students develop the skills they will need to be successful in the more competitive and freer atmosphere of the high schools to which they next move.

High Schools and Junior High Schools

The culminating program in many individuals' education experiences, especially students with disabilities, is the high school program. High schools present an entirely new challenge to students. Groups of students move between teachers who are trying to impart specific information to the students in each class. Elementary and middle school programs, which tend to have specific teachers who spend significant time with each student, are replaced by high school programs with five to eight periods a day.

Students spend time with a wide cross section of other students within each academic class, but usually within a narrow academic level. Furthermore, high schools are usually significantly larger than elementary schools in terms of number of pupils and size of the building. Another big change for all students, especially special needs students, is the rich social structure that these students encounter at this level.

Rules of dress, language, and social interaction are formally a part of these high school structures. Students entering into this milieu must not only seek out their classrooms but also determine the social structure to which they belong. Students soon join groups that are labeled as athletes, "greasers," "nerds," musicians, and "retards," to name a few. For many, these are groups that are self-selected; too often the student with a special need is placed by peers in a group with a derogatory label.

This is a complicated situation that often has not been clarified for students with disabilities or their teachers (Leone & Retish, 1978). Teachers, who are not sure how or what to teach mainstreamed children, and other students, who do not like to be thrown in with the special education children, are constantly delaying the special needs students' transition from elementary or middle schools to high school.

For many students, the idea that this is the final stage of educational opportunities is cause for concern, and at times these students become immobilized. For others, it's an exciting time, full of fun and anticipation about moving on to careers or to additional training. For students with disabilities, as will be explained later, this may be the last place where they will experience success and work with people who are concerned with their welfare.

Adulthood invades the lives of all high school students, and their preparation for independence represents an important aspect of their education. Yet for many teachers, the curriculum taught does not represent competence. Rather, curriculum is a set of ideas and facts that all students should know regardless of their individual needs.

When describing changes in education, Ernest Boyer (1983) stated,

In 1981, only 52 percent of all white families had school-age children (under 18 years of age). In contrast, 71% of all black and 75% of all Hispanic households had children in this category. With fewer school-age children, the commitment of white American families to public education may well decline. And while minority parents have a growing stake in education, historically, they have limited power to help the nation's schools. (p. 5)

Shifting demographics are important for classes of special needs students because of "the fact that black and Hispanic young people are primarily those with whom our schools have been least successful" (Boyer, 1983, p. 5). Thus minority students still constitute a disproportionately large component of special education, and if population trends continue, their numbers will increase rather than decrease. Boyer (1983) also noted that great disparities exist between high schools. Certain groups of high schools send the bulk of their graduates to college and/or snare a disproportionate amount of the academic awards.

Transition issues and processes in high school are important both to the students and to the school programs. One hopes that the issues and processes of transition are addressing the best interests of students and their success after they leave school.

The importance and potential impact of these transition processes was highlighted when Will (1984) indicated that our most important business is to get the total spectrum of students (including those with disabilities) ready to enter into the world of work. Students need to be adequately prepared, and communities should be ready to assist them in being useful. Out of Will's plan came private industry councils (PICs) made up of local business people who offer their assistance in transition processes. Though the evidence has not been published, informal contacts (W. Hitchings, personal communication, March 6, 1986; B. Schmalle, personal communication, March 6, 1986) indicate that local organizations do not know what their roles can or should be and cannot effectively change employers' attitudes. There also is a serious lack of jobs in rural America during the 1980s, which is made even more of a problem by the fact that many workers who previously held mid-level jobs are now seeking entry-level jobs.

Therefore, transition is not an easy problem to define, but more important, it is getting to be more difficult to teach skills that will assist special needs individuals to succeed in the work force and as adult citizens.

Yet progress is being made by educators who are modifying their schools' curricula in the hope that all special needs learners will become aware and prepared for the opportunities that exist outside of schools. For example, teachers are being trained to understand the skills necessary to assist special needs students to function successfully outside of school (Brolin, 1982; Retish et al., 1987). One of the most important developments for students with disabilities is that schooling, training, and learning do not have to end at graduation from high school. Now there are a number of postsecondary programs and services that cater to special needs individuals (Brown & Retish, 1987).

Postsecondary

Traditionally, for the non-college-bound population, postsecondary opportunities existed primarily in the armed forces and trade schools. Both of these options still exist and are now being complemented by programs in two-year colleges that are geared to special needs learning (Anderson, personal communication, April 6, 1985; Kirkwood Community College, 1986). These facilities serve many purposes. They can provide training in specific skills or enhance students' generalizable skills, which can be used in a variety of settings. They also give special needs children the opportunity to do as their peers do, that is, go to "college." This feeling of belonging may, in the long run, be just as important as the actual process of going to college.

Yet many of these postsecondary institutions continue to encounter problems related to personnel, funding, direction, peer relationships, and knowing what skills should be taught (Brown & Retish, 1987). One can say that there are opportunities at the postsecondary level as well as all other levels, and it's up to educators to assist special needs learners to be successful.

A special attribute of post-high school programs is their ability to use data from the workplace to assist special needs individuals to be better workers. Many students have had work experience prior to enrolling in postsecondary programs. If these institutions collect and analyze these data, there may be an opportunity to assist special needs workers in remediating problems in the workplace.

Postsecondary opportunities are being increasingly examined in terms of their implications for persons with disabilities. Some programs have been established for learning disabled students who are believed capable of coping with these situations (Retish, 1979). Fortunately, many of these institutions are now exploring opening their doors for a variety of special needs learners. Persons who are retarded, physically handicapped, and/or emotionally handicapped are now beginning to have programs designed for them that are vocationally oriented and include on-the-job training (e.g., Iowa Lakes Community College, 1981). If these opportunities continue, the spirit of Public Law 94–142 and other laws, which were designed to let all students become all they are capable of being, has the possibility of reality.

Transition in the Schools

Curriculum
According to the Holmes Report (1986), curricula that teachers need to teach effectively should focus on a broad spectrum of possibilities for students. In

transition-related curricula for special needs learners, a series of correcting steps, based on the knowledge we have, should be taken and then the outgrowth should become an integral part of the curriculum.

Ceiling Effect

Many researchers (e.g., Bellamy, Horner, & Inman, 1979; Gold, 1975), have reminded us that evidence indicates that the population we label as special needs, regardless of the severity of their disabilities, can function at much higher levels than has often been assumed possible, required, or even attempted in the schools. Some studies (Beez, 1968; Retish, Hitchings, & Hitchings, 1987; Rosenthal & Jacobsen, 1968) have shown that low expectations, can *cause* low performance and high expectations can *cause* high performance.

Brolin (1982) and Rush and Mithaug (1980) have developed curriculum guidelines that assist teachers to raise expectations and to develop curricula based on the needs of special learners. These curricula discourage academics for academics' sake and stress functional curricula that enhance transition processes mentioned in the first section of this chapter.

Instructor's Role

According to recent publicity, education, teachers, and teacher training programs are at a crossroads. The basic consideration of whether or not curricula reflect the needs of students has been addressed in reports by the Carnegie commission (1986) and the Holmes group (1986). The conclusion that instructors are not prepared to teach modern students has been loudly proclaimed. This lack of preparation becomes clear when one examines the difficulties that emerge when attempting to infuse transition concepts among all special needs students. More often than not, teachers are satisfied to continue using very traditional teaching practices, that is, to teach straight academic and school behavior. Though this is comfortable for teachers, it does not meet the needs of students with disabilities and other special learning characteristics.

Infused into all levels of curricula should be those skills, experiences, and discussion opportunities that will ultimately give the student the necessary skills to move through all aspects of transition processes. Materials, resources, and field trips, to name only a few, should be provided as experiential encounters with the skills necessary to cope with all of an individual's transition needs. Teachers are the key to the development of understanding, examination skills, and strategies concerning transition in an environment that encourages this behavior.

Job Development

Work is one of the end products to which most students are trained to aspire. No matter what level of skills each individual has, programs are designed to assist individuals to become the best workers possible. There has been a great deal of criticism of many job training programs. Some have said that sheltered workshops and in-school experiences take advantage of special needs students by paying them little or nothing (Gold, 1975; Retish, 1979). Others have indicated that work experience training does not develop skills and does not enhance job-seeking success skills (Retish & Eigenbrood, in press). Yet others consider any experience worthwhile, as long as it is productive and teaches some skills (Brolin, 1982; Kolstoe, 1972).

When one reads research published on follow-ups of special needs students working after graduation (Hasazi, Gordon, & Roe, 1985; Mithaug, Horiuchi, & Fanning, 1985), a clear picture emerges of a lack of correlation between work experiences and job attainment for special needs students. Questions arise about other explanations for the lack of success or possible leads to assist in employment opportunities. Retish and Eigenbrood (in press) indicated a relationship between those employers willing to use their businesses for work-study programs and later employment.

Unfortunately, the findings on this issue do not suggest exact remedies. Clearly, educators should do a better job of educating the public regarding the employment of special needs students. There is also the need to teach special needs individuals what to do with themselves when they are not working, cannot get a job, and have dim job prospects.

All these paths are transition-related, and schools should take into consideration all the possibilities, especially with the great changes going on in work habits and job availability. Success outside of school is the measurement yardstick to use in determining if a program has any long-term impact. Success out of school needs to be defined broadly and from the perspective of special needs students trying to be self-actualizing in the situations in which they must live.

Program and Student Evaluation

The need to evaluate what we have and need to accomplish has never been more of an issue than it has been recently. The Colorado study (Mithaug, Horiuchi, & Fanning, 1985) and the Vermont study (Hasazi, Gordon, & Roe, 1985), plus the Carnegie Report (1986), have strongly noted a discrepancy between what we say we are trying to do and what follow-up research says we have accomplished.

Teacher evaluation, as used in Florida and Houston, has been severely criticized. What we, as teachers, are suggesting be used as standards is unclear and hidden by verbal clouds that seem only to inhibit the operation of programs. School districts often use evaluations processes as a club to dismiss, demote, or threaten teachers so that advancement may be limited and, thus, budget expenses reduced. Yet teacher evaluation is a necessary mechanism for ensuring growth, performance, and salary-based reward systems. Furthermore, evaluation is a positive way of providing useful feedback regarding educators' strengths and weaknesses, which can ultimately be of benefit to students.

Furthermore, as far as transition processes are concerned, evaluation can be used to add new ideas and encourage professionals to seek out advances, implement new concepts, determine community needs, and understand resources. Teacher evaluation processes can be a positive mechanism that encourages change and creates an atmosphere in which teachers can respond to concepts like transition and updating their curricula as needed.

These evaluation procedures will prove beneficial for students as well. Ongoing, updated curricula that include the newer concepts of transition programming can only have a positive effect on whatever future plans students might have or want to develop.

Obviously, one of the goals of teacher education programs is to upgrade the quality of teachers and to reward those who are doing the best job.

In light of the studies done on follow-ups of special education classes, evaluation of students' progress, once out of school, should provide valuable information to teachers and school programs. Feedback regarding quality of work performance on the job and in the community can be used to evaluate curricula and to make appropriate changes. These evaluations can also help educators evaluate specific job sites that are being used and to compare their relative merits. Further use of specific skills that students have or are lacking can be identified by follow-up studies and then analyzed and translated into program content in school classrooms.

Schools, teachers, and administrators have been too lax in understanding the merits of evaluation. For too long we have done things because they felt good rather than on the basis of solid evidence that identifies the strengths and weaknesses of personnel and programs.

TRANSITION

One of the positive outgrowths of the marriage of many support organizations, such as Mayor's Youth Programs and CETA/JTPA, has been the development of Private Industry Councils (PICs). On paper, this innovative group taps community business leaders to give advice, open doors, and serve as general resources to schools as they seek to address community needs. Though there have been various levels of success with PICs, the general framework of these structures points out an ongoing need of the schools, that is, a close school-to-community understanding, with both groups understanding how positively to affect the other.

In an ever-changing world of employment and job-related skills, there is an enormous need for schools to evaluate programs to ensure that the special needs students are truly prepared to make the transition from school to work (West, 1986). The changing employment patterns of assembly-line workers, either advancing their skills or moving into the service industries, will have a dramatic effect on the jobs that will be available to special needs individuals. To continue to prepare the special needs students for the jobs of the 1960s and

1970s is to create a group bound for failure. Furthermore, if Farber's (1984) theory that we have a surplus population built into our society is correct, then we, as vocational and special educators, rehabilitation specialists, and adult service providers, should prepare students to develop realistic job and transitional skills; moreover, these skills should also include strategies about what students should do when they are unemployed or underemployed. Only when we recognize these changes will we truly have put together an evaluation system leading to comprehensive, up-to-date programs.

Curriculum and evaluation are energy-producing concepts that are forever going through review and change. Each of these processes, once institutionalized, should be continually evaluated, with updating, change, and evaluation being the natural outgrowth of the process. Therefore, teachers and administrators need constant updating based on new and proven methods and ideas—an expensive but necessary process in order to provide a quality education for all students who are constantly in a state of transition. One might conclude that a large portion of transition is evaluation. Self-evaluation of goals, strategies, opportunities, and support systems affect how individuals understand transition and contribute to the development and implementation of innovative curricula that produce qualified graduates.

Parent and Family

In any system, it is highly unusual for an individual to stand alone. Usually, each individual has many outside systems supporting what is going on and what is being planned. For students with disabilities and other special learning needs, this concept does not appear to be different from anyone else, except that one component of the supporting structure can also be a source of stress. The support system has many faults, but the following section will concentrate on one aspect—the family.

Support

Saenger (1957), in an early work, talked about the effect on a family of having a special needs child. Later work done by Gallagher, Beckman, & Cross (1983) and Retish, Hitchings, and Hitchings (1987) indicated the positive and negative forces that can stem from a family. In the mid-1950s, families of special needs students banded together to form parenting groups that could act as advocacy and support models for both parents and students in terms of their school needs and their efforts to obtain community agency support. That movement continues today. In the schools, these groups have scrutinized classes, teachers, laws, and outside help in ways that have caused the schools to become better prepared to teach all children.

In transition processes at all levels, parents have combined their strength to see that programs and support staffs were available, that the programs were taught by qualified personnel located in the appropriate settings, and that students have quality learning experiences (Kirp & Jensen, 1986). As a result of court actions and out-of-court settlements, a broad array of special education programs now exist in the schools.

Yet in some ways parents and advocacy groups and educators were short-sighted when they organized elementary school classes and did not quickly turn their attention to the later years of education and postsecondary education. Therefore, a lag in the development of programs and sophistication has occurred for older (high school age and above) special needs individuals.

The latest studies on postsecondary adjustment (Hasazi, Gordon, & Roe, 1985; Mithaug, Horiuchi, and Fanning, 1985; Retish, Hitchings, & Hitchings, 1987), suggested that adult life for special needs students is not what it could be. Once again, the parents (relatives and friends) are the biggest source of support. These groups are the predominant employers of special needs individuals, or as Retish, Hitchings, and Hitchings (1987) noted, they wish only security for their children rather than a job. This mixed message from parents seems to describe the only actual support system generally available to many special needs students as they leave school and try to fend for themselves in their communities.

Agencies and organizations geared to assist employment or transition (Vocational Rehabilitation, Job Training Partnership Act, and Social Services) are heavily overloaded, underfunded, or more interested in cases that promise a higher possibility of continuing employment. This void is being primarily filled by parents.

The pressures of advocacy have pressed programs to look at job sites, on-job experiences, follow-ups, and social welfare cases, to name a few. Advocacy efforts have also pressured schools to provide opportunities that prepare for the real-life situations as they arise outside of school.

Yet for some who have severe disabilities, there is evidence that parents' aspirations are focused primarily on guardianship and care rather than on skills or independence (Retish, Hitchings, & Hitchings, 1987). Pressure to not raise employment expectations has come from parents and educators. Although these attitudes and behaviors must be changed, parents' acknowledgement of the lack of job opportunities for students with severe and profound or moderate disabilities may sometimes be more realistic than those educators who speak of quality independent working lives for all special needs individuals, regardless of level of disability. We need much more research to develop plans based on realistic expectations rather than rejecting all prior practices and not learning from prior errors.

Advocacy by parents of special needs individuals is, to many educators, a mixed blessing (W. Hitchings, personal communication, March 12, 1985). Clearly, schools have a history of not providing services for special needs individuals or for providing services with a minimum of effort and support. On the other side of the ledger, parents have had unreasonable expectations of some children in terms of performance, attention, total care, and responsibility. This imbalance has left many educators to wonder if the rest of their lives will be devoted to paperwork regarding accusations of inadequate school programming combined with meeting the requirements of Public Law 94-142.

There definitely needs to be a watchdog system to ensure that the content of programming for special needs students includes what is necessary for their success out of school. The evidence, as stated earlier, suggests that there may be more concern focused on services that have already been established and/ or are easier to implement rather than stressing what is necessary. Therefore, advocacy systems have been developed that should be staffed by objective leaders who demand quality at all levels of service delivery. Too many issues may be addressed only from parents' or educators' perspectives. Collaborating efforts among schools, special needs students, and parents should result in the establishment of quality curricula that give students all the basic skills they need to learn, as well as the social and self-help skills that are necessary to make the transition from one stage of their lives to another.

Preparing Educators for the Transition Process

Minimum competency, merit raises, levels of teaching, and vertical or horizontal momentum are all issues with which classroom teachers have to cope. All that is in addition to their various regular classroom duties, committees, and selection of books and curricula, which also dictate the development of curricula and other innovative concepts. Into this debate comes a new idea for special needs individuals called transition programming. Teachers may respond, "What is there that makes this concept important?" "What has to be deleted?" "Who will do it?" "When will it be implemented?" "I am already overloaded." "I can't add anything here." All are issues faced by educators as they are once again asked to insert another new fad into their curricula. But is this just another fad? Are teachers prepared to handle these new concepts? What experiences and background do teachers need to do an adequate job in preparing their students to go through appropriate transition processes?

The evidence that transition processes are occurring and that teachers and schools need to be better prepared to implement these ideas is quite clear. Not as evident is whether the schools and teachers are prepared to implement these concepts for special needs students.

Research by Goldstein, Moss, and Jordan (1965) raised many questions regarding curricula taught by special educators. Also raised was the question of whether teachers are willing to shift from traditional teaching roles to innovative modes that transition programming requires (Leone & Retish, 1978). Complicating this changing process is the lack of flexibility in teacher training models. The Carnegie Commission's report was quite straightforward in criticizing training programs, which do not prepare future teachers with sufficient breadth to create innovative and dynamic schools and curricula.

With all these stagnant habits, new approaches have been implemented to get professionals to look at alternative programming for special needs individuals. Project Discovery evaluated a project that tried a variety of exploratory procedures to assist special needs students in making the transition from school to work (Retish & Jepsen, 1978). Bellamy, Horner, and Inman (1979) discussed task analysis, and Brown and colleagues (1971) examined many aspects of job exploration and job placement that could have major impacts on training and curricula. Recent efforts by Stodden and others (1987) stated,

> The direct relationship between vocational assessment and work-study placement is the most strongly demonstrated relationship in this study, and provides clear evidence for the impact for vocational assessment information. It is also a further indication that the correct role which vocational assessment plays in IEP planning and subsequent classroom planning could be enhanced by creating more specific annual goals and objectives on the IEP. (p. 22)

Therefore, evidence is being gathered that points to new programs, new training needs, and new skills for future teachers.

One could conclude that teachers participating in special needs programs and transition planning efforts should be fully aware of the community needs and the skills necessary for being successful in their communities. Therefore, training programs should include an emphasis on community work, understanding, and communication. Resources for jobs, support systems, and leisure activities should be part of the repertoire of contemporary teachers. Fully integrated curricula, at all levels of schooling, should include programs to assist students in activities inside and outside of school. Cognizance of the developmental stages of special needs students, and how they affect transition programming, should be an integral part of curricula. Teaching strategies focused solely on being successful in school have been proven to be inadequate after students leave school and try to be successful in other postschool environments.

Furthermore, experiences in teaching before becoming a full-time teacher, though still important, need to be complemented with field work with community agencies and employers to develop insights regarding expectations, problems, and resources that exist in those settings. These experiences may be used as precursors for entry into training programs leading to certification and licensing to teach special needs students. These requirements should be based on the recognized needs of special students for assistance in out-of-school programs as well as within school. Many teachers have had few experiences (besides going to school) and therefore need practical experiences. Furthermore, this need is exacerbated by the fact that many teachers come from middle-class backgrounds and that special needs students are disproportionately from lower socioeconomic settings. Therefore, job aspirations, knowledge, community background, and resources tend to be very different for the middle-class teachers and lower socioeconomic students.

Yet the everchanging nature of communities regarding opportunities, problems, and support systems forces educators to continue to investigate new developments that will affect their students in transition efforts and, therefore, the impact of these changes on their curricula. Curricula evolve, mirroring many of society's changes. With increased numbers of businesses closing, shifting patterns of employment, and new needs in skills, curricula and teachers are evolving (West, 1986). Therefore, teachers and administrators cannot develop particular curricula and think their job is completed. Once new curricula are implemented, they, too, should begin to evolve. Teachers and administrators should continue to monitor new needs and developments and to respond according to the needs of their students.

Implicit in all these changes and developments is the constant idea that what we think we know today becomes the falsehoods of tomorrow. Marc Gold (1975) indicated that our dependence on standardized tests, normative data, and comparisons to what is perceived as a standard have led us to put an artificial ceiling on the accomplishments of special needs persons. A comment that I once heard comes to mind: "I have a lot of answers, no one has ever asked me the right questions." Maybe the latter part of this statement is the real definition of effective educators—determining what the child knows, wants, and dreams of, and opening up those avenues by teaching the skills that will assist individuals through all their transition phases.

Dependence on traditional education systems and methods has not led to fruitful outcomes for special needs students. They have been marked by labels that society cannot remove, and thus, they are not allowed to become full-fledged members of their communities. We continue to tell special needs individuals to aspire high, yet we help them to do less. We attribute to them such characteristics as lack of interest, need for repetition, and uncontrollable outbursts, which explains why education and society have not been forthright with special needs individuals but does not explain the high skill levels many researchers have found when appropriate opportunities and training were provided (e.g., Bellamy, Horner & Inman, 1979; Brown et al., 1971; Gold, 1975).

CONCLUSION

Separate but equal, segregation, and isolation are concepts that have been declared illegal, proven wrong, or not countenanced any longer. For special needs students, not recognizing their lives outside of school, ignoring the processes of transition they are going through, or continuing to use outdated curricula are practices as archaic as the separate-but-equal concept. There are many individuals and groups who want to go back to old ways rather than go forward. With budgets always in question, costly staffing, and inadequate support from the literature, we are clearly mandated to advocate a renovated curriculum with ongoing research, which teaches ways to improve, moderate, and change.

Yet some components of the education system need to remain constant. Education personnel have to be advocates for students. Clear relationships between school and communities should be established and reinforced, and the willingness to discover new directions and processes should always be present.

Education is not a concept that arbitrarily ends with a slip of paper. Education is like transition, in that both go on throughout an individual's lifetime. We should recognize that these two processes are ongoing, and we need to be prepared to deliver what is necessary when it is necessary. Furthermore, education and transition are not just the responsibility of the schools but require the cooperation of every agency, group, and citizen.

REFERENCES

Beez, V. (1968). *Influences of biased psychological reports on teacher behavior.* Unpublished manuscript, Indiana University, Bloomington.

Bellamy, T., Horner, R. H., and Inman, D. P. (1979). *Vocational rehabilitation of severely retarded adults.* Baltimore: University Park Press.

Boyer, E. (1983). *High School.* New York: Harper & Row.

Brolin, D. (1982). *Vocational preparation of persons with handicaps* (2nd ed.). Columbus, OH: Charles E. Merrill.

Brown, L., Johnson, S., Gadberry, E., & Fenrick, N. (1971). Increasing individual and assembly line production rates of retarded students. *The Training School Bulletin, 67,* 206–212.

Brown, J., & Retish, P. (1987). Postsecondary institutions and support systems for special needs learners. In G. D. Meers (Eds.), *Handbook of Special Vocational Needs Education* (2nd ed.). Rockville, MD: Aspen Systems.

Carnegie Task Force on Teaching as a Profession. (1986). *A nation prepared: Teachers for the 20th century.* New York: Carnegie Forum on Education and the Economy.

Clark, G. (1979). *Career education for the handicapped in the elementary classroom.* Denver: Love Publishing.

Farber, B. (1984). Families with mentally retarded members: An agenda for research, 1985–2000. Presentation at the S. Kirk Colloquium, University of Illinois, Urbana.

Gallagher, J., Beckman, P., & Cross, A. (1983). Families of handicapped children: Sources of stress and its amelioration. *Exceptional Children, 50*(1), 10–19.

Gold, M. (1975). Vocational training. In J. Wortis (Ed.), *Mental retardation and developmental disabilities: Vol. 7* (pp. 254–264). New York: Brunner Mazel.

Goldstein, H., Moss, J. W., & Jordan, L. J. (1965). *The efficacy of special class training on the development of mentally retarded children.* Urbana: University of Illinois, Institute for Research on Exceptional Children.

Hasazi, S. B., Gordon, L. R., & Roe, C. A. (1985). Factors associated with the employment status of handicapped youth exiting high school. *Exceptional Children, 51,* 455–469.

Holmes Report. (1986). *Tomorrow's teachers.* East Lansing, MI: Holmes Group.

Hoyt, K. B. (1973). *Series of monographs on career education.* Washington, DC: U.S. Government Printing Office.

Iowa Lakes Community College. (1981). *Curriculum and college goals.* Estherville: Iowa Lakes Community College.

Jencks, C. (1972). *Inequality.* New York: Basic Books.

Kirkwood Community College. (1986). *Kirkwood statement of purposes.* Cedar Rapids, IA.

Kirp, D. L., & Jensen, D. N. (1986). *School days, rule days* (Stanford series on education and public policy). Philadelphia: Falmer Press.

Kolstoe, O. P. (1972). *Mental retardation: An educational viewpoint.* New York: Holt, Rinehart & Winston.

Leone, P., & Retish, P. (1978). A handicapped kid in my class? *The Social Studies, 69*(1), 18–20.

Marland, S. (1971). Career education now. Speech presented before the annual convention of the National Association of Secondary School Principals, Houston.

Mithaug, D. E., Horiuchi, C. N., & Fanning, P. N. (1985). A report of the Colorado follow-up survey of special education students. *Exceptional Children, 51,* 397–404.

Red Oak Community School District. (1971). Red Oak, Iowa.

Retish, P. (1968). The effect of positive overt teacher verbal reinforcement on peer acceptance. Unpublished doctoral dissertation, Indiana University, Bloomington.

Retish, P. (1979). Career education for the culturally different. *Career Development for Exceptional Individuals, 2*(2), 107–108.

Retish, P., & Eigenbrood, R. (in press). Work experience: Employers' attitudes regarding the employability of special education students. *Career Development for Exceptional Individuals.*

Retish, P., Eigenbrood, R., Schmalle, B., & Hitchings, W. (1987). Secondary methods text. Manuscript submitted for publication.

Retish, P., Hitchings, W., & Hitchings, S. (1987). Parent perspectives of vocational services for moderately retarded individuals. *Journal of Career Development, 13*(4).

Retish, P., & Jepsen, D. (1978). *Final report: EBCE.* Des Moines: State Department of Public Instruction.

Rosenthal, R., & Jacobsen, (1968). *Pygmalion in the classroom.* New York: Holt, Rhinehart & Winston.

Rush, F. R., & Mithaug, D. E. (1980). *Vocational training for mentally retarded adults: A behavior analytic approach.* Champaign, IL: Research Press.

Saenger, G. (1957). *The adjustment of retarded adults in the community.* New York: International Department of Health Resources Board.

Stodden, R., Meehan, K, Hokdell, S., Bisconer, S., & Cabebe, S. (1987). *Vocational assessment research project: A report of findings for project year 1985–1986.* Honolulu: University of Hawaii, Department of Special Education.

U.S. Commission on Civil Rights. *Racial isolation in the schools* (Vol. 1). (1967). Washington, DC: U.S. Government Printing Office.

West, J. (1986). *Executive development session.* Iowa City: University of Iowa, College of Business.

Will, M. (1984). *Bridges from school to working life: Programs for the handicapped.* Washington, DC: U.S. Department of Education, Office of Information and Resources for the Handicapped.

CHAPTER 6

Collaboration Among Clients, Families, and Service Providers

Lloyd W. Tindall and John J. Gugerty*

INTRODUCTION

In reviewing recent legislation dealing with education, vocational rehabilitation services, and job training for individuals with disabilities, two themes emerge. The first is collaboration. Laws such as the Job Training Partnership Act (P.L. 97–700), the Carl D. Perkins Vocational Education Act (P.L. 98–524), and the Education of the Handicapped Act Amendments of 1986 (P.L. 99–457) encourage or mandate state program administrators and local service providers to establish and carry out administrative, fiscal, and service linkages with other organizations dealing with the same individuals. The second theme is accountability. These laws spell out specific steps that state and local agencies must take to evaluate the impact of their services.

This chapter will focus on the first theme—collaboration—and its role in developing and sustaining structures and procedures required for youths with disabilities to make timely and appropriate transitions to greater personal, social, financial, and vocational independence. Collaboration at the federal level will be discussed first, followed by a discussion of state level collaboration

*Lloyd W. Tindall is a director of vocational special needs research at the Vocational Studies Center, School of Education, University of Wisconsin–Madison. He received his Ph.D. in vocational education from Michigan State University. His research interests are the education and employment of youth and adults with disabilities.

John J. Gugerty is a senior outreach specialist at the Vocational Studies Center, University of Wisconsin–Madison. His research interest focuses on the development of effective approaches to the vocational preparation of youths and adults who are disabled.

issues. Factors in local collaboration will then be addressed. The chapter will conclude with a look at the role of leisure activities in the transition process and a summary of recommendations for policy makers, administrators, teachers, other direct service personnel, parents, and advocates.

TRANSITION IMPLEMENTATION: KEY ACTORS AT THE FEDERAL LEVEL

Key actors at the federal level include the U.S. Department of Education, the U.S. Department of Health and Human Services, and the U.S. Department of Labor. These agencies may choose to collaborate in the implementation of transition processes for a number of reasons. The most common reason is that federal agency policies on collaboration usually develop as a result of the legislation that creates or funds these agencies. National advocacy organizations are interested in improving the transition processes and outcomes, and they may view collaboration as a means to accomplish this goal. Whatever the reasons that collaboration occurs, key actors at the federal level can affect transition at the state and local levels.

Federal Agencies

At the federal level the key agency in the development and implementation of transition is the U.S. Department of Education and offices within the department. Two key offices are the Office of Special Education and Rehabilitative Services (OSERS) and the Office of Vocational and Adult Education. The offices of Special Education and Vocational Rehabilitation are combined under OSERS. Several other federal agencies provide support and services to disabled youths and are involved directly or indirectly in transition. A key support agency important to transition is the Social Security Administration and its Social Security Disability Insurance (SSDI) and Supplemental Security Income (SSI) programs. Other key agencies are the Department of Health and Human Services and several smaller but important and highly visible agencies such as the President's Committee on Employment of the Handicapped.

The U.S. Department of Labor funds the $3 billion-plus Job Training Partnership Act (JTPA). According to the President's Committee on Employment of the Handicapped (1987), approximately 12 percent of the youths receiving employment and training services from the JTPA are disabled. JTPA, through the Private Industry Councils (PIC), is playing an increasing role in collaboration at the local level. Knight (1987) states,

> More appropriate to the business orientation of PICs would be a broad based review or comprehensive planning approach to the problems of the local labor market. This strategy will place PICs at the center of education and job training policy considerations as the nation confronts the economic and demographic

changes of the coming decade. The PIC is a unique body for bringing the private and public sectors together and is becoming, in many communities, the forum for elected, education, and community business and industry leaders to share information and to develop the means to address community employment and human resource challenges. (p. 11)

A major issue at the federal level is the lack of coordination of overlapping pieces of legislation and a workable national policy on collaboration. Schalock (1986) described the service delivery system to persons with disabilities as duplicative, fragmented, and inefficient. He claimed that the fragmented nature of current services to persons with handicaps is the result of

1. Overlapping legislation and lack of a clear national policy,
2. Multiple funding sources without financial coordination,
3. Multiple planning bodies accompanied by inadequate control and responsibility,
4. Lack of reliable data on program benefits and effectiveness. (p. 115)

Part of the problem is the shear enormity of the array of federal services for persons with disabilities. Federal agencies disperse funds and operate agencies according to the legislation that set up the agencies and that provides guidelines on the use of these funds. Many federal agencies are involved in disbursing funds to programs that serve disabled youth. A perspective on the coordination problems and the collaboration needed at the federal level can be gained by reviewing Table 6.1. Table 6.1 lists many of the federal agencies and their programs that serve youths and adults with disabilities, Catalog of Federal Domestic Assistance Number (CFDA), funding levels, and in some cases the number of persons with disabilities served. The statistics were compiled by the National Council on the Handicapped (1986).

National Advocacy Organizations

This maze of federal agencies contains other key actors such as national advocacy agencies. The list of advocacy agencies is as long and varied as the types of persons with disabilities that they serve. Advocacy agencies, as a group, are usually successful in providing leadership to their constituents at the state and local levels. Nearly every disability group has a nationally recognized professional advocacy organization. Included in the list of influential advocacy organizations are the Association for Retarded Citizens, the Association for Children and Adults with Learning Disabilities, the Council for Exceptional Children, and the American Foundation for the Blind.

These and other agencies offer a wide range of services to the persons they represent, to their parents, and to service providers. Services provided include

130 COLLABORATION: CLIENTS, FAMILIES, AND SERVICE PROVIDERS

TABLE 6.1. FEDERAL AGENCIES HAVING A DIRECT OR INDIRECT ROLE IN TRANSITION

Disabled Persons U.S. Department of Education Served	CFDA	1986 Budget
Education of Handicapped Children 4,200,000	84.027	1,164,000,000
Vocational Rehabilitation 931,800	84.126	1,100,000,000
Vocational Education (10 percent setasides) 490,000	84.048	72,000,000
National Institute of Handicapped Research	84.133	39,000,000
Rehabilitation Services—Service Projects	84.128	29,300,000
Centers for Independent Living 26,000	84.132	27,000,000
Handicapped Media Captioned Films	84.026	16,500,000
Handicapped—Innovative Development	84.023	16,000,000
Deaf Blind Centers 6,100	84.025	12,000,000
Secondary Education and Transitional Services	84.158	6,330,000
Client Assistance Program	84.161	6,300,000
Handicapped—Regional Resource Centers	84.028	6,000,000
Postsecondary Education Programs	84.078	5,300,000
Social Security Administration		
Social Security Disability Ins. 3,900,000	13.802	19,566,567
Supplemental Security Income 1,927,000	13.807	6,400,000
Department of Health and Human Services		
Developmental Disabilities—Basic Support and Advocacy	13.630	64,000,000
Developmental Disabilities—University Affiliated Facilities	13.632	9,000,000
President's Committee on Mental Retardation	13.613	800,000
Developmental Disabilities—Special Projects	13.631	2,700,000
Architectural and Transportation Barriers Compliance Board	88.001	1,930,000
Small Business Administration		
Handicapped Assistance Loans 164	59.021	30,000,000
National Council on the Handicapped	NCH	750,000
President's Committee on Employment of the Handicapped	PCEH	2,000,000

1. Lobbying for improved or new legislation
2. Awareness information
3. Legal advice
4. Publications for parents, service providers, employers, and others on needs of their disabled youths and adults and how to meet these needs
5. Advocacy techniques
6. Organized collaborative activities to meet needs

Most advocacy organizations publish newsletters and periodicals designed to enhance services for their target populations. Persons seeking information about advocacy groups in their communities can obtain it from special and vocational special needs educators or rehabilitation counselors.

Advocacy agencies at the national level are often influential when working with legislators in the development of needed legislation. These agencies were instrumental in shaping the All Handicapped Children's Act, Public Law 94–142; in shaping the Carl D. Perkins Vocational Education Act; and in modifying the Job Training Partnership Act to serve students with disabilities. Collaborative activities of the advocacy organizations have been instrumental in the implementation of legislation at both the state and local levels.

Congressional and Presidential Cabinet Committees

The U.S. Senate, the House of Representatives, and the president's cabinet have oversight committees to address the needs of persons with disabilities. The president's cabinet has secretaries in the Departments of Health and Human Services, Education, Labor, Housing and Urban Development, and Transportation. These departments fund and monitor the legislative programs listed in Table 6.1. Collaboration and access to Congressional committees is usually coordinated through the senators and representatives who serve on these committees. Advocates can communicate with members of these committees by correspondence or telephone.

National State and Local Media

Collaborative efforts to serve disabled populations need to consider the influential role of the media. National media such as newspapers, magazines, radio, and television networks have a long record of favorable attitudes toward persons with disabilities. There is a daily flow of news relating to the needs and successes of such persons. The television and movie industries produce a constant variety of shows whose themes are built around the successes, trials, and needs of various disability groups. State and local media promote activities designed to improve the education, employment, and quality of life for persons with disabilities. Collaborative activities at any level should surely include these friendly resources.

Influential Organizations

Collaboration between influential organizations and education and business is a common occurrence. An example is Louis Harris and Associates, Inc. (1986). This firm is a nationally recognized pollster in the education field, and its poll results are widely quoted and respected. The recent poll on disabled

Americans in 1986 provided an insight into the needs of disabled persons and suggested solutions.

Congress funds several influential organizations. Three of these are the President's Committee on Employment of the Handicapped, the National Council on the Handicapped, and the President's Committee on Mental Retardation. The National Association of Private Industry Councils collaborates with education and business in serving the needs of persons with disabilities, as does the National Association of Counties.

Another influential organization strong in advocacy and interagency collaboration is the National Clearinghouse on Postsecondary Education for Handicapped Individuals, which publishes *Information from Health.*

Role of Federal and Other National Actors

There are literally hundreds of public and private agencies and organizations at the national level that collaborate in assisting youths and adults with disabilities. Yet comprehensive national collaboration policy does not exist. The huge number and diverse nature of key actors at the federal level may prohibit the formation of a comprehensive collaborative approach. The role of these key influences at the federal level is twofold: (1) to concentrate on a few key issues that require new or improved legislation, and (2) to develop a collaborative approach for use at the state and local levels. Collaboration at the federal level is probably the most difficult to achieve. Collaboration improves at the state level as actors pick and choose the services of agencies and organizations to meet their objectives. Collaboration is perhaps the most efficient at the local level, where well-informed agency personnel develop specific collaboration activities to serve specific persons with disabilities. Accountability is measured most quickly and accurately at the local level, where people in local communities are quick to note the success or failure of collaborative efforts to serve people with disabilities.

KEY ACTORS WHO BRING ABOUT EFFECTIVE IMPLEMENTATION OF TRANSITION AT THE STATE LEVEL

Key actors at the state level are responsible for the development of policies to serve disabled persons within their respective organizations and agencies. Collaboration and strong leadership at the state level will assist local service providers by (1) providing a mandate or examples to follow, (2) speeding up the implementation and delivery of services, (3) providing for effective and efficient use of resources, and (4) smoothing the transition of persons with disabilities from school to work and the adult life.

State Agency Collaborative Activities and Mandates

Several federal mandates to the states have tended to increase collaboration at the state level. The federally funded Secondary Transition Intervention Effectiveness Institute at the University of Illinois works with and provides technical assistance to over 100 federally funded transition projects. These transition projects promote collaboration among special and vocational educators, vocational rehabilitation personnel, and employers. State Departments of Special Education, in implementing the All Handicapped Children's Act, Public Law 94–142, have spawned collaboration with vocational education, vocational rehabilitation, and advocacy organizations. Vocational education is included in Public Law 94–142's definition of special education, if the vocational education provided consists of specially designed instruction at no cost to the parent(s) and its purpose is to meet the unique needs of the handicapped student.

The Rehabilitation Act of 1973 (P.L. 93–112, as amended) mandates that all rehabilitation clients have Individual Written Rehabilitation Plans (IWRPs). The IWRP and the Individualized Education Plan (IEP) mandated by Public Law 94–142 are similar in that they both serve as a plan of action for the improvement of a disabled person's education and employment. State advisory committees are mandated by the Carl D. Perkins Vocational Education Act, which requires that state vocational education plans be developed and made available for review by the State Job Training Coordinating Councils (SJTCC). Individual SJTCCs have no legal authority over the plan but do coordinate JTPA and Perkins Act activities.

The Carl D. Perkins Act mandates that handicapped youth be provided with (1) information on the availability of vocational education offerings; (2) vocational assessment; (3) special services, that is, curriculum modification, equipment, facilities, and so on; (4) guidance, counseling, and career development; (5) counseling for transition; (6) equal access; (7) least restrictive environments; and (8) programs offered in collaboration with special education, as is appropriate.

Section Two of the Carl D. Perkins Act mandates collaboration at the state and local levels. Specifically these mandates address

1. Collaboration between public agencies and the private sector in preparing individuals for employment, in promoting the quality of vocational education in the states, and in making the vocational system more responsive to the labor market in the states.
2. Part B, State Organizational and Planning Responsibilities, Section III, states, "The responsibility of the State Board shall include the adaptation of such procedures as the State Board considers necessary to implement State level coordination with the State Job Training Coordinating Council to encourage cooperation in the conduct of their respective programs."

State boards of vocational education will be reviewed by the JTPA State Job Training Coordinating Council.

3. Section III (B) states that the "planning periods required by paragraph (1) of this subsection shall be coterminous with the planning program periods required under this section 104(a) of the Job Training Partnership Act." Other Perkins Act coordination-oriented activities include the linkage of authorized data systems, occupational information systems, and information basis of such systems. The act also allows the use of complementary funds in the development of vocational programs.

Many areas of the U.S. Department of Labor's Job Training Partnership Act mandate and/or imply collaborative activities. The need for collaboration between JTPA and other agencies can be seen in JTPA's purpose, which is to "establish programs to prepare youth and unskilled adults for entry into the labor force and to afford job training to those economically disadvantaged individuals and other individuals facing serious barriers to employment, who are in special need of such training to obtain productive employment," as noted in Section 2 of the act.

Fundable activities under Title IIA of JTPA include job search assistance, employment counseling, basic skills training, vocational skills training, work habits, education to work activities, work experience, on-the-job training, job development, and several other areas. In addition, JTPA, under Title IIB, offers a summer training program for disadvantaged and handicapped youths.

All areas of the United States fall within one of the approximately 600 Service Delivery Areas (SDA). Service Delivery Areas must consist of a local government with a population of 200,000 or more or any consortium of contiguous units of general local government with an aggregate of 200,000 or more. The administrative structure of the SDA is the Private Industry Council (PIC). Private Industry Councils comprise a broad range of community members, 51 percent of whom must be from the private sector. Agencies competing for JTPA funds must describe their collaboration activities in their proposals to the PICs.

In most states the amount of federal funds spent in training handicapped youths under the Job Training Partnership Act is three to four times the amount spent in the education of handicapped youths under the Carl D. Perkins Vocational Education Act, in which 10 percent of the funds are set aside for the education of handicapped youths.

A Summary of Agency Mandates

Legislation at the federal level places an emphasis on collaboration at the state and local levels. Opportunities for collaboration are virtually unlimited. A list of some of the reasons for collaboration follows:

1. The IWRP and IEP have similar objectives
2. The Office of Special Education and Rehabilitative Services, the Carl D. Perkins Act, JTPA, and the Vocational Rehabilitation Act all require a transition plan with similar objectives and outcomes.
3. Vocational education and JTPA curricula and training programs are similar and overlapping.
4. Private Industry Councils require secondary and postsecondary schools and other agencies to collaborate in the delivery of services.
5. The State Vocational Education Plan must be reviewed by the JTPA State Job Training Coordinating Council.
6. The Carl D. Perkins Vocational Education Act and JTPA promote business and education partnerships.

Meaning to Key Actors at the State Level

Responsibility for putting all these mandates into perspective should be taken seriously at the state level. The shunning of this responsibility by state agencies casts an unnecessary burden on agency personnel at the local level. Cooperative agreements among vocational and special education, vocational rehabilitation, programs funded by JTPA, and other agencies should be worked out at the state level. An example of such a successful agreement is the Cooperative Agreement Plan among Vocational Rehabilitation, Vocational/Technical Education, Secondary Vocational Education, and Special Education (Minnesota Department of Education, 1986). See Table 6.2.

Key actors at the state level should also exhibit collaborative approaches that can be followed at the local level. Open communications and mutual trust among key personnel are extremely important to the implementation process. State level collaborative efforts can provide examples of cooperation and give leadership and technical assistance to local level efforts.

Tindall and colleagues (1982) listed activities that state level teams can use to help implement and maintain local collaborative efforts.

1. Prepare and distribute information on the state level negotiated agreements to local interagency teams.
2. Design and develop a monitoring and evaluation system to assess process and product outcomes of local linkages.
3. Organize state level interagency linkage teams to give inservice and provide technical assistance to local level personnel.
4. Maintain communication with local level interagency teams.
5. Periodically review state level agreements and adjust appropriately.
6. Develop plans designed to increase the number of local interagency agreements and cooperating teams.
7. Evaluate the effectiveness of state and local agreements to insure that em-

ployment and training opportunities of handicapped individuals are being improved.

Initiating Collaboration

Although several agencies have received mandates to collaborate with other agencies, it is the responsibility of individual agency personnel to take the first step and make the initial efforts to achieve such goals. Numerous potentially important leadership opportunities exist for individuals and groups of individuals to work collaboratively. However, a close examination of successful collaboration efforts at the state and national levels usually identifies single individuals who function as the key actors in initiating and maintaining collaboration activities.

Collaboration activities at the state level can be initiated by personnel in almost any of the agencies having roles in the education and employment of persons with disabilities. Although legislation may mandate certain collaborative activities, no overall mandate has been established. Someone must take the initiative and the responsibility of leading the collaborative process. The National Council on the Handicapped (1986) realized this problem and recommended that Congress direct the U.S. Department of Education to designate State Education Agencies as having the responsibility for starting, developing, and carrying out transition processes.

Problems Facing the Key Actors

The ability to implement collaborative activities depends, to a great extent, on the ability to eliminate or cope with barriers that face disabled populations. Halloran and colleagues (1986) reported on barriers that have formed, in part, because of a lack of coordination of efforts in assisting students with severe disabilities. Among the barriers that he identified were the following:

1. The limited availability of community-based services,
2. Competition with other clients for available programs,
3. The lack of effective coordination between schools and adult service agencies within the community,
4. Parental concern over situations they and their children encounter in the transition from school to adult services,
5. The need to address the importance of leisure and community arrangements in transition planning, and
6. Lack of state legislation to expand community-based services.

Several earlier authors have provided insight and identified factors that contribute to the development and implementation of collaborative plans. Levine and White (1961) listed the resources necessary for achieving an agency's objectives as clients, labor, equipment, knowledge about the services to be

TABLE 6.2. 1984–86 IMPLEMENTATION PLAN FOR THE COOPERATIVE AGREEMENT BETWEEN VOCATIONAL REHABILITATION, VOCATIONAL/TECHNICAL EDUCATION, SECONDARY VOCATIONAL EDUCATION AND SPECIAL EDUCATION IN MINNESOTA

GOAL: To develop, promote, and implement standards for the continued provision and coordination of vocational rehabilitation (VR), vocational/technical education (VTE), vocational education (VE), and special education (SE) services in Minnesota so that a transition from school to work system for all handicapped persons is established or improved at the community level.

OBJECTIVES: A. To continue to promote:

   1. The coordination of referrals, assessments and program services to students/clients who are beginning to make their transition from school to work.

   2. The involvement of vocational rehabilitation counselors and all other involved agencies in the staffings of LEA secondary school-age students/clients eligible for transition services, and

   3. The joint development of individual education plans (IEP) and individual written rehabilitation programs (IWRP) with other interested agencies and parents so that each student/client has an individualized transitional plan.

   B. To clarify the definition of transition services for Minnesota's handicapped students/clients.

   C. To clarify overlapping eligibility criteria for agencies.

   D. To reevaluate, clarify and coordinate the provision of services as outlined in Attachment A of the Interagency Cooperative Agreement in terms of the new emphasis on transition services.

   E. To promote the establishment of local interagency committees which include Local Education Agencies (LEAs), Vocational Rehabilitation (VR), Vocational/Technical Education (AVTIs), Job Training Offices (JTPA), State Services for the Blind (SSB), Developmental Achievement Centers (DACs) and other Developmental Disabilities grant recipients, parents, rehabilitation facilities and other providers of services to handicapped youth/adults.

   F. To promote the development of local cooperative agreements between providers of transition services.

   G. To establish and implement an evaluation mechanism that will monitor the effectiveness of this agreement.

TABLE 6.2. Continued

Activity	Time Line	Who Responsible	Materials/Resources Needed	Evaluation Criteria
1. To assist and facilitate agencies' applying for "Transition from School to Work" federal grants	Summer, 1984	Interagency Committee	Federal Grant	All grants were submitted in a timely manner according to Federal Regulation
2. To establish an on-going Advisory Committee utilizing members of the Interagency Committee to assist those projects funded under "Transition" federal grants	December, 1984	Expanded Interagency Committee	Grant Project Materials	Project evaluation is completed
3. To co-sponsor the "Bridging the Gap from Home to School to Work", a Minnesota Association for Persons with Severe Handicaps (MNASH), the Developmental Disabilities Program Office and the State Job Training Office	November 15–16, 1984	Interagency Committee and other agency representatives	National and local speakers and information	Conference Evaluation results indicate transition information was disseminated
4. To expand the membership of the Interagency Committee to include representatives from the Developmental Disabilities Program Office, the State Job Training Office, State Services for the Blind, and a parents' organization to review and revise the Cooperative Agreement	Fall, 1984 to June, 1986	Interagency Committee	Cooperative Agreement	Cooperative Agreement is revised
5. To plan, prepare and support all activities regarding a Transition Partnership Conference whose goals are to: 1) define Transition;	January 16–18, 1985	Expanded Interagency Committee	Goal statements and local data	Minnesota Transition policy is set and plans disseminated

138

2) identify problems and strategies
3) provide policy direction/redirection; and
4) plan for local/regional/state service delivery

Objective/Activity	Timeline	Responsible Party	Data Source/Method	Outcome
6. To explore methods for making Education and Rehabilitation data systems for handicapped persons more compatible with each other and to become aware of other agencies' data systems	Spring, 1984 to June, 1986	Norena Hale (SE); Ron Koebnick (VE); Ken Lundquist (VR); Lloyd Petri (SBVTE); Kim Rezek (VR)	Agency data	Data systems are revised to reflect coordination efforts
7. To assess and/or survey the extent and nature of local arrangements between all agencies involved in providing Transition services to handicapped youth	Spring, 1984 to June, 1986	Expanded Interagency Committee	On-site visits and Survey Instrument	A catalog of local programs is developed
8. To provide technical assistance as requested to LEAs, VR, AVTIs, JTPA, DACs and other interested agency staff who are, or may be involved in providing transition services to handicapped youth	On-going as requested	Designated Committee members	As needed	Local agreements are developed and disseminated
9. To continue clarifying/revising the Agreement to provide direction to all agencies providing services to handicapped youth/adults	Meet ten times per year	Designated Committee members	Agreement and its Attachments	Modifications, information completed and disseminated on a regular basis
10. To process necessary amendments to Agreement and/or its Attachments	As needed	Designated Committee members	Agreement and its Attachments	Modifications, information completed and disseminated in a timely manner

delivered, and funds. An agency possessing all these assets would not have a need to collaborate. However, it is unlikely that an agency would adequately control all these resources; therefore, collaboration becomes more necessary and desirable.

Agencies that do collaborate were found to possess the following characteristics (Research Utilization Laboratory, 1977):

1. They were more complex, in the sense of having more staff with specialized functions, and more different types of activities within the organization.
2. They were more innovative. That is to say, they had more new programs.
3. They had more active internal communication systems, as measured by the number of committees and frequency of meetings.
4. They were slightly more decentralized, as measured by staff input into decision-making. (p. 18)

Baumheier, Welch, and Mohr (1978) identified several characteristics of exemplary collaborative relationships that vocational rehabilitation agencies had with collaborating agencies. These characteristics, which are listed below, may be relevant to collaborative efforts at both state and local levels.

1. One agency or an external coordinator should assume leadership in putting together and maintaining linkage networks.
2. All agencies involved should recognize the authority of one case manager, who is responsible for coordinating services.
3. The orientation and motivation of senior administrators may have a profound effect on the success of linkages.
4. Interagency councils or committees with power to negotiate policy or procedural changes are helpful.
5. It is necessary to allocate staff time, as well as sufficient funding levels, for linkages.
6. Client and consumer advocacy groups may assist by bringing about increased pressures for dealing with problems.
7. Organizational structures and settings may affect the success of cooperative agreements.

Advocacy Organizations

Advocacy organizations at the state level are in a position to collaborate with state and local agencies. Such collaboration may be directed toward the following areas:

1. Providing information about education and employment needs,
2. Suggesting and helping formulate legislation,

3. Promoting cooperation between parents and educators,
4. Providing feedback on the success, failure, or efficiency of programs to serve youths and adults with disabilities,
5. Cooperating in joint projects to assist specific youths and adults with disabilities,
6. Providing information to local level advocacy organizations researching how to collaborate and advocate on specific programs and issues.

The Association of Retarded Citizens and the Association for Children and Adults with Learning Disabilities are examples of national level agencies that have significant impact at the state and local levels. Conferences and workshops are often jointly developed by these and other advocacy agencies and the education and business communities. Members of advocacy agencies should establish and maintain collaborative activities with key education and employment agencies and be readily available to provide assistance and information.

Influential Organizations

Many influential organizations assist in the transition process. It is important that these organizations be involved in collaborative efforts. An example of an influential organization is the President's Committee on Employment of the Handicapped (PCEH). The PCEH is active in promoting legislation to improve services to individuals with disabilities and in providing information, ideas, and developments on national and state levels regarding the employment of disabled persons. Counterparts of the PCEH are found in each state. The California Governor's Committee on Employment of the Handicapped is one of the nation's most active Governor's Committees (1986). Services provided by this committee to persons with disabilities and service providers in California include

1. Technical assistance to employers on job placement
2. Public forum for education on employment and disability
3. Quarterly newsletter
4. Awards and recognition program for employers
5. Media access awards
6. Innovative training curriculum entitled "Windmills"

A Wisconsin advocacy organization that provides services and information to parents and service providers is the United Cerebral Palsy's Parent Education Project (1987) in Milwaukee. This project provides information to parents on legislation, implementation of legislation, advocacy, and meeting the needs of disabled youths. Project staff members conduct in-service meetings for parents, educators, and other interested groups.

THE ROLE OF COLLABORATION IN CREATING AND SUSTAINING EFFECTIVE TRANSITION SERVICES AT THE LOCAL LEVEL

Factors in Effective Collaboration

At the local level, legislation is not enough. Communities that establish and maintain effective transition services exhibit the following characteristics:

1. The sustained involvement of key individuals
2. A focus on goals that address the education and training needs of those served, coupled with a stress on activities that provide tangible progress toward those goals; this focus contrasts with a procedural-compliance orientation
3. The establishment and implementation of a clear process of collaboration between service delivery systems and advocacy groups
4. The use of a documentation mechanism that specifies goals, time lines, activities, and persons responsible for carrying out those activities

The following portions of this section will discuss these factors and provide examples of each.

Involvement of Key Individuals

Many people feel that one individual can have little impact on the direction or activities of organizations. Because of this perception, they often fail to expend sufficient effort to become effective change agents. Persons who combine intense effort with effective organizational change techniques demonstrate the power of the single committed individual. One such individual was described in an article entitled "Discover exceptional parents: Barbara Gear" (1987).

> Barbara Gear, a graduate of Cook County School of Nursing in Chicago, holds an Associate Degree in Art. Her husband is a naturopathic and chiropractic physician. Their two sons attend Arizona State University, and their 16-year-old mentally handicapped daughter, Christy, is in high school.
>
> "I had searched for help and support since Christy was three and, early on, I found it only in private sources. She entered kindergarten in the public school system, was tested and diagnosed as being borderline learning disabled (LD)/educable mentally retarded (MH), and was then placed in an EMH class where learning was minimal. After 1-1/2 years, I realized that Christy was not in the right placement and began another search. This time, with the help of many people, I became a more informed parent. Two years later, Christy was placed in a self-contained LD class where she actually began learning more than I was teaching her. I joined the Arizona Association for Citizens with Learning Disabilities (AACLD) in April 1979.
>
> "I didn't realize how desperate the local AACLD chapter was for new mem-

bers when I indicated that I wanted to be an 'active' parent. I was immediately asked to fill a vacancy as trustee of the local chapter, which meant that I was their representative to the state AACLD meeting. A month later, I was state executive secretary and chairperson of the annual AACLD conference, which I had never before attended. This conference has since grown from 200 attendees to more than 700 and is the major source of income for AACLD.

"I was president of AACLD for two years and made it clear that parents of special needs students were welcome as members. Currently, I'm a board member and chairperson of the AACLD Professional Advisory Board. I'm also in my second year as a member of the State Special Education Advisory Committee, the Graduation and Promotion Subcommittee, Corrections Subcommittee, Comprehensive System of Personnel Development Subcommittee, and chairperson of the LD Criteria Subcommittee.

"An important opportunity occurred when the Arizona Department of Education asked me to represent Arizona parents at a meeting of the Western Regional Resource Center (WRRC) in San Francisco. I have since attended every WRRC semi-annual meeting, serve on the WRRC Advisory Board and its Technology Task Force, and act as Secretary of Westlink, the WRRC's parent-professional partnership group.

"After attending the WRRC meetings, I saw the need for a working coalition in Arizona, and ultimately the Arizona Alliance for Children with Disabilities evolved. It took a while to establish goals, but now we have a brochure, three parents with not much time, some dedicated professionals to give advice, no money, no staff, and no office. . . .

"We have also written to legislators, provided speakers for groups, and sent newsletters. Future possibilities include providing a center for disseminating information to parents, tracking unmet needs in order to recommend legislative changes, and providing for respite care, summer camp, and social activities. All we need are time and funding!" (p. 6)

This individual's story illustrates the power of one dedicated person. Note the approach that she used. First, after experiencing great difficulty altering the "system" as an individual, she became part of an organized group whose members shared her concerns. Second, she volunteered to help build the organization. Third, from her leadership position at the local and state levels, she helped direct the organization's energies toward the attainment of specific goals. Fourth, she not only recognized the value of existing mechanisms, such as advisory committees and task forces, but also joined several that served agencies whose activities related to the AACLD's goals. Fifth, she recognized the need to involve other advocacy and professional organizations and helped establish a coalition. Such coalitions can help prevent advocacy groups from working at cross purposes to one another. Coalitions also lessen the likelihood that organizations will be played off against one another by those who prefer an inadequate status quo to the fear-provoking possibility of change. Sixth, she made sure that the organization and its members informed legislative decision makers about their concerns and recommended options for their consideration. Last, parent needs such as respite care and recreational opportunities for their children were addressed. Barbara Gear demonstrates how powerful a committed individual who applies effective organizational change techniques can be.

Focus on Goals

Organizations and individuals who collaborate effectively focus on specific goals. This focus is coupled with a strong emphasis on conducting only those activities that provide tangible progress toward the desired goals. Either implicitly or explicitly, two questions are asked of any proposed activity: "So what?" and "Now what?" If a proposed activity does not contribute to the attainment of a goal, it is not done. In addition, activities are not proposed nor performed in a vacuum. Each specific step is tied to the previous one, and future goals and activities are sketched out and discussed. This process provides tentative answers to the "Now what?" questions that are applied to each activity as it nears completion. This goal-directed focus contrasts with a procedural-compliance orientation often present in work groups that seldom seem to accomplish anything of substance.

The Vocational Committee of the Association for Retarded Citizens (ARC) in Dane County, Wisconsin, provides an example of how parents and professionals can collaborate to develop and maintain a goal-directed focus. The committee, co-chaired by a parent and a professional advocate who is also secretary-treasurer of the Dane County Association for Children and Adults with Disabilities, decided that vocational and transition services at both the secondary and the adult levels for youths with disabilities were not adequate. To address this problem, the committee developed a fourfold strategy:

1. Inform local decision makers about the committee's goals, solicit their views concerning their organizations' role in meeting those goals, and request their commitment to work with the committee in addressing those goals.

To accomplish this, the ARC Vocational Committee scheduled individual meetings with administrators of appropriate local organizations. These included the head of the Dane County Community Support and Health Services Department (responsible for vocational and residential services to developmentally disabled and mentally ill adults), the local office supervisor of the Division of Vocational Rehabilitation, the head of Adult Basic Education at Madison Area Technical College, the assistant director for instructional services at Madison Area Technical College, the superintendent of the Madison Public School system, a coordinator from the Integrated Student Services Department of the Madison Public School system, the Dane County Executive, and his chief assistant.

2. Obtain data regarding the status of vocational services available to learning disabled, mildly mentally retarded, and emotionally disturbed youths and adults.

The ARC Vocational Committee requested that the school districts in Dane County conduct a follow-up of former learning disabled, emotionally disturbed, and mildly mentally retarded students, if they had not done so recently, and share the results with the ARC Vocational Committee. Not all school districts have provided these data, but the Madison School District, by far the county's largest, has done so. The committee also requested data, from Dane County's adult service system and from the Division of Vocational Rehabilitation. The former has provided information regarding the number of individuals on waiting lists for vocational services, budget allocations, and the cost-per-person of various service options. The latter has provided a detailed breakdown of the types and percentage of clients served, as well as the outcomes achieved with each disability group.

3. Influence policies, service priorities, and procedures by providing feedback to agencies responsible for the education and vocational preparation of youths and adults with disabilities.

   The committee addresses this goal in three ways:

   a. Monitor advisory and oversight bodies, such as the state Department of Public Instruction's Public Law 94–142 Advisory Committee, the Wisconsin Jobs Council, and the Dane County Community Support and Health Services Department.

   b. Join advisory and oversight bodies, including the Planning Committee of the Dane County Community Support and Health Services Department, the Consumer Advisory Council of the local Division of Vocational Rehabilitation office, the special needs advisory committees of two high schools in the county, the state ARC Vocational Committee, the Steering Committee for the Madison School District's 1987–1988 evaluation of its K–12 programming for individuals who are mentally retarded, and the Advisory Committee for a Master's Level Transition Specialist training program offered by the Special Education Department of the University of Wisconsin–Whitewater.

   c. Provide verbal and written feedback concerning proposed policies, services, and regulations. Members have provided feedback on proposals to update implementation of Public Law 94–142, Chapter 115 (Wisconsin's state version of P.L. 94–142), the Governor's Coordination and Special Services Plan (used to set policy for JTPA), JTPA eligibility determination policies, JTPA 6 percent incentive grant policies, and county priorities for vocational services. Committee members also provide verbal and written feedback to state legislators on policies, priorities, and procedures that affect the vocational preparation of youths and adults with disabilities.

   d. Provide training to parents to help them understand their options, develop more effective strategies to obtain appropriate vocational preparation for their children, and facilitate their children's transition from junior high school to the secondary system and from the secondary system to adult service options and/or employment.

Because the ARC Vocational Committee is a volunteer organization, and because many individuals with disabilities need help to obtain vocational preparation and make a smooth transition from dependence to greater vocational and personal self-sufficiency, the committee sought the cooperation of other parent groups and service delivery systems. This cooperation was evident in the design and implementation of an annual parent training workshop. The host site rotates among participating school districts, and local school administrators help publicize it. Figure 6.1 illustrates the format and topics covered in the spring 1987 workshop. The committee's goal is to have the county's school districts sponsor such a workshop annually.

In addition, the committee wishes to use parent needs assessment data to improve local programming and influence both state and local policies, priorities, and procedures. To address this goal, the committee requested and received permission from the authors of a Parent Needs Assessment Instrument (Jorgensen, McCreadie, & Johnson, 1987) to share it with all school districts in the county. The ARC Vocational Committee suggested that they survey the parents of their students with this instrument or modify it to fit local conditions. The committee also suggested that districts use the results to help structure local parent meetings and staff in-service training days. The Parent Needs Assessment Instrument was first used in the Madison School District during spring 1987. Data from this survey helped shape the topics addressed in the fall 1987 parent training workshop co-sponsored by several school systems and advocacy groups. The data were also presented during the Madison school system's staff in-service training day held in October 1987 and incorporated into the Madison School District's K–12 program evaluation to be carried out during the 1987–1988 school year. Figure 6.2 illustrates this Parent Needs Assessment Instrument.

Establishment of a Clear Collaboration Process

In addition to the sustained involvement of key individuals and the adaptation of a goal-directed focus, effective collaboration requires the establishment of clear processes to achieve desired goals. This process may or may not be formally established, recorded, and signed by key decision makers. However, if it is totally informal, collaboration is jeopardized if one or more key people stop participating. In their absence, the history of the collaborative effort, as well as the mechanics of the working relationship, are lost. Written agreements, in themselves, do not guarantee that collaboration among service providers will occur, but written agreements cement the commitment of those who wish to work together and provide continuity in the event of turnover among key participants.

Figure 6.1. Parent Training Workshop

The Third Annual Workshop for Parents
Middleton High School Student Center
7400 North Avenue
Middleton, WI 53562

March 5, 12, & 19, 1987   6:00–9:30 PM

Sponsored by the Association for Retarded Citizens in Dane County (ARC), the Middleton-Cross Plains School District, the Wisconsin Association for Children and Adults with Learning Disabilities (WACLD), and Cooperative Educational Services Agency Number Two

Session I: Thursday, March 5, 1987, 6:00–9:30 PM

Speaker: Dr. Lou Brown, UW–Madison Behavioral Disabilities Department
Topic: "The Importance of Vocational Education for all Exceptional Needs Students"
Discussion: Vocational Education for the Child with Special Needs: Parents' Perspective

Session II: Thursday, March 12, 1987, 6:00–9:30 PM

Speaker: Rick Lombard, University of Wisconsin–Whitewater
Topic: "Vocational Paths in the Secondary School System"
Carousel Topics:
—Industrial Arts Education (high school)
—Business Education (high school)
—The Designated Vocational Instruction Approach and Transitioning (high school and after high school)
—Supported Work for Persons with Severe Intellectual Disabilities (middle, high school, and after high schoool)
—DVR: Services and Choices (high school and after high school)

Session III: Thursday, March 19, 1987, 6:00–9:30 PM

Speaker: Liz Irwin, Parent Education Project, Milwaukee
Topic: "Parents' Rights and the Individual Education Plan (IEP)"
Discussion: What Is an Effective IEP? Planning for Your Child

THIS PROGRAM WILL GIVE PARENTS THE OPPORTUNITY TO ASK QUESTIONS OF SPECIAL EDUCATORS, VOCATIONAL EDUCATORS, SUPPORT SERVICES EXPERTS, AND OTHER PARENTS REGARDING VOCATIONAL PLANNING FOR THEIR CHILD. PLEASE FEEL FREE TO CALL IF YOU HAVE ANY QUESTIONS. HOPE YOU CAN ATTEND!!

Who's Invited? Either or both parents.

Pre-registration required. . . . . REGISTRATION LIMITED TO 60
Send pre-registration before February 28, 1987 to:
Diane Szymanski
WACLD
5218 Century Ave.
Middleton, WI 53562

Name _____

Street _____

City _____ State _____ Zip _____

Telephone _____/_____

Will one or both parents attend? _____

Figure 6.2. Parent Needs Assessment

The Madison Metropolitan School District would like to know how our programs for mentally retarded students can better respond to your needs and those of your son or daughter. Please answer all of the following questions.

Type of child's program: _____ EMR   _____ TMR

Level of Program: _____ Early Childhood (0–5 years)
　　　　　　　　 _____ Elementary (grades K–5)
　　　　　　　　 _____ Middle (grades 6–8)
　　　　　　　　 _____ High School (grades 9–12)

DIRECTIONS: Check the specific items you would like to know more about.

1. I WOULD LIKE TO LEARN MORE ABOUT MEETING MY CHILD'S INDIVIDUAL NEEDS:
   _____ helping my child make friends
   _____ getting involved with neighborhood activities and peers
   _____ language boards, picture books, sign language, voice machines or other communication systems used by non-verbal children and adults
   _____ dealing with my child's developing sexuality
   _____ my son's/daughter's disability
   _____ dealing with my son's/daughter's behavior
   _____ setting goals for my son/daughter

2. I WOULD LIKE TO LEARN MORE ABOUT INCREASING MY CHILD'S INDEPENDENCE IN:
   _____ bathing/hygiene
   _____ cleaning his/her room
   _____ dressing

3. I WOULD LIKE TO LEARN MORE ABOUT TRANSITIONS DURING AGES 0–21 YEARS:
   _____ getting my child ready for elementary school
   _____ middle school opportunities and expectations
   _____ high school
   _____ vocational opportunities in high school

4. I WOULD LIKE TO LEARN MORE ABOUT COMMUNITY SUPPORT SERVICES:
   _____ where will he/she live?
   _____ what kind of work will he/she do?
   _____ what resources are available to help?
   _____ the post graduate training, ages 18–21
   _____ how to help my son/daughter get a job after high school
   _____ how to secure respite services

5. I WOULD LIKE TO LEARN MORE ABOUT:
   _____ the Handicapped Children's Law
   _____ my rights as a parent
   _____ the Individual Education Plan (IEP)
   _____ advocacy training
   _____ education from birth to 21 years of age

148

Figure 6.2. Continued

DIRECTIONS: Complete the following by placing a check in the appropriate space or answering the questions.

6. I TALK WITH OTHER PARENTS OF DISABLED CHILDREN:

  _____ frequently _____ sometimes _____ never

7. I WOULD LIKE TO GET TOGETHER WITH OTHER PARENTS FOR DISCUSSIONS:

  _____ monthly _____ every other month _____ not interested

8. I WANT INFORMATION ABOUT AGENCIES THAT CAN PROVIDE SUPPORT/ADVOCACY:

  _____ Family Support _____ Adult Service _____ Recreation
  _____ Youth ARC _____ ARC _____ Advocacy Groups
  _____ Respite Care _____ Special Olympics

9. HOW DO YOU FEEL YOUR CHILD WOULD BENEFIT FROM SPENDING MORE TIME IN REGULAR EDUCATION?

  _____

  _____

10. WHAT SCHOOL PROGRAMS HAVE HELPED YOUR SON OR DAUGHTER DURING THE SUMMER?

  _____

  _____

11. MY SON/DAUGHTER USES SKILLS LEARNED AT SCHOOL WHEN HE/SHE IS HOME:

  _____ always _____ sometimes _____ never

12. MY CHILD USES SKILLS LEARNED IN SCHOOL WHEN HE/SHE IS IN THE COMMUNITY:

  _____ always _____ sometimes _____ never

13. HOW WOULD YOU RATE COMMUNICATION BETWEEN HOME AND SCHOOL?

  _____ very effective _____ somewhat effective
  _____ somewhat ineffective _____ very ineffective

14. WHAT WOULD YOU SUGGEST TO IMPROVE COMMUNICATION BETWEEN HOME AND SCHOOL?

  _____

  _____

  ADDITIONAL COMMENTS: _____

  _____

Thank you for your response! Please return the completed form to Jack Jorgensen in the self-addressed, stamped envelope by May 4, 1987.

Figure 6.3 provides an example of a written collaborative agreement that includes representatives from the school system, vocational rehabilitation, the developmental disabilities system, and a parent organization. Note that "first dollar" issues are addressed directly and that the parent group is an equal participant. This agreement was signed by administrators representing each system and is currently being implemented.

Developing and Using a Documentation Mechanism

In addition to the involvement of key individuals, the establishment of precise goals, and the use of a specific collaboration process, a fourth characteristic of effective transition efforts is related to effective documentation. This documentation frequently consists of one or more sheets that are filled out on each individual to be served. These records specify who is being served, the goals to be attained, time lines, and persons responsible. Some schools incorporate these records into each individual's IEP. Others use an individual service plan. Still others set up separate transition plans. The most effective approaches tend to display certain similarities: goal specificity, concrete time lines, specific responsibilities assigned to those involved, and a cross categorical focus on the varied needs of those served. Figure 6.4 illustrates the approach used by the School Board of Leon County, Tallahassee Florida (1987) to develop and document special education students' transition plans.

Summary

Effective collaboration to provide vocational training and transition services to individuals with disabilities most often occurs when key individuals commit themselves to establishing and sustaining this process. Without the involvement of energetic, committed individuals, collaboration will exist, if at all, only on paper. The most efficient and productive among these individuals often demonstrate a goal-directed focus; involve representatives from key agencies; communicate with local and state level decision makers; and strive to influence policies, service priorities, and procedures in a systematic way over extended periods of time. Documentation, whether in the form of interagency agreements, written transition plans, or similar mechanisms, provides continuity and accountability among those involved in the process.

LEISURE ACTIVITIES AND THEIR ROLE IN TRANSITION

Collaboration to assist persons with disabilities to make the transition to adult life and the world of work should be more comprehensive than merely focusing on preparing for and acquiring employment. Persons with disabilities should also learn to use their leisure time appropriately. They should not be

Figure 6.3. Collaboration Process

Memorandum of Understanding Between the Division of Vocatlonal
Rehabilitation (DVR), DSHS the Division of Developmental
Disabilities (DDD), DSHS Washington Parents Advocating for
Vocational Education (P.A.V.E.) and _____
School District # _____

The Region 5 Division of Vocational Rehabilitation (DVR), the Region 5 Division of Developmental Disabilities (DDD), Washington Parents Advocating for Vocational Education (P.A.V.E.), and _____ School District # _____, agree to cooperate in initiating a pilot project for improving the transition of handicapped students into work in accordance with P.L. 94–142, Section 504 of the Vocational Rehabilitation Act of 1973 (P.L. 93–112), the Vocational Education Amendments of 1976 (P.L. 94–482), and the Washington State DVR/DDD/Superintendent of Public Instruction Cooperative Agreement of 1984. This pilot project will test the assumption that the transition of handicapped secondary students from school to work can be improved through a closer working relationship between the disciplines of special/general education, vocational education, vocational rehabilitation, developmental disabilities, and parent organizations.

To this end, each discipline and/or organization agrees to the following:

Special/General Education

1. Provide consultation necessary to assure the initiation of cooperative programs for identified handicapped learners in accordance with the state and local plans for special education and (PL 94–142).
2. Cooperate with appropriate vocational education, vocational rehabilitation, and developmental disabilities staff in identifying students with disabilities who are eligible for services.
3. Take responsibility for developing Individualized Education Programs (IEPs) for identified handicapped learners.
4. Assist in determining eligibility for DVR services in conjunction with vocational rehabilitation counselor. Assist in determining eligibility for DDD services in conjunction with DDD case manager.
5. Cooperate with vocational education, DDD staff and DVR staff in development of Individualized Written Rehabilitation Plan (IWRP).
6. Cooperate with vocational education, vocational rehabilitation and developmental disabilities in developing the Individual Service Plan (ISP).

151

Figure 6.3. Continued

7. Provide identified handicapped learners with the full range of special education services as outlined in the IEP, ISP, or IWRP, keeping in mind first dollar responsibility. (In cases where rehabilitation, developmental disabilities, and education can offer the same service, education has first dollar responsibility).

8. Cooperate with vocational education, vocational rehabilitation, and developmental disabilities in assessing and utilizing available labor market information for the purposes of providing appropriate supplemental instruction.

9. Cooperate with Washington P.A.V.E. in a joint effort to encourage parents to take advantage of training, information, and support in the transition process.

Vocational Education

1. Provide consultation necessary to assure the initiation of cooperative programs for identified handicapped learners in accordance with the state and local plans for vocational education and the Vocational Education Amendments of 1976 (P.L. 94–482).

2. Cooperate with appropriate special education, vocational rehabilitation, and developmental disabilities staff in identifying students with disabilities who are eligible for services.

3. Provide vocational program information (goals, objectives, assessment of essential prerequisite skills, modifications, etc.) necessary to assist in the development and implementation of the Individualized Education Programs (IEPs).

4. Assist in determining eligibility for DVR services in conjunction with vocational rehabilitation counselor. Assist in determining eligibility for DDD services in conjunction with DDD case manager.

5. Cooperate with special education, developmental disabilities and DVR staff in development of Individualized Written Rehabilitation Plan (IWRP).

6. Cooperate with special education, vocational rehabilitation, and developmental disabilities in developing the Individual Service Plan (ISP).

7. Provide identified handicapped students with the full range of vocational education services as outlined in the IEP, ISP or IWRP, keeping in mind first dollar responsibility. (In cases where rehabilitation, developmental disabilities and education can offer the same services, education has first dollar responsibility.)

8. Cooperate with special education, vocational rehabilitation, and developmental disabilities in assessing and utilizing available labor market information for the purpose of providing appropriate vocational instruction.

9. Cooperate with Washington P.A.V.E. in a joint effort to encourage parents to take advantage of training, information, and support in the transition process.

Vocational Rehabilitation

1. Assign a vocational rehabilitation counselor (VRC) to the project.

2. Cooperate with appropriate special education and vocational education staff in identifying pilot project students who may be eligible for DVR services as early as the student's sophomore year.

Figure 6.3. Continued

3. Provide vocational consultation for these potentially eligible students with disabilities to assist in the development of the Individual Education Plan (IEP) in the sophomore and junior year.

4. Determine eligibility for DVR services for those students deemed appropriate by the VRC to have a reasonable expectation for transitioning into employment as a result of DVR services in or before the student's last year in school.

5. Cooperate with special education, developmental disabilities and vocational education staff in the development of the Individual Written Rehabilitation Plan (IWRP).

6. Cooperate with special education, vocational education, and developmental disabilities staff in the development of Individual Service Plan (ISP).

7. Provide eligible students with the full range of vocational rehabilitation services as outlined in the IWRP, keeping in mind DVR first dollar responsibility. (In cases where rehabilitation and education can offer the same services, education has first dollar responsibility.)

8. Cooperate with special education and vocational education in accessing available vocational and labor market information and programs for the purpose of reaching vocational goals of eligible handicapped students.

9. Assume the sole responsibility for DVR eligible students after age 21 or when they graduate from high school.

10. Cooperate with Washington P.A.V.E. in a joint effort to encourage parents to take advantage of training, information, and support in the transition process.

Division of Developmental Disabilities

1. Cooperate with appropriate special education, vocational education and DVR staff in identifying pilot project students who may be eligible for, and request, DDD services.

2. Provide an overview of DDD services including eligibility requirements and services offered to school personnel, students and families.

3. Cooperate with special education, vocational education, and DVR staff in developing Individual Educational Plan (IEP).

4. Cooperate with special education, vocational education, and DVR staff in developing Individual Written Rehabilitation Plan (IWRP).

5. Cooperate with special education, vocational education, and DVR staff in developing Individual Service Plan (ISP).

6. Pursue possibility of service development when DDD services are not available for eligible students whose needs have been forwarded to Pierce County Developmental Disabilities coordinator.

7. Assume responsibility for initiating residential or support services when needed by DDD eligible students.

8. Cooperate with Washington P.A.V.E. in a joint effort to encourage parents to take advantage of training, information, and support in the transition process.

Figure 6.3. Continued

Washington Parents Advocating for Vocational Education (P.A.V.E.)

1. Provide publicity through newsletters about policies, activities and programs in place to encourage coordination among vocational rehabilitation, developmental disabilities, and schools.
2. Provide training for parents and others about such topics as:
   a. The purpose and process of parent involvement in the IEP/IWRP/ISP.
   b. How parents can help ensure vocational planning in their young adult's future.
   c. Understanding DDD/DVR eligibility requirements for services.
   d. How to bring vocationally related information/resources into their young adult's plan.
   e. Awareness of employment trends, testing results, local post secondary training opportunities, etc. for students with special learning needs.
3. Provide publicity in the community through parents in order to increase the employment of persons with disabilities.
4. Connect community resources which can assist student and planning team, such as training in independent living, peer support groups, equipment repair, transportation and housing assistance.
5. Provide information to parents, vocational rehabilitation, developmental disabilities, and schools about proposed regulatory and/or statutory changes affecting education and/or rehabilitation.
6. Participate in team planning meetings as a parent support person (only when invited by parent or adult student).

The terms of this agreement may be modified or revised by mutual consent. Notification shall be given to all concerned parties in advance of any modifications with opportunity of consultation. The agreement may be terminated for cause by any party upon thirty days written notice to other cooperating disciplines/organizations within Pierce County.

Signatures:

_____	_____
Superintendent Date	DVR Region 5 Date
	Administrator
Representing Dist. # _____	
Address _____	Address _____
_____	_____
_____	_____
DDD Region 5 Date	Washington P.A.V.E. Date
Administrator	Director
Address _____	_____
_____	_____

Figure 6.4.

LEON COUNTY SCHOOLS
The Best Place to Learn

LCS-ESE ————
Approved: ————
Expiration: ————

THE SCHOOL BOARD OF LEON COUNTY, FLORIDA
EXCEPTIONAL STUDENT EDUCATION
INDIVIDUAL TRANSITION PLAN

Conference Date: _____

Last Name First M	School	DOB	Student Number
Parent's Name	Diploma Option Grad. Date	AGE	Social Security No.
Address		Phone	

TRANSITION PLANNING AREAS	STATUS	RECOMMENDATIONS Anticipated Services, Placement, Other Options	RESPONSIBILITIES Parent/Student School/Agency	TIME LINE Initiated/ Completed
Personal/ Family Relationship				————
Medical Needs/ Resources/ Other				————
Personal Management Leisure/ Recreation				————
Vocational Training/ Assessment/ Placement/ Work Experience/ Post Sec. Ed.				————
Transportation				————
Financial/ Income				————
Agency Eligibility/ Resources				————
Living Arrangements				————

Comments: _____

Participants/Title Signature	Participants/Title Signature

White-Cumulative/ESE Folder   Yellow-ESE Office   Pink-Parent   Goldenrod-ESE Teacher allowed to begin employment without acquiring skills in the meaningful use of their nonworking time. For example, how will they use their leisure time, especially weekends and vacations?

Leisure skills training will enhance social development. Young adults with disabilities often exhibit immature behavior because they are treated as though they are years younger by their parents and the rest of society (Hedberg, 1979). Specifically, youths with disabilities are overpatronized, overindulged, over-avoided, and underestimated. They are not informed of the appropriateness of their actions, and this distortion of interpersonal feedback often leads to inadequate development of social skills.

Help Is Available

Researchers have been working in the field of therapeutic recreation for many years. Frye and Peters (1972) noted that "Recreation really re-creates. It affects the individual deeply, is somewhat akin to therapy, but is more positive than therapy. Recreation is pointed less toward the correction of disorder than toward the elevation of the quality of living."

Kraus (1983) noted that all recreation should be seen as therapeutic. Without question, recreation is a health-related area of human services and contributes directly to personal well-being. However, in a more specific sense, the term *therapeutic recreation service* is used to describe recreation programs and experiences that are provided for individuals who have special impairments that limit involvement. Kraus suggested that other treatment modalities, generally described under the broad heading of activity therapies, be considered when developing and designing services for clients with disabilities. Some of these areas are occupational therapy, physical therapy, corrective therapy, and adapted physical education. Other well-developed therapies to consider are in the areas of music, art, dance, play, and horticulture.

A vast array of services exists in the area of leisure and therapeutic recreation to assist persons with disabilities. Durgin, Lindsay, and Hamilton (1985) provided an extensive list of sports and recreation organizations and national information clearinghouses addressing the needs of persons with disabilities.

An example of a successful recreation program for people with disabilities is the Madison, Wisconsin, School Community Recreation Program for disabled youths (Madison Metropolitan School District, 1987). The goals of this program reflect the services offered to students with disabilities and the collaborative activities conducted. The program's statements of philosophy and goals are listed below.

Statement of Philosophy School Community Recreation

To understand the importance of developing leisure appreciations and skills throughout one's lifetime by providing opportunities to participate in a wide variety of school-related recreation activities, to explore broad community recreation resources, and to participate in related classroom discussion, activities or projects.

Recreation for People with Disabilities

The philosophy of recreation for persons with disabilities is to provide comprehensive services in order to facilitate individual development and greater participation of disabled students and adult members of the community in their leisure time pursuits.

Goals:
A. To provide individualization in services including:
   1. Assessment
   2. Leisure Education
   3. Leisure Counseling
   4. Participation Opportunities
B. To coordinate and cooperatively work with existing community agencies providing like services to persons with disabilities.
C. To provide information on accessible facilities as well as advocating for necessary changes to existing facilities or to foster improvement in transportation services, or other need areas, relevant to an individual's successful participation in a specific program.
D. Achievement of satisfaction, fun, enjoyment or self expression by each participant at the highest level of independence possible.
E. Achievement of equality in opportunity in recreation services.
F. Advocacy for opportunities that promote a normal lifestyle in all aspects of the lives of persons with disabilities in areas that would impact on the recreation participation of those individuals.

Techniques and strategies for the development and implementation of leisure activities for persons with disabilities are well established. It also is important that leisure activities be included as part of the transition from school to work.

Where to Begin

Transition teams should include persons who are familiar with and trained in the leisure and therapeutic recreation areas. This would include teams associated with Individualized Education Plans and Individual Written Rehabilitation Plans and transition teams formed in conjunction with the delivery of vocational, special education, rehabilitation, or JTPA programs and services. The normalization of persons with disabilities will be significantly improved if leisure activities are a regular part of the transition process.

Most special education programs currently include leisure in their curricula. These existing programs can be strengthened at the upper secondary level. Youths with disabilities have a critical need for recreation and the appropriate use of leisure time as they make the transition into their adult life periods. Activities to assist in the appropriate use of leisure time should be a part of any collaborative effort designed to assist youths with disabilities to make the transition from school to work and adult life.

RECOMMENDATIONS

Recommendations for enhancing the transition of youths with disabilities to work and to their adult lives are made for four groups of key actors in transition processes. It has been stated several times in this chapter that the key to the development of successful collaborative action depends on individuals. One specific individual is usually responsible for the implementation of a collaborative effort. Therefore, it will depend on an individual to initiate each of the recommendations below.

Policy Makers and Administrators at the Federal Level

- Develop a national policy to coordinate the overlapping pieces of legislation and form a workable policy on collaboration.

Policy Makers and Administrators at the State Level

- Develop, implement, and maintain state level collaborative agreements that are exemplary for local level leaders to follow.
- Mandate collaboration as a prerequisite to funding local programs.
- Provide in-service and technical assistance to assist in the development and implementation of local level collaborative efforts.

Teachers and Other Direct Service Personnel

- Develop a collaborative approach involving vocational and special educators, vocational rehabilitators, regular educators, parents, other service providers, and employers to enhance the transition of students with disabilities from school to work and the adult life.
- Collaborate on the development of follow-up approaches to provide assistance to persons with disabilities during their postschool careers.

Parents and Advocates

- Take an active role as a personal and group advocate.
- Conduct advocacy efforts as part of an organized group. Insist on the establishment of concrete goals, definite time lines, and individual accountability.
- Collaborate with other organized groups to improve the transition process and outcomes.

REFERENCES

Baumheier, E. C., Welch, H. H., & Mohr, J. (1978, June). *Cooperative arrangements and interagency linkages in vocational rehabilitation.* Denver: University of Denver, Regional Rehabilitation Research Institution.

California Governor's Committee for Employment of the Handicapped (1986). *Annual Report to the Governor.* Sacramento, California.

Carl D. Perkins Vocational Education Act, 20 U.S.C., 2301 et seq. (1984).

Discover exceptional parents: Barbara Gear. (1987, February). *Counterpoint,* p. 6.

Durgin, R. W., Linsday, M. A., and Hamilton, B. S. (1985). *A guide to recreation, leisure and travel for the handicapped* (Vol. 1. Recreation and sports). Toledo, Ohio: Resource Directories.

Education of the Handicapped Act Amendments of 1986, 20 U.S.C., 1401 et seq. (1986).

Frye, V., & Peters, M. (1972). Therapeutic recreation: Its theory and practice. In R. D. Ray, & K. E. Allen, Eds. *Serving recreation needs of special populations in Wisconsin communities.* Madison: University of Wisconsin, Department of Continuing and Vocational Education.

Halloran, W., Engelke, S., Donehey, L., Lewis, L., & Walsh, S. (1986). *Severely handicapped youth exiting public education: Issues and concerns.* Washington, DC: National Association of State Directors of Special Education.

Hedberg, S. (1979, March). Teaching the learning disabled teens to socialize: A must for survival. International Conference of the Association for Children and Adults with Learning Disabilities, San Francisco.

Job Training Partnership Act, 29 U.S.C., 1501 et seq. (1982).

Jorgensen, J., McCreadic, V., & Johnson, F. (1987). Parent needs assessment. Unpublished survey. Madison, WI: Madison Metropolitan School District.

Knight, R. (1987, Spring). Private industry councils: Partner and critic; a better understanding of their role. *The Journal for Vocational Special Needs Education,* 9(3).

Kraus, R. (1983). *Therapeutic recreation service: Principles and practices.* Saunders College Publishing.

Levine, S., & White, P. E. (1961, March). Exchange as a conceptual framework for the study of interorganizational relationships. *Administrative Quarterly,* 5.

Louis Harris and Associates, Inc. (1986). *Disabled Americans' self perceptions: Bringing disabled Americans into the mainstream.* No. 854009.

Madison Metropolitan School District. (1987). *Recreation programs for people with disabilities staff manual.* Madison, WI: Madison School-Community Recreation.

Minnesota Department of Education. (1986). Implementation plan for the cooperative agreement between Vocational Rehabilitation, Vocational/Technical Education, Secondary Vocational Education and Special Education. St. Paul, Minnesota.

National Council on the Handicapped. (1986, February). *Toward independence: An assessment of federal laws and programs affecting persons with disabilities—with legislative recommendations.* Washington, DC.

Parent Education Project. (1987, March). *The PEP Rally.* Milwaukee: United Cerebral Palsy of Southeastern Wisconsin.

The President's Committee on Employment of the Handicapped. (1987). Memorandum: Participation of disabled people in Job Training Partnership Act (JTPA). Washington, DC.

Research Utilization Laboratory. (1977, May). *RVL Number 6: Guidelines for interagency cooperation and the severely disabled.* Chicago: Jewish Vocational Services.

Schalock, R. L. (1986). Service delivery coordination. In F. R. Rusch, *Competitive employment issues and strategies.* Paul H. Brooks.

School Board of Leon County, Tallahasee, FL (1987). Individual transition plan. Unpublished planning document.

Tindall, L.W., Gugerty, J., & others (1982). *Vocational education models for linking agencies serving the handicapped: Handbook on developing effective linking strategies.* Madison: University of Wisconsin, The Vocational Studies Center.

CHAPTER 7

Job Development, Placement, and Follow-up Services

David R. Johnson, Gary J. Warrington, and Marna Lee Mellberg

Recent studies and reports that examine the status of graduates of special education programs (Halpern, Close, & Nelson, 1986; Hasazi, Gordon, & Roe, 1985; Mithaug & Horiuchi, 1983; Wehman, Kregel, & Seyfarth, 1985) and adults with disabilities (Greenleigh Associates, 1975; U.S. Department of Labor, 1977, 1979) reveal the serious difficulties these individuals are experiencing in becoming employed and deriving satisfaction from that employment. Although these reports tend to challenge the efficacy of special education, rehabilitation, and adult community service programs in general, specific criticism is directed at the ineffective manner in which public agencies have designed and made available job development, placement, and follow-up services. Criticisms are directed at:

David R. Johnson is Associate Program Director of the University Affiliated Program on Developmental Disabilities at the University of Minnesota. He received his Ph.D. in special education administration from the University of Minnesota. His research and program development interests are in special education transition services, vocational education policy, supported employment, and interagency cooperation.

Gary J. Warrington is presently an assistant principal in the Minneapolis Public Schools. He has worked in the field of special education for many years, focusing his interests on the development of community-based employment options for students with severe disabilities. He received his MA from the University of Minnesota in special education. He has lectured widely on the topic of job placement strategies for persons with disabilities.

Marna Lee Mellberg is director of human resources for Minnesota Diversified Industries. She received her Ph.D. in vocational education from the University of Minnesota. She has worked extensively in the areas of management, training, and supported employment with an emphasis on employer relationships and trainer preparation.

1. The moderate benefits of work-study programs (Bullis & Foss, 1983; Hasazi, Gordon, & Roe, 1985);
2. Inadequate vocational education programs that do not directly prepare individuals with disabilities for meaningful employment (Comptroller General of the United States, 1974; Olympus Research Corporation, 1974; U.S. Office of Civil Rights, 1980; Wehman, Kregel, & Seyfarth, 1985)
3. Limited effectiveness of work evaluation and work adjustment preplacement services in rehabilitation facilities (Berven & Maki, 1979; Chun & Growick, 1983; Cook, 1983; Stolarski, 1985);
4. Nonplacement of sheltered workers into competitive employment (Greenleigh Associates, 1975; Loosemore, 1980; U.S. Department of Labor, 1979);
5. Lack of attention given job placement activities by rehabilitation counselors (Murray, 1981; Usdane, 1976; Zadny, & James, 1977)
6. Limited development effective job follow-up and support services (Ford, Dineen, & Hall, 1984; Hanley-Maxwell et al., 1986; Rusch, 1986; Shrey, 1980).

This chapter addresses the information needs of job developers and placement personnel. The purposes of this chapter are (1) to emphasize the need and importance for developing higher levels of sophistication and expertise in providing job development, placement, and follow-up services; and (2) to present procedures involved in the placement process.

TRADITIONAL PLACEMENT SERVICES

In a recent review of job placement research Vandergoot (1986) noted that traditional job placement efforts seem to do very little to help clients get jobs, much less good jobs. It is disappointing to realize that most persons with disabilities find their own jobs with minimal assistance from special educators, vocational educators, or rehabilitation personnel. Rehabilitation counselors, for example, are reported to spend only 7 percent of their time on job placement activities with their clients (Usdane, 1976). The major part of this problem is due to the lack of attention given to job development, placement, and follow-up services by professionals.

Job placement has traditionally been viewed as an "event" and not a "process" (Vandergoot, Jacobsen, & Worrall, 1979; Wehman, 1981). Once individuals accept job offers, the rehabilitation process essentially ends. Thus, although there is a rehabilitation process leading to placement, there is not a distinct placement process (Vandergoot, Jacobsen, & Worrall, 1979).

Over the years, special education and rehabilitation programs have concentrated their energies on the development of an array of preplacement services, that is, work evaluation, work adjustment training, work experience programs, skill training programs, and job seeking skills. Such services were viewed as essential in leading clients to the point of job "readiness." So much emphasis is focused on the development of preplacement service that persons with disabilities are often unassisted when seeking and maintaining their own employment. Society certainly stresses values related to self-reliance and personal independence; however, studies show that even persons with mild handicaps can and do experience substantial difficulties in initially obtaining, as well as maintaining, employment over time (Hasazi, Gordon, & Roe, 1985; Wehman, Kregel, & Seyfarth, 1985).

Two of the most neglected, yet important functions of the placement process are job development and follow-up services. Recently, a number of competitive and supported employment model conceptualizations have been put forth (Mithaug, Hagmier & Harring, 1977; Rusch & Mithaug, 1980; Rusch & Schutz, 1979; Wehman & Hill, 1981). These conceptual models apply learning and behavior principles to job training and employment for persons with moderate and severe disabilities and stress the importance of job development and follow-up services as factors contributing to successful job placement and job retention.

TRENDS IN JOB PLACEMENT

Until recently, vocational rehabilitation programs predominantly served persons with physical disabilities or mild mental retardation (U.S. Department of Labor, 1977, 1979; Whitehead, 1979). Special education and vocational education programs that expanded during the 1970s and 1980s similarly emphasized the development of programs for students with mild disabilities. These individuals were viewed as persons who, with appropriate exposure to and involvement in preplacement evaluation and training services, could become job-ready and enter the labor market without much assistance. Job placement models developed during this time reflect similar assumptions about the individuals who were receiving and would continue to receive rehabilitation and special education services.

Recent judicial decisions and legislative enactments have increasingly emphasized the benefits of community participation by persons with moderate and severe disabilities. The Education for All Handicapped Children Act of 1975 (P.L. 94–142), the Rehabilitation Act of 1973 (P.L. 93–112), and the Carl D. Perkins Vocational-Technical Education Act of 1984 (P.L. 98–524) are components of the recent legislative trend intended to expand community-based service options for persons with more severe disabilities. These and other federal and state actions place special emphasis on providing effective job training and employment services to persons who in previous years would not have been considered for such services. Many of these individuals do not fare well in traditional job training and placement programs. These clients often do not acquire needed skills through counseling or just being in a sheltered environment, but rather they require intensive training, coordinated placement efforts, and long-term follow-up to move from sheltered rehabilitation settings or directly into competitive employment (Rusch & Mithaug, 1980).

Research has contributed substantially to the more recent changes in professional outlook regarding job development, placement, and follow-up services for persons with disabilities. By the mid-1960s, researchers began investigating the application of learning principles to the vocational training of persons with moderate and severe mental retardation (Crosson, 1969; Evans & Spradlin, 1966; Gold, 1973, 1974); later research focused on the application of behavioral principles in work settings (Rusch & Mithaug, 1980; Schutz, Vogelsberg, & Rusch, 1980; Zimmerman et al., 1969) and recent research has investigated environmental factors that influence the successful integration of persons with moderate and severe disabilities in community-based employment (Chadsey-Rusch, 1985; Schalock, 1985; Schalock, Harper, & Genung, 1981). Emerging from this research is a new technology for job training and placement that places a special emphasis on job development and follow-up services.

Although recent research has enabled an increasing number of individuals with disabilities to participate successfully in competitive employment, there remains a dearth of information that can be made available to job developers regarding the placement process itself. It is argued that job developers and placement personnel should become more knowledgeable than ever about how to work effectively with members of the business community when seeking meaningful employment opportunities. Procedures for creatively analyzing labor market trends, communicating with employers, analyzing work environments, maintaining positive relationships with job supervisors and co-workers, and providing follow-up services should be thoroughly understood by these professionals. The following sections provide personnel involved in job development, placement, and follow-up services with recommended procedures for effectively working with employers when attempting to create new employment opportunities for persons with disabilities.

THE JOB DEVELOPMENT
AND PLACEMENT PROCESS

Job placement consists primarily of a process that matches individuals' capabilities and interests to the requirements of specific full- or part-time competitive community jobs (Martin, 1986). Job development refers to specific strategies that job developers apply directly in the labor market to identify, negotiate, analyze, and secure employment options that meet the needs of workers with disabilities. Effective job development efforts begin with an analysis of labor market conditions and follow with initial contacts with business and industry representatives. Once desired placement sites have been initially secured, job developers evaluate the range and nature of job opportunities that exist within sites. Traditionally, this step involves the application of job and task analysis techniques to identify the skill requirements and working conditions of jobs. This information is used to match workers to jobs and to design on-the-job training programs. A sometimes overlooked step is to define formally the roles and responsibilities of employers and agency placement representatives. Questions that typically need to be addressed regard when performance reviews will occur, who will evaluate client progress, how co-workers should relate to workers with disabilities, and numerous other issues. In addition, job developers should initiate discussions with employers to articulate formally areas of responsibility.

One of the major weaknesses of job placement services typically offered by schools, rehabilitation programs, and other community service agencies is related to the limited application of business marketing principles and strategies to placement processes. This problem is most obvious in placement approaches that tend to serve only clients' needs, without adequate concern for assisting employers to meet their needs and business objectives. This chapter stresses the importance of using business marketing principles and strategies in approaching employers with placement objectives.

Labor Market Opportunities

On June 10, 1986, the National Alliance of Business hosted a national leadership meeting, Youth: 2000, sponsored by the Departments of Labor and Health and Human Services, with the participation of the Department of Education. The purpose of the meeting was to focus on complex and challenging economic, social, and educational issues facing today's youths. When William E. Brock, secretary of labor, addressed the meeting, he said, "Unless the economy stagnates, there will be a job for every qualified person who wants one. . . . the question is, are we going to have the people to fill them, with the kinds of skills that are requisite to those jobs." The statement that Secretary Brock offered is a telling one for all our nation's youth. What he is alluding to is that the U.S. economy is systematically being restructured, with a shift from manufacturing and agricultural labor to rapidly expanding service, information processing, and telecommunications industries. This suggests that many more new jobs will become available in the future. Thus, when securing these new jobs for individuals with disabilities, job developers will need to familiarize themselves with current labor trends and conditions and anticipate employer needs for present and future labor resources.

A second point in Secretary Brock's statement was that from now to the year 2000, demography will be on the side of people who want jobs. For years, employers have been accustomed to the availability of a large labor source, predominantly consisting of youths 16 to 25 years of age. This will radically change in the next few years. Major service industries that have relied on an abundance of youths to fill typically minimum wage positions will be scurrying for new labor sources. This means that there will be many more opportunities to provide individuals with disabilities their first job experiences within new and emerging industries. The authors of Chapter 8 comment more specifically on labor market trends that will influence future job development and placement services. The major point here is that job developers should seek out and use detailed information on labor market trends and conditions available through various federal and state employment service agencies.

Employers as Partners

Changes in the business economy and demographic factors will offer job developers increased opportunities to establish productive partnerships with the business community. These partnerships cannot, however, be struck in casual terms. The mere fact that labor market trends indicate that the employment outlook for persons with disabilities may be brighter in the future does not necessarily mean that employers will automatically perceive these individuals as the most desirable candidates for present and future positions. Owen B. Butler, retired chairperson of the Board of Proctor and Gamble, in addressing the Youth: 2000 leadership conference, commented that "a reduction in the supply of labor will not do much to solve unemployment problems . . . , in fact, in a free market society, the number of jobs created will be equal to the number of productively employable people who are available in the labor force . . . the unemployed consist primarily of people in transition between jobs, and people who are unemployable" (National Alliance of Business, 1986). Stereotyped images of persons with disabilities as being potentially unemployable and unproductive should be corrected. It is unlikely that employers will be rushing to our doorsteps in search of qualified workers with disabilities until this occurs.

Employers should be viewed as partners in efforts to create job opportunities. Partnerships with employers should be established on the basis of understanding and mutual need. Job developers should be as clear in their understanding of employers' needs to meet business objectives as they are about their clients' needs for meaningful employment. Enhancing the awareness of employers and the public regarding the capabilities of persons with disabilities to work productively, as well as taking additional initiatives to increase their level of sophistication in marketing placement services to employers, will be an ongoing responsibility of job developers.

Marketing Approach to Placement

The American Marketing Association (1985) defined marketing as a process of planning and executing the conception, pricing, promotion, and distribution of ideas, goods, or services to create changes that satisfy individual and organizational objectives. Ebert (1986), in addressing marketing strategies in rehabilitation programs, commented that successful marketing should include (1) effective planning and preparation, (2) quality products and services at competitive prices, (3) persistence, and (4) attentive customer services. These key marketing factors are the essence of effective job placement practices. First, effective planning and preparation require job developers to know their clients. The job interests and capabilities of individuals whom they are seeking to place should be well understood before job development activities are initiated. Effective planning and preparation also require job developers to be actively involved in labor market research to identify potential job leads. Second, job developers seeking to secure job placements in the business community should adequately package the services they intend to market to employers. In other words, prior to actually contacting employers, job developers should specifically define the type, level, and amount of evaluation, training, and follow-up services they will make directly available to those employers. Third, "persistence" means that job developers will need to make long-term commitments to employers. In many instances, several contacts and meetings will be required to secure placements. Some employers may simply need additional time to analyze information communicated by job developers or to examine individual concerns. Job developers who accept failure following an initial rejection by an employer miss many job placement opportunities. It is well known that employers contacted the most tend also to hire the most people (Zadny, 1980). Fourth, job developers should be continuously attentive to the ongoing needs and concerns of employers and disabled workers. Job developers should consider the needs of individuals with disabilities, as well as those of employers who are customers and consumers of the placement services that agencies offer. These points are discussed in the following sections.

Market Research Plans: Identifying Potential Job Placements

The primary purpose of marketing research plans is to identify potential job placement sites. Initial job search activities should be based on a comprehensive understanding of clients' interests, needs, and capabilities. The basic criterion that should be considered first is the desire of individuals to be trained and, ultimately, placed (Rusch & Mithaug, 1980). Once this is known, labor market research can be undertaken.

Marketing research is the systematic and complete design, execution, and

reporting of investigations to solve product, price, distribution, and promotion problems (Nelson, 1985). Nelson operationalized this definition in the
following examples of industry marketing research:

1. Scripto investigated consumer attitudes and behaviors, competitive prices
   and sales volume, and company production capabilities before introducing
   its 98-cent erasable pen in 1980.
2. Wendy's measures who buys what in their restaurants, in addition to how
   often customers eat at Wendy's, how often they eat at competitors' restaurants, and what they like and dislike about Wendy's and its competitors.
3. A. C. Nielsen audits sales of consumer packaged goods (foods, health, and
   beauty aids) in over 1,300 supermarkets across the country every two
   months, then reports the results to interested manufacturers.

Research of this nature helps marketing decision makers operate more
effectively and assists managers to plan and control operations with more confidence and efficiency. The basic purpose for presenting these examples is to
illustrate that business personnel know how to analyze their needs by planning
and executing effective marketing research. How then does this apply to the
type of research job developers should conduct in the labor market? Princi-
pally, job developers should conduct research to determine what the market
will bear. Local economic conditions, hiring trends, high-growth industries,
and emerging fields need to be surveyed.

There are many individual factors that should be considered in conducting effective labor market research. Three major factors are: (1) source of job
leads used, (2) characteristics of local industries (e.g., union versus nonunion,
small versus large industries, and location of the business of the community),
and (3) knowing how to make initial contacts with employers.

Job Lead Sources

Expanding the number of job lead sources eventually enhances opportunities
for job developers to be more selective when seeking out potential employment
options for persons with disabilities. Some of the best job developers rely extensively on job information networks. These networks typically consist of
friends, family, business associates, and acquaintances. The use of job information networks has long been recognized as the most effective method of
securing placements (Jones & Azrin, 1973; Sheppard & Belitsky, 1966), and
other methods, such as using want ads and the local job service office, are
much less effective (Dunn, 1974). Developing exhaustive lists of possible job
lead sources, which include formal sources (e.g., want ads and job service
announcements) and informal sources (e.g., friends, family, and acquaintances), provide job developers with additional flexibility when identifying job
leads. The following is a list of several formal and informal sources of job
leads:

1. Want ads
2. Job service announcements
3. Scanning yellow pages and business directories
4. Membership in local chambers of commerce
5. Participation in professional and business associations
6. Establishing a placement advisory committee
7. Informal networking with friends, family, and acquaintances
8. Requesting assistance from agency boards of directors
9. Conducting cold calls
10. Communicating placement needs to consumer advocacy organizations
11. Observing new business developments in the community

Job developers should continually expand their job lead sources and maintain updated and active files on all job leads.

Assessing Industry Characteristics

Marketing research also involves the careful assessment of industry character-istics. This is usually undertaken before initially contacting employers. During this phase of marketing research, job developers evaluate factors such as the size of industries, union versus nonunion conditions, and location of busi-nesses within communities. Each of these factors is important to the develop-ment of placement strategies.

Company size is a factor that appears to have an influence on job devel-opment and placement decisions. Small businesses employ the largest portion of the labor force, and this share is increasing (Vandergoot, 1986). The growth of small businesses in the United States has followed expansions in informa-tion processing, telecommunications and service industries. Although place-ment personnel need to learn more about conducting marketing efforts with smaller companies, several cautions appear warranted. Many small business operations today are short-lived, operate with tight profit margins, and place high demands on personnel for productivity. Others tend to be loosely struc-tured and offer minimal or no employee benefits. However, job developers are encouraged to continue placement activities in small businesses even though job stability and security may pose problems for some clients.

Rehabilitation personnel traditionally have placed most of their clients in large companies (Zadny, 1980). Galloway (1982) offered several arguments for considering large employers first: (1) A large work force is often associated with better potential for economic and status advancements (upward mobil-ity), (2) large employers often have better fringe benefits, (3) large employers are often more likely to have organizational policies devoted to employee de-velopment and training, and (4) large employers are more likely to be sensitive to internal and external policy influences regarding nondiscriminatory hiring practices. Gade and Toutges (1983) also found that large employers felt that they could more easily overlook disability-related factors than small employers. Unfortunately, large companies pose other types of problems for workers with disabilities. Because of larger and more complex organizational structures, the response time needed for management to resolve worker-related difficulties tends to be slower. Further, in large companies it is sometimes more difficult for workers to develop a personal sense of belonging.

The American labor movement has worked for decades to achieve improved services and benefits for all workers and their dependents, including those with disabilities (Corthell & Boone, 1982). Over the years, several national unions have developed policy statements specifically addressing the employment of persons with disabilities (e.g., National Restaurant Association, AFL-CIO, etc.) Other labor unions have been less accepting of efforts to employ persons with disabilities. Part of this resistance has evolved historically as a function of unions assuming responsibility for the economic welfare of its members. Perceptions of disabled individuals as potentially weakening the hard-fought-for wage structures, being less qualified than nondisabled persons in parallel job classifications, and/or not quite fitting into existing job classifications have been difficult barriers to overcome.

Several strategies should be used in overcoming these barriers in union-organized businesses. Like other organizations, local labor unions observe certain elements of protocol, tradition, and authority (Corthell & Boone, 1982). Thus, job developers need to be sensitive to these issues. Also, the involvement of local labor union representatives during early discussions regarding placement plans should be encouraged. If individuals with disabilities do not meet all the prerequisite criteria for employment in union job classifications, other means may be temporarily used to secure the job. Government civil service structures, for example, typically have job classifications referred to as fixed-term, nonclassified positions. These positions are used to employ workers on a temporary basis to meet overload production needs and usually last from a few weeks to several months. The employment of individuals in fixed-term, nonclassified positions can be used as a means to buy additional time while negotiations continue with leaders to reclassify positions to a permanent status or until individuals with disabilities prove themselves capable of handling jobs under a different classification. The fact remains, however, that most job developers continue to use nonunion business sites for the majority of their placements.

The location of a business within a community is another important consideration in job placement. In many cases, public transportation may not be available to certain industry sites. Also, in many rural areas public transportation is nonexistent. Various options exist to overcome transportation barriers. Selected examples of these options include (1) ensuring that placement sites are near clients' residence to allow for walking or bicycling to work, (2) identifying employee car pools, (3) requesting parent or guardian assistance, or (4) gaining access to special transportation vehicles that are used to transport elderly persons or preschool children.

Making Initial Contacts with Employers

Various authors emphasize the use of mail surveys and telephone canvassing to secure job leads (Martin, 1986; Rusch & Mithaug, 1980). Mail surveys are typically used to canvass large numbers of employers in a community.These procedures involve sending employers introductory letters regarding the availability of placement services at a given agency. Returned mail surveys are then followed up with phone calls. Relying on mail surveys to establish employer contacts may not, however, be time- or cost-effective (Vandergoot, 1976). In his study on mailing approaches Vandergoot (1976) reported a meager return of 4 percent on appeal letters sent to 100 managing personnel of manufacturing businesses. Gordon (1979) suggested that job development represents a persuasive form of communication. Hence, a number of factors that affect the impact of persuasion are relevant: source of message, content, message, channel (media or modality) by which the message is transmitted, characteristics of the receiver, and the nature of the issue contained in the message (Roessler & Hiett, 1983). The use of personal contacts instead of mail surveys and telephone canvassing has also been strongly advocated by others (Garzan & Mansolo, 1981; Sands & Zalkind, 1972; Usdane, 1976; Zadny, 1980).

Employers today are becoming increasingly inundated by mass mail appeals from placement agencies. The recent, rapid expansion of competitive and supported employment services in schools, rehabilitation programs, and adult day habilitation services means that an increasing number of agencies are competing for jobs from employers. There is simply more and more traffic in the marketplace. Marketing research plans, if well conceived and executed, should identify several promising businesses to contact. The authors of this chapter suggest that better results will be obtained by personally contacting employers and by requesting face-to-face meetings. Vandergoot (1976) reported that person-to-person contact is probably necessary to activate the motivational appeal implicit in one of his experimental approaches (see also Fairweather, Sanders, & Tornatzky, 1974; Roessler & Hiett, 1983).

Communicating with Employers

Marketing principles can be efficiently used by job developers when communicating with employers. Effective communications are an indication that job developers are sensitive to the motivations, needs, and expectations of employers. Specific procedures can be used to determine who should be approached in business hierarchies; what will be communicated during placement appeals; and, if placements are secured, what follow-up steps should be undertaken to assess systematically the job options being made available.

Employer Motivations and Expectations

Understanding the needs and motivations of employers is an important part of a job developer's role. Job development should be viewed as a process of seeking mutual benefits for individuals with disabilities and for their employers. It is a process in which employers' business objectives and clients' needs are both satisfied. Agencies that fail to recognize the importance of assisting employers to meet their business objectives often discover a short-lived welcome in the marketplace (Barrett & Lavin, 1987). Some placement strategists suggest emphasizing employers' concerns about making a profit (Texas Rehabilitation Commission, 1975). Others stress the importance of presenting information on the positive attitudes, motivation, and work productivity of clients (Wehman, 1981, p. 81). Whatever approach is taken, placement professionals should recognize employers' financial objectives and discuss with employers how potential employees (clients) will make a financially acceptable contribution (Shroka & Schwartz, 1982).

A study conducted by Mellberg (1984) identified several critical factors that affect employers' decisions to hire or not hire individuals who are mentally retarded. The results of this study show that (1) employers generally feel that the training and employment of individuals who are mentally retarded is the responsibility of someone other than employers, (2) employers would rather contribute in terms of money or contract work rather than employment of individuals who are mentally retarded, and (3) the primary factor affecting the decision to hire or not hire individuals who are mentally retarded is not based on altruism. The cost-effectiveness of hiring mentally retarded employees is the factor stated most often as the concern for hiring.

The implications of these findings for job developers are clear. In the area of training, for example, employers expect that the selection of individuals, their training, and the cost of these services are assumed by someone else (the placement agency). Employers also report that they do not feel competent to train individuals who are mentally retarded. Further, these employers hold high expectations that the training services for placement agencies will see each employment situation through to its satisfactory end. One of the major disincentives for hiring workers with disabilities is related to fears about firing workers who are mentally retarded. Employers express concern for not wanting to hurt individuals, as well as concerns about potential lawsuits that would result from firing workers with disabilities. Job developers should recognize the importance of employers' business objectives, employers' need for worker productivity, profit, and support that is needed during screening, training, placement, and follow-up. This is especially true when performance and/or behavior problems indicate that employees may need to be fired. Job developers who are aware of these needs tend to communicate their understanding and sensitivity of these issues to employers during placement appeals and negotiations.

Top-Down Versus Bottom-Up Contacts
Based on their past experiences, various job developers adopt differing strategies regarding whom to contact first in business. One of the most widely used,

but not consistently effective, methods stresses communication with personnel offices during initial contact efforts. Within many large corporations, personnel officers have very little direct decision-making power related to policies that affect the employment of persons with disabilities. In addition, job development actions are sometimes thwarted by personnel workers who are reluctant to make hiring commitments or even to communicate the idea to upper management.

Some job developers routinely try to identify individuals far up in an organization's hierarchy, such as chief executive officers, vice presidents, plant managers, or members of boards of directors as the targets for their first contacts (Galloway, 1982). Upper-level managers are in obvious positions to establish policies that support the hiring of persons with disabilities. Top-down strategies appear to be of particular importance in employing persons with moderate and severe disabilities. Job developers seeking to establish enclaves where several individuals will be placed in businesses will need the support of upper management. Personnel officers, first-line supervisors, and co-workers should feel that upper-management personnel are supporting their involvement in these specialized placement situations.

Job developers' initial choices between upper- or middle-level managers during initial contacts are based on their personal judgment. We suggest conveying first-contact placement messages to upper management, especially for job developers seeking to place individuals who will require special accommodations at their work sites.

Setting Up Person-to-Person Contacts

Setting up initial person-to-person contacts with employers is a straightforward procedure. As emphasized earlier, personal contacts appear to be more effective than mass mail surveys or phone canvassing. Initial labor market research efforts should yield lists of several key employers to contact. Personalized letters (not a standard form letter) of introduction should be sent introducing job developers and their placement agencies. These letters should communicate job developers' intent to call employers in the near future. It is suggested that these letters be limited to one or two clearly written paragraphs. If the employer that is being contacted was recommended by another business contact, it is appropriate to mention the referral in the letter. It is suggested that these letters not specifically address intentions to place persons with disabilities at employers' businesses. This general rule of thumb should also be used when making introductory phone calls. The primary goal is to interest employers enough so that initial meetings can be conducted. Following phone contacts, letters should be drafted and immediately sent to employers thanking them for their willingness to meet, confirming dates and times. Even if employers reject job developers' requests for initial meetings, send letters thanking them for their consideration and indicate that they will be contacted again in the future.

The Placement Appeal

Job development personnel should realize that first contacts with employers are as much an opportunity for job developers to screen employers as they are for employers to screen the competence of job developers and placement agencies. Often, job developers enter this first contact situation with specific information on clients for whom they are seeking employment. Job developers who proceed in this manner often fail to recognize what employers are looking for during this initial contact. It is more likely that employers are assessing the personal qualities of individuals making presentations and the types of training and follow-up services that could be made by placement agencies.

Job developers' purpose for initial contacts is simply to ensure that a second meeting will occur in the future. This challenge is greater than it might appear. Job development usually requires several meetings with employers prior to the placement of any clients at these sites. Galloway (1982) suggested the following goals for first meetings with potential employers:

1. Explanation to employers of available services and positive responses by developers to questions, objections, and stalls
2. Identification of employers' key decision makers
3. Collection of useful information about employers' products and services, hiring policies and procedures, operations, and labor-management environment
4. Creation of procedures for follow-up negotiations
5. Agreement on times for tours of employers' operation
6. Referrals to other potential employers
7. Clarification of employers' interests in working with job developers and their agencies

It is helpful for job developers to role-play initial contact situations with other agency staff members. Initial meetings should last no more than 20 minutes, and if time passes beyond this point, it should be due to the interest employers are expressing in job developers' services. If employers remain interested, subsequent meetings will occur. As negotiations progress, opportunities for job developers to enter employment environments to analyze work stations for specific clients may result. During the later stages of negotiation with employers, it is best to establish formal written agreements between job placement agencies and businesses. This agreement is in no way a legally binding document. This step is usually accomplished by drafting a letter of commitment and understanding between both parties.

Communicating Tax and Wage Incentives

Several federal subsidy programs provide incentives to potential employers to hire workers with disabilities. In recent years, the federal government has maintained special tax and wage subsidy programs for employers. The federal

Targeted Jobs Tax Credit program is used to promote the hiring of economically disadvantaged, minority individuals, as well as persons with disabilities. Special wage certificates can also be obtained in cases where substantially lower productivity is expected of workers with disabilities. Job developers interested in these programs should contact their state vocational rehabilitation agencies.

Although these incentives are important to overall marketing plans, some caution is warranted in their use. Galloway (1982) suggested that job developers who dwell too much on the issue of being able to provide tax incentives as marketing strategies risk having employers focus on an apparent contradiction: "If your clients would make such wonderful employees, why is the government prepared to bribe me to hire them?" The point is, these tax benefits and wage subsidy programs should be introduced after the employers express an interest in employing individual clients. Some job developers overstate the importance of these incentive programs to the extent that employers become more interested in tax breaks than the actual hiring of capable and qualified workers with disabilities.

Assessing the Range and Nature of Job Options

When jobs are targeted for individuals with disabilities, the requisite skills specific to the placements should be properly identified (Schutz & Rusch, 1982). A wide variety of systematic techniques for effectively analyzing work environments are available (Mithaug, Hagmeier, & Harring, 1977; Rusch & Mithaug, 1980; U.S. Department of Labor, 1982; Wehman, 1981). There are several categories of information that are commonly addressed when analyzing work stations.

Job Analysis Survey

Job analysis surveys enhance training programs by acquiring information about new work environments, tasks to be completed, conditions of employment, and worker requirements (Rusch & Mithaug, 1980). Job developers typically use structured recording systems to collect information regarding specific job requirements and characteristics. Several strategies can be used to collect this information. Rusch and Mithaug (1980) pointed out that the analysis of work sites should be completed by (1) interviewing people who will be direct supervisors, (2) having a conversation with the workers who are currently doing the tasks, (3) observing workers in their work environments while touring job sites, and (4) actually doing the job for a period of time. Ideally, one or two days should be reserved for observing and interviewing persons who are currently doing the job. Job developers should also request first-line supervisors to review the information collected during analysis of work sites. This will help confirm the accuracy of the information obtained.

Specific sets of information that should be collected include the following:

Type of Skills Required for the Position

1. Are the skills required realistic for the job?
2. Are skills within the ability level of the people to be included for the placement?
3. Are duties clearly defined?
4. Is supervision clearly prescribed?
5. Are available job descriptions consistent with tasks performed by the worker?
6. What are the prerequisite skills and competencies of the job?
7. What are minimum productivity requirements?

Working Conditions

1. Are normal safety procedures observed?
2. Is the business site accessible?
3. Does the work environment promote opportunities for normal interactions with nonhandicapped co-workers?
4. Does it appear that co-workers will be supportive and friendly?

Conditions of Employment

1. Are the hours scheduled at a regular time each week or does the employee operate on a flextime schedule?
2. Is the job during the day shift or the night shift?
3. Does the employer offer full-time and part-time opportunities?
4. Are available wages and benefits satisfactory?
5. Is the company viewed favorably by employees?
6. Are there opportunities for upward mobility from the initial position?
7. Are workers' travel requirements for getting to and from work reasonable?

It should be emphasized that job analysis is regarded as a component of overall marketing and placement plans. All prior information obtained from job developers' research and initial contacts with employers should be included with on-site job analyses. Job developers should maintain a comprehensive file on all job development activities. Once work sites have been analyzed, the next step is to match available individuals with jobs.

Matching Candidates to Jobs

Efforts to match candidates to jobs successfully require accurate and up-to-date information about individuals as well as specific jobs. This information needs to cover not only vocational data (e.g., clients' interests and abilities) but also medical information and personal data. Planning for the total individual should be emphasized during the job-matching process. Intended jobs should be meaningful to individuals and make sense in individuals' lives. If job matches are made on this basis, workers with disabilities should experience higher levels of job satisfaction, which should also positively influence individual workers' job retention levels. The actual matching of available positions to candidates is both an objective and a subjective process (Martin, 1986). It should be noted that there is never a perfect match between clients and job situations. There are simply too many variables to control.

There are some general strategies that can be used when attempting to make the best possible match. The first step in the job-matching process is to review objective information, or bottom line issues, related to potential placements. Objective information includes location of the job in the community, availability of transportation, client's interest in the work, job skills and ability levels required, time of the day and week work is scheduled, and other factors. These objective criteria are weighed and decisions made regarding the feasibility of the placement. Any one or a combination of these factors can affect a decision to accept or reject a placement opportunity.

The second level of decision in the job-matching process is more subjective. Professional judgment, clients' preferences, and family perspectives become primary decision-making criteria. Decisions made at this point are difficult to express in actual terms. The most important issues that should be addressed at this point are related to whether or not the work is meaningful and if the job is likely to make sense in an individual's life.

Job Development Strategies

When there is a discrepancy between the abilities of a worker and the requirements of a particular job, other strategies may be used to overcome areas of difficulty. Job restructuring, compartmentalizing work routines, and developing paired work stations are commonly used procedures. Redesigning jobs to meet the needs of individuals requires the cooperation and approval of employers. It is advisable to propose changes in work environments and/or routines in writing directly to first-line supervisors or employers. The most important individual to involve in decisions regarding proposed job modifications is the first-line supervisor. The first-line supervisor is the primary person responsible for the day-to-day management of workers. Job developers should request supervisors to participate directly in planning job modifications. This makes sense because first-line supervisors are the individuals who will be most affected by job modifications.

Job Restructuring

Job restructuring involves modifying in some way job descriptions, environments, and/or supervision levels. There are numerous examples of job restructuring procedures. Job descriptions can be altered to reduce task complexity; picture cues and coding systems can be used to sequence work tasks; work schedules can be altered and prosthetic devices can be used to improve the functioning of individuals with disabilities within work environments. Whatever restructuring procedures are used, employers and supervisors will need to be involved and assured that the changes will only help to increase productivity and not reduce workers' responsibilities for the work to be accomplished. Most job modifications are inexpensive and can be made quite easily.

Compartmentalizing Work Routines

Compartmentalizing is the process of breaking down jobs into a series of fairly homogeneous units, which makes tasks easier for an individual to learn and remember. For example, in a laundry, the job of folding linens and towels can be compartmentalized so a worker folds only towels or pillowcases or sheets. What job developers are attempting to do is to isolate a part of a job routine that individuals may be able to accomplish satisfactorily. If workers with disabilities are folding only towels, for example, other workers in the laundry would shift their work load to folding items other than towels.

Paired Work Stations

This strategy can be used when two or more individuals are placed at the same business site. Each individual is essentially employed in the same job classification and does basically the same tasks. The assumption underlying this approach is that each worker with disabilities presents certain strengths and weaknesses in the performance of job duties. Work tasks are reviewed by job developers, and those duties that match a client's strengths are assigned to that client. For example, two clients are placed in an electronics industry where the job requirements are quite simple and require only, first, the measuring and cutting of wire to specified lengths, and second, stripping insulation from both ends of the wire. In this situation, the individual who is better at measuring and cutting wire would be assigned that task, and the one who is more skilled at stripping insulation would be assigned that task. This job development strategy has been used effectively in situations where several individuals are placed at a single business site.

The Job Developer's Ongoing Role

Job developers' ongoing roles should address disabled workers' needs for systematic follow-up services at job placement sites. One fundamental reason for establishing follow-up services is to identify problems that prevent targeted employees from losing their jobs (Rusch, 1986). The role and importance of follow-up services are discussed in the final section of this chapter.

FOLLOW-UP SERVICES

Job development and placement services are only part of a comprehensive process that supports the employment of persons with disabilities. A sound marketing plan for placement efforts also includes planned strategies for how job developers and agency training staffs will remain attentive to the needs of clients and employers over time.

Information relevant to job development was gleaned from a recently completed study that identified the rehabilitation services most desired by employers who had previous experience with rehabilitation programs (Young, Rosati, & Vandergoot, 1986). These employers were asked to indicate how well their needs for services were met. Providing postplacement follow-up services including work adjustment, personal and social adjustment, and opportunities for phone consultation was cited as a highly valued service. Although this service was expressed as being highly valued, employers felt that their needs for follow-up services were not being met.

In this same study, a striking disparity was found between employers' needs and rehabilitation responses in the area of follow-up services. Only about a third of the sample was able to use these services, whereas on average, about 90 percent of the employers felt they needed the services (Young, Rosati, & Vandergoot, 1986). Meeting the needs of employers is likely to have a direct impact on clients' placement successes (Vandergoot, 1986). A lack of attention to the ongoing needs of clients and employers may ultimately result in needless job losses.

A variety of postplacement services should be developed to meet the ongoing needs of workers with disabilities for evaluation, training, and counseling. The literature reflects differing views and procedures concerning the types of follow-up services that should be provided and their appropriate frequency. Historically, follow-up services offered by vocational rehabilitation programs were intended to serve persons with physical disabilities and mild mental retardation. The assumption made for these individuals was that extensive follow-up services would not be necessary because of the capacities of these individuals to adjust satisfactorily once placed. Follow-up services are typically time-limited, with periodic on-site or phone contacts being made by rehabilitation counselors. Sinick (1962) suggested that postplacement services be provided during the first three months of work. In most cases, 60 to 90 day follow-up periods were offered, and case closures typically occurred at the end of this time.

The Role and Importance of Extended Follow-Up Services

Over the past decade, competitive and supported employment programs have become available for persons with severe disabilities. These programs evolved quickly, largely because of the refinement and adoption of specialized training technologies used in preparing persons with severe disabilities for employment (Bellamy, Horner, & Inman, 1979; Moss, 1980; Rusch & Mithaug, 1980; Wehman, 1981). Ford, Dineen, and Hall (1984) pointed out that although vocational training and job placement are closely important facets of preparing individuals for living independent, satisfying lives, experience indicates that competitive placements are only the beginning of the services needed for many individuals. Extended follow-up services have been found to be of particular importance when assisting persons with severe disabilities to maintain acceptable levels of productivity and appropriate social behaviors.

A recent study by Crimando, Belcher, and Riggar (1986) noted that productivity problems account for about 38 percent of job failures, and social problems account for about 23 percent. A second study also reported that productivity and social problems, alone or in combination, cause clients with severe disabilities to lose their jobs (Hanley-Maxwell et al., 1986). Rusch (1986) commented that follow-up services after clients have been placed are necessary for several reasons, including (1) identifying problems early, (2) establishing follow-up schedules, (3) providing on-the-job intervention, (4) seeking validation by significant others, (5) planning interventions by others, (6) withdrawing follow-up, and (7) evaluating adjustment. Failure by job developers to address these areas systematically may result in needless job losses for clients.

Interventions at Employment Sites

Certainly, not all individuals with disabilities who become employed will require extensive follow-up services. Others with more severe disabilities will, however, require extensive ongoing support to maintain their employment. Follow-up services are typically provided by job developers, placement specialists, rehabilitation counselors, and other specialized staffs, such as job coaches. Follow-up contacts with persons at work sites should be carefully planned and executed. For example, schedules should be developed to indicate when job site visits will occur. Other specific follow-up procedures have been suggested by several authors (Mithaug, Hagmeier, & Harring, 1977; Mithaug & Rusch, 1980; Rusch, 1986; Wehman, 1981). Some of these procedures consist of the following components: (1) assessing skills required to complete a job, (2) reviewing and monitoring behaviors expected by supervisors, (3) socially validating training requirements, (4) specifying and verifying client reinforcement systems, (5) evaluating conformity to rules, (6) assessing skill levels relevant to jobs, (7) specifying behavioral objectives for each identified deficiency, and (8) providing additional training as required.

The systematic identification of postplacement problems is also essential. It is suggested that structured evaluations be used to obtain feedback from supervisors, co-workers, and other individuals who are aware of clients' performance levels (White & Rusch, 1983).

Withdrawing Follow-Up Services

The amount of follow-up services required by workers will vary as a function of individuals' disability levels and the complexity of jobs to be performed. The goal of placement services is to ensure that workers can manage all their assigned job duties and adjust satisfactorily to work environments. Traditional procedures for maximizing clients' levels of independence on jobs have included developing advocacy approaches that reinforce employers' cooperation and parental involvement (Wehman, 1981), gradually withdrawing job trainers from employment sites (Rusch and Mithaug, 1980; Rusch, 1986; Wehman, 1981), using co-workers as trainers (Shafer, 1986), partially withdrawing components of training programs (Rusch & Kazdin, 1981), and fading reinforcement schedules (Rusch, Connis, & Sowers, 1978). Many of these procedures are included in client training plans, with job coaches assuming responsibility for their implementation.

Procedures for withdrawing follow-up services should be routinely evaluated to ensure their effectiveness and impact on efforts to increase workers' levels of independence at work sites. Wehman (1981, p. 102) developed a data collection system that monitors the amount of training time spent on individual clients. He advocated collecting measures of direct intervention time provided to workers versus total number of hours spent by trainers at employment sites. Direct intervention time includes only the total hours and minutes spent directly assisting clients with performance or behavior problems. Monitoring direct intervention time provides a more sensitive analysis of the actual training requirements of individuals at work sites.

Use of Co-Workers and Supervisors

Little research has been undertaken to systematically investigate the important role that co-workers and supervisors sometimes play in supporting the employment of workers with disabilities. Researchers involved in the development of competitive and supported employment programs uniformly communicate that many of the follow-up activities routinely performed by job trainers can be assumed by nonhandicapped co-workers and supervisors (Rusch & Mithaug, 1980; Rusch & Schutz, 1981; Wehman, 1981). Rusch (1983) and White (1986) suggested that co-workers can serve as normative references to compare clients' behaviors and performance levels to nonhandicapped employees and provide subjective evaluations of clients' overall performance levels. Social comparisons and subjective evaluation procedures stress the overall importance of evaluating how well workers with disabilities perform assigned tasks relevant to others and how they are perceived by others. Simple measures of workers' overt behavior cannot adequately address these crucial areas; hence the importance of social validation (White, 1986).

Shafer (1986) contended that co-workers can be effectively utilized as advocates, observers, and trainers who support job placements of workers with disabilities. Advocacy can take the form of helping clients complete particularly troublesome or new parts of jobs, speaking up for individuals with their supervisors, or shielding clients from antagonistic peers (Shafer, 1986; Wehman, 1981). Co-workers can also assist workers with disabilities by observing and monitoring their levels of work performance (Kazdin & Polster, 1973; Rusch & Menchetti, 1981). These informal assessments made by co-workers can be communicated during follow-up visits to work sites. There are also many ways in which co-workers can assist workers with disabilities as they are learning work routines (DeMars, 1975; Shafer, 1986). These efforts offer promising directions in the development of follow-up procedures and services.

CONCLUSIONS

This chapter has addressed the basic components of job development, placement, and follow-up processes. Despite the obvious value and importance of job placement, it remains an elite "art" form that few master with any degree of sophistication, skill, or consistency. Job placement efforts lack a conceptual, theoretical, and empirical foundation. This is a curious dilemma, considering that the major job placement agents in vocational rehabilitation, vocational education, and now, special education and adult day habilitation services depend largely on reports of placement outcomes to judge the efficacy of their programs. It should be no surprise to professionals that the vast studies in each of these fields over the past two decades have reported major difficulties in securing meaningful employment outcomes for persons with disabilities.

In recent years, numerous advances have been made in the design of effective instructional technologies and service models that now enable individuals with severe disabilities to participate in community development. Although these frontiers are moving forward, little attention is given to improving job placement processes. It is disappointing that these advancements in training don't have a clearer relationship to placement processes. Further, rehabilitation and special education programs need to exert conscious and well-planned efforts to encourage the active involvement of employers in creating employment opportunities for persons with disabilities. This will require that strong commitments be made by placement agencies to create open environments in which the mutual interests and needs of workers with disabilities and employers can be communicated and met.

REFERENCES

American Marketing Association. (1985, March). American Marketing Association approves new marketing definition. *Marketing News*, p. 1.

Barrett, J., & Lavin, D. (1987). *The industrial work model: A guide to developing transitional and supported employment.* Menomonie: University of Wisconsin–Stout, Materials Development Center.

Bellamy, G. T., Horner, R. H., & Inman, D. P. (1979). *Vocational habilitation of severely retarded adults: A direct service technology.* Baltimore: University Park Press.

Berven, N. L., & Maki, D. R. (1979). Performance on Philadelphia JEVS samples and subsequent employment status. *Journal of Applied Rehabilitation Counseling, 10,* 214–218.

Bullis, M., & Foss, G. (1983). Cooperative work study programs in vocational rehabilitation: Results of a national survey. *Rehabilitation Counseling Bulletin, 26,* 349–352.

Carl D. Perkins Vocational Education Act (October 19, 1984). Public Law 98–524, 98 Stat. 2435, 20 USC 2301.

Chadsey-Rusch, J. G. (1985). Community integration and mental retardation: The ecobehavioral approach to service provision and assessment: In R. H. Bruininks and K. C. Lakin (Eds.) *Living and learning in the least restrictive environment* (pp. 245–260). Baltimore: Paul H. Brookes.

Chun, R. T., & Growick, B. S. (1983). On the congruence of training and placement. *Rehabilitation Counseling Bulletin, 27,* 113–116.

Comptroller General of the United States. (1974). *Federal programs for education of the handicapped: Issues and problems.* Washington, DC: General Accounting Office.

Cook, D. W. (1983). The accuracy of work evaluator and client predictions of client vocational competency and rehabilitation outcome. *Journal of Rehabilitation, 49,* 46–49.

Corthell, D. W., & Boone, L. (1982). *Marketing: An approach to placement.* Menomonie: University of Wisconsin–Stout, Research and Training Center, Stout Vocational Rehabilitation Institute.

Crimando, W., Belcher, K., & Riggar, T. F. (1986). Job retention problems of clients served in rehabilitation facilities. *Journal of Job Placement, 2,* 10–12.

Crosson, J. E. (1969). A technique for programming sheltered workshop environments for training severely retarded workers. *American Journal of Mental Deficiency, 73,* 814–818.

DeMars, P. K. (1975). Training adult retardates for private enterprise. *The American Journal of Occupational Therapy, 29,* 39–42.

Dunn, D. J. (1974). *Placement services in the rehabilitation program.* Menomonie: University of Wisconsin–Stout, Research and Training Center, Stout Vocational Rehabilitation Institute.

Ebert, T. (1986). Marketing issues in rehabilitation. *Western Industrial Record, 2,* 2–15.

Education for All Handicapped Children Act of 1975 (November 29, 1975). Public Law 94–142, 20 U.S.C. 1412.

Evans, G., & Spradlin, J. (1966). Incentives and instructions as controlling variables in productivity. *American Journal of Mental Deficiency, 71,* 129–132.

Fairweather, G. W., Saunders, D. H., & Tornatzky, L. G. (1974). *Creating change in mental health organizations.* New York: Pergamon Press.

Ford, L., Dineen, J., & Hall, J. (1984). Is there life after placement? *Education and Training of the Mentally Retarded, 19,* 291–296.

Gade, E., & Toutges, G. (1983). Employers' attitude toward hiring epileptics: Implications for job placement. *Rehabilitation Counseling Bulletin, 26,* 353–356.

Galloway, C. (1983). *Employers as partners: A guide to negotiating jobs for people with disabilities.* Sonoma, CA: Sonoma State University, Institute on Human Services.

Garzan, R., & Mansolo, R. (1981). Texas unit develops job opportunities for blind and visually impaired people. *American Rehabilitation, 7,* 25–26.

Gold, M. W. (1973). Research on the vocational rehabilitation of the retarded: The present, the future. In N. Ellis (Ed.), *International review of research in mental retardation* (Vol. 6). New York: Academic Press.

Gold, M. W. (1974) Redundant cue removal in skill training for the retarded. *Education and Training of the Mentally Retarded, 9*, 5–8.

Gordon, J. (1979). Empirically-based technologies for job development. In D. Vandergoot and J. Wornall (Eds.), *Placement in Rehabilitation* (pp. 103–125). Baltimore: University Park Press.

Greenleigh Associates. (1975). *The role of the sheltered workshop in the rehabilitation of the severely handicapped.* Washington, DC: Department of Health, Education, and Welfare, Rehabilitation Services Administration.

Halpern, A. S., Close, D. W., & Nelson, D. J. (1986). *On my own: The impact of semi-independent living programs for adults with mental retardation.* Baltimore: Paul H. Brookes.

Hanley-Maxwell, C., Rusch, F. R., Chadsey-Rusch, J., & Renzaglia, A. (1986). Reported factors contributing to job terminations of individuals with severe disabilities. *The Journal of the Association for Persons with Severe Handicaps, 11*, 45–52.

Hasazi, S. B., Gordon, L. R., & Roe, C. A. (1985). Factors associated with the employment status of handicapped youth exiting high school from 1979 to 1983. *Exceptional Children, 51*, 455–469.

Jones, R. L. & Azrin, N. H. (1973). An experimental application of a social reinforcement approach to the problem of job-finding. *Journal of Applied Behavior Analysis, 6*, 345–353.

Kazdin, A. E., & Polster, R. (1973). Intermittent token reinforcement and response maintenance in extinction. *Behavior Therapy, 4*, 386–391.

Loosemore, F. (1980). Surveys of sheltered workshops and activity therapy centres in Australia funded under the Handicapped Persons Assistance Act. *International Journal of Rehabilitation Research, 3*, 228–229.

Martin, J. E. (1986). Identifying potential jobs. In F. R. Rusch (Ed.), *Competitive employment issues and strategies* (pp. 165–174). Baltimore: Paul H. Brookes.

Mellberg, M. L. (1984). Factors affecting private sector employers' decision to hire individuals who are mentally retarded. Unpublished doctoral dissertation, University of Minnesota, MN.

Mithaug, D. E., Hagmeier, L. D., & Harring, N. G. (1977). The relationship between training activities and job placement in vocational education of the severely and profoundly handicapped. *AAESPH Review, 2*, 89–109.

Mithaug, D. , & Horiuchi, C. (1983). *Colorado statewide follow-up survey of special education students.* Denver: Colorado State Department of Education.

Moss, J. W. (1980). *Post-secondary vocational education for mentally retarded adults.* Reston, VA: ERIC Clearinghouse on Handicapped and Gifted Children.

Murray, R. A. (1981). Rehabilitation experience of service recipients related to achieving and maintaining competitive employment. *Dissertation Abstracts International, 42*, 1964. (University Microfilms No. AD681-23928.)

National Alliance of Business. (1986, June). *Youth: 2000: A call to action.* Washington DC: U.S. Department of Labor, Health and Human Services and Education.

Nelson, J. E. (1985). *Exercise in marketing research.* Boston: Kent Publishing Company.

Olympus Research Corporation. (1974). *An assessment of vocational education programs for the handicapped under Part B of the 1968 Amendments to the Vocational Education Act.* Salt Lake City.

Roessler, R. T., & Hiett, A. (1983). *A comparison of job development strategies in rehabilitation.* Fayetteville: Arkansas University, Rehabilitation Research and Training Center.

Rusch, F. R. (1983). Competitive vocational training. In M. Snell (Ed.), *Systematic instruction of the moderately and severely handicapped* (2nd ed., pp. 503–523). Columbus, OH: Charles E. Merrill.

Rusch, F. R. (1986). Developing a long-term follow-up program. In F. R. Rusch (Ed.), *Competitive employment issues and strategies* (pp. 225–232). Baltimore: Paul H. Brookes.

Rusch, F. R., Connis, R. T., & Sowers, J. (1978). The modification and maintenance of time spent attending to task using social reinforcement, token reinforcement, and response cost in an applied restaurant setting. *Journal of Special Education Technology, 2,* 18–26.

Rusch, F. R., & Kazdin, A. E. (1981). Toward a methodology of withdrawal designs for the assessment of response maintenance. *Journal of Applied Behavior Analysis, 14,* 131–140.

Rusch, F. R., & Menchetti, B. M. (1981). Increasing compliant work behaviors in a nonsheltered setting. *Mental Retardation, 19,* 107–112.

Rusch, F. R., & Mithaug, D. E. (1980). *Vocational training for mentally retarded adults: A behavior analytic approach.* Champaign, IL: Research Press.

Rusch, F. R. & Schutz, R. P. (1979). Nonsheltered employment of the mentally retarded adult: Research to reality? *Journal of Contemporary Business, 8,* 85–98.

Rusch, F. R., & Schutz, R. P. (1981). Vocational and social work behavior research: An evaluative review. In J. L. Matson & J. R. McCartney (Eds.), *Handbook of behavior modification with the mentally retarded* (pp. 247–280). New York: Plenum Press.

Sands, H., & Zalkind, S. S. (1972). Effects of an educational campaign to change employer attitudes toward hiring epileptics. *Epilepsia, 13,* 87–89.

Schalock, R. L. (1985). Comprehensive community services: A plea for interagency collaboration. In R. H. Bruininks & K. C. Lakin (Eds.), *Living and learning in the least restrictive environment* (pp. 37–63). Baltimore: Paul H. Brookes.

Schalock, R. L., Harper, R. S., & Genung, T. (1981). Community integration of mentally retarded adults: Community placement and program success. *American Journal of Mental Deficiency, 85,* 478–488.

Schutz, R. P., Vogelsberg, R. T., & Rusch, F. R. (1980). A behavioral approach to community integration of mentally retarded persons. In A. R. Novak & L. W. Heal (Eds.), *Integration of developmentally disabled individuals into the community.* Baltimore: Paul H. Brookes.

Shafer, M. S. (1986). Utilizing co-workers as change agents. In F. R. Rusch (Ed.), *Competitive employment issues and strategies* (pp. 215–224). Baltimore: Paul H. Brookes.

Sheppard, H., & Belitsky, A. (1966). *The job hunt: Job seeking behavior of unemployed workers in a local economy.* Baltimore: Johns Hopkins University Press.

Shrey, D. E. (1980). Post-employment needs of the rehabilitated client: A skilled assessment approach. *Rehabilitation Counseling Bulletin, 24,* 266–272.

Shroka, J. S., & Schwartz, S. E. (1982). Job placement of handicapped persons: A positive approach. *Career Development for Exceptional Individuals, 5,* 116–121.

Sinick, D. (1962). Placement training handbook. San Francisco: U.S. Department of Health, Education, and Welfare.

Stolarski, A. C. (1985). The success rate of vocationally handicapped individuals using psychometric data in job placement. *Dissertation Abstacts International, 45,* 2299. (University Microfilms No. ADG84–23043.)

Texas Rehabilitation Commission. (1975). *Participant's handbook for conference on placement and follow-up of severely disabled persons.* Austin, TX.

U.S. Department of Labor. (1977). *Sheltered workshop study: Workshop survey* (Vol. 1). Washington, DC.

U.S. Department of Labor. (1982). *Sheltered workshop study: Study of handicapped clients in sheltered workshops and recommendations of the secretary* (Vol. 2). Washington, DC.

U.S. Department of Labor. (1982). *A guide to job analysis: A "how-to" publication for occupational analysis.* Menomonie: University of Wisconsin–Stout, Materials Development Center.

U.S. Office of Civil Rights. U.S. Office of Civil Rights Report. (1980). Washington, DC: U.S. Department of Health, Education, and Welfare, Office of Education.

Usdane, W. (1976). The placement process in the rehabilitation of the severely handicapped. *Rehabilitation Literature, 37,* 162–165.

Vandergoot, D. (1976). A comparison of two mailing approaches attempting to generate the participation of businessmen in rehabilitation. *Rehabilitation Counseling Bulletin, 20,* 73–75.

Vandergoot, D. (1986). *Review of placement research literature: Implications for research and practice* (Contract No. 300–84–0007). Washington, DC: The Catholic University of America, DATA Institute.

Vandergoot, D., Jacobsen, R., & Worrall, J. D. (1979). New directions for placement practice in vocational rehabilitation. In D. Vandergoot & J. D. Worrall (Eds.), *Placement in rehabilitation* (pp. 2–41). Baltimore: University Park Press.

Vocational Rehabilitation Act of 1973 (September 26, 1973). Public Law 93–112, 87 Stat. 355, 29 U.S.C. 722.

Wehman, P. (1981). *Competitive employment: New horizons for severely disabled individuals.* Baltimore: Paul H. Brookes.

Wehman, P., & Hill, J. W. (1981). Competitive employment for moderately and severely handicapped individuals. *Exceptional Children, 47,* 338–345.

Wehman, P., Kregel, J., & Seyfarth, J. (1985). Transition from school to work for individuals with severe handicaps: A follow-up study. *Journal of the Association for Persons with Severe Handicaps, 10,* 132–136.

White, D. M. (1986). Social validation. In F. R. Rusch (Ed.), *Competitive employment issues and strategies* (pp. 199–214). Baltimore: Paul H. Brookes.

White, D. M., & Rusch, F. R. (1983). Social validation in competitive employment: Evaluating work performance. *Applied Research in Mental Retardation, 4,* 343–354.

Whitehead, C. (1979). Sheltered workshops in the decade ahead; Work and wages, or welfare. In G. T. Bellamy, G. O'Connor, & O. C. Karan (Eds.), *Vocational rehabilitation of severely handicapped persons—Contemporary service strategies.* Baltimore: University Park Press.

Young, J., Rosati, R., & Vandergoot, D. (1986). Initiating a marketing survey by assessing employer needs for rehabilitation services. *Journal of Rehabilitation, 52,* 37–41.

Zadny, J. J. (1980). Employer reactions to job development. *Rehabilitation Counseling Bulletin, 24,* 161–169.

Zadny, J. J., & James, L. F. (1977). Time spent on placement. *Rehabilitation Counseling Bulletin, 21,* 31–38.

Zimmerman, J., Stuckey, T., Garlick, B., & Miller, M. (1969). Effects of token reinforcement on productivity in multiply handicapped clients in a sheltered workshop. *Rehabilitation Literature, 30,* 34–41.

CHAPTER 8

Factors Affecting Employers' Roles in the School-to-Work Transition of Persons with Disabilities

James M. Brown, Diane Fjeld Joseph, and Joseph W. Wotruba*

INTRODUCTION

Far too frequently in the past, educators have guided and encouraged special needs learners and then abandoned these students when they graduated or reached the age of 21, assuming that they would succeed because of all the long hours of special help they had received during their school years. High school programs for students with disabilities often focus on math and communications skills with little or no emphasis on the skills that they will need to function effectively after leaving school. The federal transition initiative

---

*James M. Brown is an associate professor of vocational and technical education and is director of the Vocational Special Needs Research Program at the University of Minnesota. He received his Ph.D. at Bowling Green State University and is past president of the National Association of Vocational Education Special Needs Personnel. His research interests are identification and monitoring of potential dropouts, educational applications of microcomputers, influence of attitudes and motivation on learning, and development of training systems for business and industry personnel who hire disabled workers.

Diane Fjeld Joseph is a graduate student at the University of Minnesota, working on her Ph.D. in educational psychology and special education. She received her master's degree in education for the hearing impaired at Lewis and Clark College, Portland, Oregon, and completed her undergraduate degree in psychology and education at the University of Washington.

Joseph W. Wotruba is a psychologist currently attending the graduate program in educational psychology at the University of Minnesota. He completed his masters in educational psychology in 1977 at the University of Minnesota and specialized his clinical practice in the area of families of developmentally and emotionally disabled children. Present research interests are in motivation and developmental and acquired disabilities as contributing factors in the transition of special need populations into independent living and gainful employment.

that emerged in the early 1980s has caused many educators and agency personnel to realize that job-related skills are critical to the long-term survival of people with disabilities. Thus, many new well-designed and implemented efforts to enhance the quality of life many persons with disabilities have emerged. Also, increased attention has been focused on who should carry out this broad range of activities.

In 1979 the University of Minnesota's Research and Development Center for Vocational Education (MRDC) began a long-term research project designed to identify and analyze transition-related practices, policies, and preferences both within Minnesota and nationally (Brown & Kayser, 1982). The small number of transition practices identified tend to be very informal, lack consistency, are of questionable validity, and are of limited impact. However, most cooperating educators expressed strong support for the development of a well-designed transition-enhancement system that could help special needs learners to obtain meaningful, productive careers.

Brown and Kayser (1982) found that in order for transition-enhancement systems to function effectively, they should be based on the major concepts that affect institutions, communities, and students and clients. Transition models should focus on secondary school programs, postsecondary vocational training (where feasible and appropriate), interagency collaboration, pretraining activities, and posttraining activities in community employment settings.

Who Should Provide Long-Term Transition Assistance?

Just whose responsibility is it to provide long-term support to disabled workers? Obviously many workers have permanent disabilities, which need to be identified and accommodated throughout their working lives. Since (1) special education program services seldom go beyond a student's twenty-first birthday, (2) vocational education program services stop soon after students graduate and are placed in related employment settings, and (3) vocational rehabilitation agency services tend to terminate 30 to 120 days after clients are successfully placed in jobs, questions about the apparent lack of long-term services for workers with disabilities beg for a response from society. Many employers' personnel (e.g., supervisors, managers, and trainers) represent a major resource that could be used much more effectively to provide long-term transition-related services for workers with disabilities.

PRIOR EFFORTS

After developing an early transition-enhancement model, the University of Minnesota entered into a collaborative project with the University of Washington to develop an expanded transition-enhancement system that could be implemented in a variety of educational and business settings (Brown & Field,

1983). Many of the issues discussed in this chapter were identified and developed as a result of a joint Minnesota-Washington postsecondary transition project that was funded by a grant from the Office of Special Education and Rehabilitative Services (OSERS), U.S. Department of Education. Thus, an effective transition-enhancement system was developed that can address both education- and employer-related transition processes. Many of the concepts presented in this chapter stress helping job applicants (would-be workers) and previously hired workers to attain and/or maintain gainful training-related employment. We gratefully acknowledge the people and ideas of the Minnesota-Washington transition project, as well as similar projects elsewhere for the ideas and insights that have helped make this chapter possible.

IMPACT OF A CHANGING SOCIETY ON TRANSITION–ENHANCEMENT EFFORTS

A number of sociocultural phenomena influence the changing labor market. One trend that is presently affecting many labor-intensive job markets is the "mismatch effect" brought about by technological advances in the information processing industry. In addition, over the past two decades employers' needs have changed from a high demand for unskilled laborers to a greater interest in workers with higher skills and technical training. Also, hiring demands have tended to shift from manufacturing to the service industries, including such categories as clerical work, financial management, and data processing. Thus, a technological mismatch has developed between supply and demand in the labor market (Russell, 1985).

Employment Trends in the Near Future

Bowe (1984) noted that by 1990 the total supply of people who are willing to work is expected to exceed *temporarily* the number of jobs available. In addition, as the economy improves, many people who have previously dropped out of the labor force during periods of economic recession will be drawn back into the labor force. For example, after the 1974–1975 recession, the strengthened economy influenced the development of 2.9 million new jobs and 2.4 million people entered the labor market. Luckily, employment opportunities are likely to exist in specific areas of the job market until the early 1990s, in spite of an overall labor surplus. Until expected *worker shortages* occur in the mid-1990s, it will be imperative for educators, agency personnel, and business representatives to seek out these specific areas of work opportunities for persons with disabilities.

The U.S. Bureau of Labor Statistics (BLS) estimated that of the 9.1 million U.S. jobs created between 1981 and 1985, 88 percent were in service categories. The bureau also projected that by 1995, service jobs in the United

States will outnumber manufacturing positions by a ratio of 4.3 to 1 (Russell, 1985). These emerging changes within the job market should not be surprising to people in the fields of special education, vocational education, and vocational rehabilitation. For example, only 2.3 million of the 25 million new jobs created between 1970 and 1982 were in manufacturing (with 3 million manufacturing jobs *lost* between 1978 and 1980). Clearly, the major growth area for new jobs will continue to be in the *service sector*. The service sector includes a wide variety of job opportunities, including the often-mentioned and highly visible minimum wage jobs that exist in various types of fast-food restaurants. The service sector, however, also contains a broad array of high-paying jobs in areas such as law, financial management, affirmative action, environmental control, and information processing. For example, even though 50 percent of all jobs in America are already related to information processing, that figure is expected to rise to 70 percent by the year 2000.

The Baby Boom Generation

Another major trend that has been influencing the labor market for a number of decades is the impact of the "baby boom" generation. Born between the years 1945 to 1964, this generation recently celebrated the fortieth anniversary of its emergence and is now estimated to include 76 million people. As members of this generation mature, the current work force is becoming increasingly flooded with what some experts are calling the most highly educated generation ever to emerge in America (Klauda & Byrne, 1987a). As they begin to vacate many entry-level positions and unskilled jobs, those jobs will become available to a variety of other potentially qualified job seekers. These moves will occur as a result of the "boomer" generation's effort to ascend career ladders to jobs characterized by higher pay and greater responsibility. Furthermore, this generation's longevity will tend to be increased by improved medical technology, resulting in longer, healthier lives and the probability that their employability will extend beyond current retirement time lines. As these workers tend to live longer, some of the shortages of unskilled and low-skilled workers may eventually be filled by members of this aging population.

The last members of the boomer generation should reach their inevitable demise around the year 2069. The disappearance of this group from our society will make accurate projections about supply and demand in future labor markets difficult to produce. However, it seems likely that the increasing shortage of workers to fill expected employment opportunities may mean increased opportunities in the near future for minority groups and persons with disabilities and a variety of special learning needs.

As the last of the boomer generation passes through the labor force toward retirement by 2026, labor shortages in unskilled and low-skill jobs are likely to begin emerging as early as 1995. The BLS estimates that by 1990 the number of workers aged 16 to 24 will decrease by 2.7 million potential workers to a total work force of 21.3 million. An additional decrease of 1.1 million in this age group is expected by the year 1995 (Russell, 1985).

The baby boom generation has been with us for so long that it is now hard to imagine not having a large group of young people seeking jobs. For the first time in 15 years, the number of people entering the labor market will soon start to decline. The last of the baby boomers, those born in 1964, will be 24 in 1988 and will be available to enter the labor force. By the year 1990, the labor pool will be growing more slowly than the supply of jobs, and many employers will begin to struggle to obtain an adequate supply of workers.

The present labor force is highly diverse; 72 percent of the baby boom generation are employed women, and two-thirds of the married couples between the ages of 25 and 34 are members of dual-income families. Males and females in this work force are almost equally likely to be managers or professionals, with estimates of 19 percent and 18 percent, respectively (Klauda & Byrne, 1987b).

Labor Trends Specific to Persons with Disabilities

Bowe (1984) was optimistic that many persons with disabilities will find large numbers of employment opportunities during the next decade. Bowe hoped that a growing number of increasingly desirable jobs in America are going to be easier to obtain for people with disabilities than is now the case. Kiernan, McGaughey, and Schalock (1986) completed a national survey at the Developmental Evaluation Clinic, a university-affiliated program located in Boston. This survey was commissionied by the Office of Human Development Services of the U.S. Department of Health and Human Services. The clinic surveyed a large sample of vocational rehabilitation agencies, organizations, and other facilities serving persons with disabilities. Survey results indicated that 87,000 developmentally disabled (DD) adults were placed in jobs during 1984 and 1985. Of the DD persons placed in jobs, 58 percent of the adults were reported as being placed or served in sheltered employment settings. During the same period, only 5.6 percent of the DD clientele were placed in transitional training employment, 3.7 percent in supported employment, and 10.6 percent in competitive employment.

Tables 8.1, 8.2, and 8.3, adapted from a national survey of DD adults (Kiernan, McGaughey & Schalock, 1986), describe the placement of these adults in terms of occupational categories. Data summarized in Table 8.1 give the frequencies of the most reported occupational categories. For example, the food and beverage preparation and service and building (janitorial) services represent the largest occupational placement categories. Tables 8.2 and 8.3 report more detailed outcome data specifying placement by occupational category, disability level, and placements in terms of three-digit occupational categories in the *Dictionary of Occupational Titles* (U.S. Department of Labor, 1977).

TABLE 8.1. JOB PLACEMENTS BY TWO-DIGIT *D.O.T.* OCCUPATIONAL CATEGORY[a]

Category Label	Absolute Frequency	Relative Frequency[b] (percent)
Food and Beverage Preparation and Service	2,792	22.7
Building Service	2,088	17.0
Fabrication and Assembly	965	7.8
Lodging and Related Service	616	5.0
Miscellaneous Clerical	444	3.6
Packaging and Handling	426	3.5
Plant Farming	308	2.5
Production and Stock Clerk	242	2.0
Stenography, Typing, Filing	236	1.9
Miscellaneous Personal Service	199	1.6
Construction	169	1.4
Apparel Service	127	1.0
Transportation	114	1.0
Other	665	5.4

[a]As categorized in the *Dictionary of Occupational Titles* (U.S. Department of Labor, 1977).
[b]Only those job categories comprising 1 or more percent were included.

TABLE 8.2. PLACEMENTS BY OCCUPATIONAL CATEGORY AND DISABILITY LEVEL*

Occupational Category	Disability Levels			
	Severe and Profound	Moderate	Mild	70 IQ or Above
Clerical, Sales	6[a]	15[a]	80[a]	140[a]
	2.5[b]	6.2[b]	33.2[b]	58.1[b]
Service	47	240	524	427
	3.8	19.4	42.3	34.5
Agriculture, Forestry, Fishery	3.0	23	46	34
	2.8	21.7	43.4	32.1
Benchwork	18	32	96	95
	7.5	13.3	39.8	39.4
Miscellaneous	0	19	63	74
	0	12.2	40.4	47.4

[a]Number of persons within an occupational category.
[b]Percentage within an occupational category.
*Adapted from the *Dictionary of Occupational Titles* (U.S. Department of Labor, 1977).

TABLE 8.3 PLACEMENTS BY THREE-DIGIT *D.O.T.* OCCUPATIONAL CODE*

Occupation[a]	Absolute Frequency	Relative Frequency (Percent)
Food and Beverage Preparation and Service		
Host/Hostess or Steward	10	.1
Waiter	19	.2
Bartender	3	.04
Hotel, Restaurant Chef or Cook	57	.8
Miscellaneous Cook	7	.1
Meat Cutter	3	.04
Kitchen Worker	769	11.2
Miscellaneous Food and Beverage Preparation	1,926	28.0
Lodging and Related Services		
Housekeeper, Hotels	199	2.9
Housecleaner, Hotels	280	4.1
Miscellaneous Lodging Occupations	116	1.7
Building and Related Services		
Porter, Cleaner	215	3.1
Janitors	1,843	26.8
Elevator Operator	1	.01
Miscellaneous Building and Related Occupations	23	3
Fabrication and Repair of Products		
Sporting Goods	9	.1
Jewelery	9	.1
Assorted Products	947	13.8
Packaging and Materials Handling		
Packaging	116	1.6
Moving and Storing Materials	221	3.2
Miscellaneous Packing and Materials Handling	88	1.3

[a]Categories listed are those containing the highest number of placements.
*Adapted from the *Dictionary of Occupational Titles* (U.S. Department of Labor, 1977).

After analyzing their survey data, Kiernan, McGaughey, and Schalock (1986) concluded that

1. Among the facilities responding, most adults with developmental disabilities are found within shared sheltered employment environments. However, data suggest a trend toward increased movement into other employment environments, including transitional training, supported, and competitive employment.
2. Employment outcomes vary according to disability level and employment environment; higher monetary outcomes are associated with less severe disability levels and more normalized employment environments.

3. Most DD adults are likely to be placed into service, bench work, or clerical/sales occupations.

4. Competitive employment is the most common placement environment, followed by transitional training, and then supported employment. Furthermore, if a placement changes, the person is most likely to return to the environment encountered prior to placement, rather than a second alternative.

5. Of those receiving Social Security Insurance (SSI) benefits and/or Social Security Disability Insurance (SSDI), more than half are reported to have their benefits affected as a result of employment. Twenty-five percent of the people in this study's sample reported that they access SSDI 1619 (a) services, and 21.3% accessed SSDI 1619 (b) services.

6. A benefit-analysis process indicated that benefits to individuals and society from placement in employment ranged from $205 million to $280 million annually. (p. 20)

Concerns Related to the Management of a Diverse Work Force

Many personnel in business and industry are showing signs of awakening to these trends and are becoming concerned about their inability to manage a truly diverse work force. Edward Jones (1973) first developed a conceptualization of the "diversified work force," which was primarily applied to the management of black minority employees within a predominantly white labor force. That concept, however, not only applies to black minority workers but also is applicable to the management and employment of an increasingly larger number of workers with disabilities. This concept may eventually symbolize efforts to develop more effective management approaches for integrating persons with disabilities into the labor force, as projected worker shortages become a reality.

Employment Projections for Persons with Disabilities

Based on projections for 1995 and beyond, it appears likely that increased numbers of persons with disabilities may find employment in the five following job areas (Collignon, 1980):

1. *General services:* This category is intentionally broad. It includes direct services to members of the general public and to employers. Examples include secretarial and related clerical work, hotel/motel and convention services, home management services, and other services designed to assist busy people—tasks that people once did for themselves.

2. *Special services:* This grouping includes jobs in which workers provide direct services and other assistance (including devices and equipment) to persons with special needs, such as older citizens, people with chronic health conditions, and people with other disabilities.

3. *Sales:* This category is self-explanatory and includes all sales positions from groceries to sporting goods.
4. *Information services:* This grouping includes experts and other persons who are highly qualified to offer guidance and advice to corporate and individual clients, including persons with special needs.
5. *Entrepreneurship:* People start their own businesses and take advantage of two factors: (a) their own expertise and (b) market demands that are not being met by others.

LEGISLATION AND PROGRAMS
AT THE NATIONAL LEVEL

In February 1986, the National Council on the Handicapped published *Toward Independence,* which analyzed federal laws and programs affecting persons with disabilities. The council's report identified 45 major federal programs benefitting persons with disabilities and noted that approximately two-thirds of the working-age people with disabilities did not receive social security or other public assistance income. Federal disability programs emphasize income support and deemphasize initiatives focused on equal opportunity, independence, prevention, and self-sufficiency. The council's report suggested that more emphasis should be given to federal programs encouraging and assisting private sector efforts to promote opportunities and independence for individuals with disabilities.

The National Council on the Handicapped further recommended that Congress direct the Department of Education to designate individual state education agencies as leaders of efforts to start, develop, and carry out transition planning processes. The council also recommended that (1) special educators begin implementing transition-related planning processes as part of the handicapped students' individual educational programs (IEPs), (2) this planning should begin no later than the ninth grade, and (3) these processes should actively involve parents and students. Transition plans should (1) include formal written plans with long- and short-term goals and objectives identifying functional skills for employment and daily living, (2) be updated annually, and (3) be developed for all students with disabilities. The council also recommended that the Department of Education should mandate the involvement of education coordinators and vocational rehabilitation counselors in these transition processes.

The transition of persons with disabilities from schools into community-based employment settings has become an increasingly visible issue in regard to youths with disabilities. Over the last two decades federal legislation, as exemplified by the Education for Handicapped Children Act (P.L. 94–142) of 1975, the Education Amendments of 1976 (P.L. 94–482), the Vocational Rehabilitation Act of 1973 (P.L. 93–112), and the recent Education of the

Handicapped Amendments (P.L. 98–199), has focused both directly and indirectly on transition issues affecting youths with disabilities. The Office of Special Education and Rehabilitative Services (OSERS), U.S. Department of Education, prepared a document that discussed transition issues related to bridging the gap between school and work for disabled youths. It was pointed out that for many young people, the key to successful transition is the provision of a continuum of services. "The absence of appropriate transition bridges limits our ability to maximize the productivity and independence of disabled individuals." (Will, 1985, p. 1.)

In April 1987, the Minnesota Senate Education Aids Committee passed an article mandating that persons with disabilities be eligible for services from birth to age 21. This legislative action extended mandated services in Minnesota and reflects the growing awareness of how transition processes can affect youths with disabilities and their families. The Minnesota legislature also passed an article requiring that transition plans be included in all IEPs by the ninth grade or 14 years of age and calling for the formation of Community Transition Interagency Committees. Such policies clearly support the recommendations and initiatives suggested by the National Council on the Handicapped and, it is hoped, are indicative of changes that are or will soon be occurring throughout the country.

PRIOR EMPLOYMENT–RELATED STUDIES

A number of follow-up studies have focused on *post-high school* transition services for youths with disabilities and community integration and employment outcomes (Bruininks et al., 1987; Fardig et al., 1985; Hasazi, Gordon, & Roe, 1985; Hasazi et al., 1985; Holman & Bruininks, 1985; Mithaug, Horiuchi, & Fanning, 1985; Revell & Arnold, 1984; Wehman & Barcus, 1985; Wehman et al., 1985; Zigmond & Thornton, 1985). In addition, *interagency cooperation* during and after secondary school programs has been consistently viewed as being a key component of the transition-to-employment process (Johnson, Bruininks, & Thurlow, 1987; Stodden & Boone, 1987).

A review of the literature and a subsequent follow-up study by Bruininks and colleagues (in press) analyzed issues regarding how youths with disabilities make the transition from school to employment and how they are integrated into their communities. Subjects were selected from students who graduated or would have graduated in the years 1977 to 1984. Three contrast groups were established in two high schools: (1) regular education students who followed a vocational preparation coursework plan, (2) regular education students who followed a college preparation coursework plan, and (3) special education students. The proportion of persons graduating in each group was (1) 95 percent in the vocational group, (2) 98 percent in the college group, and (3) 72 percent in the special education group.

Occupational outcomes obtained by Bruininks and colleagues indicate that 79 percent of the special education group, 84 percent of the college group, and 85 percent of the vocational group are involved in paid employment. The differences in hourly earnings on the average are not substantially different among the three groups, with average hourly earnings of $7.01 for the special education group, $7.40 for the college group, and $7.85 for the vocational group. The average annual gross total wages during 1984 were $14,313 for the vocational group, $11,094 for the college group, and $12,818 for the special education group. Seventy-five percent of all groups are satisfied with their pay in comparison to the amount of work required. Less than 15 percent of the subjects obtained their jobs by using school or rehabilitation services.

Data related to the special education category descriptions and comparisons indicate that graduation rates for four categories of handicapped students, identified as being educable mentally retarded (EMR), learning disabled (LD), speech impaired (SP), and emotionally disturbed (ED), are EMR (81 percent), LD (72 percent), and SP (88 percent), with ED students displaying the lowest rate of graduation (26 percent). In addition, occupational outcome data for these four disability categories suggest that the percentages of paid employment obtained vary widely: 80 percent EMR, 80 percent LD, 73 percent ED, and 35 percent SP. Overall, it appears that postschool outcomes among these four categories of special education students are most positive for SP and LD students, and ED students have the poorest outcomes. For example, the ED students are less likely to be employed or to be involved in education activities. In addition, ED students tend to require more school services and resources than students in the other categories (Bruininks et al, 1987).

Enhancing Transition-to-Work Successes

Interagency cooperation in efforts to enhance the transition of youths with disabilities has received much attention recently in the special education literature. Stodden and Boone (1987) contended there is a need for cooperative transition planning and evaluation and that " . . . data on young handicapped adults indicate that, despite previous participation in special education programs, many experience major difficulties in bridging the gap from school to community work and living." Johnson, Bruininks, and Thurlow (1987) documented the need for more effective management strategies and suggested that many current transition efforts are less than optimal, being frequently fragmented, disorganized, and largely ineffective. They suggested that conflicting policy goals, eligibility criteria, funding patterns, and other issues regarding management of cooperative interagency planning have often inhibited, rather than facilitated, efforts to enhance the effectiveness of transition activities.

Lobbying efforts continue to draw the attention of legislators to the needs of persons with disabilities. For example, the Minnesota State Council for the handicapped has continued to draw the Minnesota Legislature's attention to quality-of-life issues. Similar problems are presumed to exist in many states; thus advocates for special needs populations are encouraged to continue to work to improve related funding allocations, priorities, and policies.

CORPORATE PERCEPTIONS OF EMPLOYMENT BARRIERS FACING WORKERS WITH DISABILITIES

One of the major business- and industry-related issues affecting the successful transition of special needs learners into gainful employment, regardless of their disability, is related to youths' sociability, the ability to "fit" into the social conventions demanded in competitive work environments. This issue often draws attention to how prospective workers are trained to carry out transition-related activities. For example, special education and secondary and postsecondary vocational special needs programs to develop students' cooperative work skills are often viewed as being ineffective.

Brolin (1978) contended that special educators should prepare students to enter vocational education programs by providing instruction focused on daily living skills, personal-social skills, occupational guidance, and general preparation to be productive workers. Specific training that stresses social and problem-solving skills related to managing conflict with authority figures is likely to enhance employability and job success. Unfortunately, curriculum modifications designed to modify maladaptive social behaviors and to avoid their negative impact on transition-related success are often ignored, poorly designed, and/or improperly implemented.

Effective Learning

There are numerous ways in which employers and educators can improve learning processes. For example, Madeline Hunter (Brandt, 1985) believed that teachers often study appropriate principles of psychology related to learning and motivation but fail to translate these principles into practices that improve their instructional efforts in the classroom. Trainers and teachers often see no similarity between principles of psychology and research and practical applications of those principles. Ysseldyke and colleagues (1982) reported that teachers often refer students for psychoeducational evaluations after observing their academic and behavioral performance in classrooms, assuming that such behaviors are caused solely by factors internal to the students. The potential contributions of learning environments to these behaviors are seldom taken into account. Similarly, teachers and trainers too often assume that students' and trainees' problems are caused primarily by learners' deficits or deficiencies. These findings support Beckman's (1976) contention that teachers accept credit for students' successes but avoid blame for students' failures by attributing their students' problems to factors outside the classroom or to dispositional characteristics.

Learned Helplessness

Ysseldyke and colleagues (1982) found a sense of "learned helplessness" that should be attributed not only to learners but also to many of their mentors. Some trainers and teachers feel they have little control over "what causes" their students' problems. In addition, they often assume that their students view themselves as suffering from "learned helplessness." This view often results in reduced personal efforts and a low sense of efficacy. Trainers and teachers often cite students' lack of ability and other environmental factors, such as the trauma of divorce and parental discipline, as the causes of students' maladaptive behaviors.

Ysseldyke and colleagues (1982) contended that when teachers attribute their instructional problems to factors external to their control (e.g., students' abilities or home environments), they often fail to implement interventions designed to *increase students' motivation*. The tendency among many persons with special learning needs, whether developmental or acquired, to lack self-initiative often continues throughout their educational experiences as habitual maladaptive behavior patterns, negatively influencing personality development and masking individuals' potential to be successfully integrated into their communities. Ysseldyke and colleagues also noted that many teachers believe they can compensate for or tolerate missing academic skills, but they expect students to be receptive to learning for teachers to be able to teach effectively. Given many trainers' and educators' inability to prepare special needs learners for their roles as members of work teams in a variety of work settings, other factors that limit the employment of persons with disabilities should also be considered.

RECOMMENDATIONS REGARDING INCENTIVES AND DISINCENTIVES

The National Council on the Handicapped (1986) addressed the issue of incentives for both the public and private sectors of business and industry and focused its recommendations on expanding the existing Targeted Jobs Tax Credit Program (TJTC) and Section 190 of the Internal Revenue Code. The council recommended that Section 190 be made permanent and that the maximum allowable deduction for removal of architectural barriers be increased to $75,000 per year for businesses that hire, reemploy, and/or assist in the employment of persons with disabilities. The council also encouraged Congress to develop other incentives, to promote return-to-work programs, and to develop model area centers for employing persons with disabilities.

Converting Disincentives to Incentives

The council recommended that Congress amend the Social Security Act, making eligibility for Social Security Insurance (SSI) and Social Security Disability

Insurance (SSDI) programs dependent on the presence of severe medical disabilities and requiring functional assessments to determine vocational potential whenever appropriate. Furthermore, the Social Security Act should also be amended to ensure that SSI and SSDI recipients who become gainfully employed will be permitted to retain benefits and have access to medical insurance. Also, the Health Care Financing Administration was encouraged to study and recommend cost-effective methods for providing health insurance coverage to persons who cannot obtain adequate insurance from private insurers at affordable rates because of preexisting conditions.

Major Disincentives

The council's examination of disincentives related to the employment of persons with disabilities resulted in the conclusion that social security laws and policies probably are the major disincentives facing persons with disabilities who are seeking full- or part-time employment. The threat of losing economic self-sufficiency under present social security legislation virtually precludes persons with disabilities from seeking employment. Many times returning to work results in a reduction of income and loss of medical and/or other benefits. Concurrently, preexisting medical conditions often make it financially prohibitive to obtain medical insurance through private insurance providers. These council recommendations, if they are implemented and if they produce the expected changes, could significantly reduce factors that limit the employment of persons with disabilities.

As business and industry personnel become increasingly aware of predicted shortages of workers in the labor market and, concurrently, aware of resources available to enhance employment opportunities for persons with disabilities, many of them may become more interested in learning how to manage these largely untapped resources. A number of major corporations identified by the National Council on the Handicapped have taken the initiative to develop programs and procedures designed to enhance efforts to employ persons with disabilities. However, the exact dynamics of how business and industry tend to respond to the employment of persons with disabilities is not yet fully understood.

Harris Survey Findings

In cooperation with the National Council on the Handicapped and the President's Committee on Employment of the Handicapped, the International Center for the Disabled (ICD) commissioned Louis Harris and Associates, Inc. (1986), a private survey company in New York City, to conduct two national surveys in 1986. One survey, published in March 1986, surveyed 1,000 people with disabilities about the quality of their lives. Respondents were asked about their work, social lives, daily activities, and educational experiences. The survey also asked questions about barriers that had prevented them from (1) working, (2) having full social lives, (3) being mobile within their communities, and (4) easily entering mainstream American life.

In regard to employment outcomes, the Harris poll reported that persons with disabilities were much poorer than nondisabled, noting that 50 percent of the respondents reported household incomes for 1984 of $15,000 or less. Only 25 percent of nondisabled households had similar income levels. In addition, 57 percent of persons with disabilities felt that their disabilities had prevented them from reaching their full potential, with two-thirds of all disabled between the ages of 16 and 64 not working. Harris also reported that only one in four worked full time and another 10 percent worked part time; however, 66 percent of working-age persons with disabilities who were not working wanted to work.

Finally, Harris reported that, in comparison to those who were not working, persons with disabilities who were employed were better educated, had higher household incomes, were generally more satisfied with life, often did not consider themselves disabled, and were less likely to state that their disabilities had prevented them from reaching their full potential.

A second survey conducted by Louis Harris and Associates, Inc. (in press), in autumn 1986 surveyed four separate samples of managers. A total of 921 interviews were conducted with 921 managers of different companies: 210 top managers of business and industry, 301 equal employment opportunity (EEO) managers, 210 department heads and line managers, and 200 top managers in very small companies employing 10 to 49 people.

The findings of this second survey suggested that persons with disabilities typically were viewed by managers as having good or excellent job performance ratings. These managers attributed the following characteristics to employees:

1. Willing to work hard: 46 percent of the production line managers rated disabled employees as better than nondisabled employees, and 33 percent rated them about the same.
2. Reliability: 39 percent rated disabled employees as better than nondisabled employees, and 42 percent rated them about the same.
3. Attendance and punctuality: 39 percent rated disabled employees as better than nondisabled employees, and 40 percent rated them about the same.
4. Productivity: 20 percent rated disabled employees as better than nondisabled employees, and 57 percent rated them about the same.
5. Desire for promotion: 23 percent rated disabled employees as better than nondisabled employees, and 55 percent rated them about the same.
6. Leadership ability: 10 percent rated disabled employees as better than nondisabled employees, and 62 percent rated them about the same.

Persons with disabilities were seen by 80 percent of the department heads and production line managers as not being any more difficult to manage than the nondisabled. Regardless of this rather positive report of the performance rating of persons with disabilities, widespread hiring of workers with disabilities is not occurring. However, larger companies are more likely to hire persons with disabilities than smaller companies, and federal contracts encourage employers to hire persons with disabilities. Unfortunately, most companies report that they have not hired larger numbers of workers with disabilities because they lack qualified applicants.

Harris concluded that most managers (1) think that their companies are already making adequate efforts to employ persons with disabilities, (2) believe there is a widespread lack of qualified applicants who are disabled, and (3) agree that employers place a lower priority on hiring the disabled than on hiring other minority groups. Thus, efforts to increase the number and nature of employment opportunities for persons with disabilities are likely to encounter substantial resistance from managers as long as such attitudes continue to exist.

FACTORS AFFECTING TRANSITION INTO EMPLOYMENT SETTINGS

In March 1987 a diverse group of representatives from public and private sector businesses, human service agencies, and rehabilitation programs met in Minneapolis. Participants in this forum identified and analyzed factors that affect workers' transition into the work force: (1) federal and state legislation; (2) interactions among education, business, and industry (primarily the private sector); and (3) self-help and empowerment for persons with disabilities.

Forum discussions focused heavily on existing federal and state legislation. Participants' comments suggested that they viewed most transition-related legislation as being cumbersome and ineffective. At least 45 special interest groups and other federally sponsored programs receive funding to provide services to specific special needs populations. Forum participants stated that interactions among these groups have been too fragmented and have often functioned with little or no coordination, Thus, it was recommended that a central bureau be established for these agencies and that lobbying efforts be more effectively coordinated to better address the employment needs of the wide range of job seekers with disabilities.

Forum participants also recommended that federal and state incentives be developed that will encourage managers in private sector businesses and industries to employ more workers with disabilities. For example, increased tax credits are potentially powerful incentives to employ specific types of workers. In addition, increasing tax credit allocations for maintaining higher employment levels of persons with disabilities could encourage business and industry efforts to hire persons with disabilities.

A majority of the forum's participants strongly supported the idea that federally mandated minimums or quotas related to the employment of persons with disabilities should be attached to existing affirmative action legislation and policies. It should also be noted that participants were aware of the difficulties associated with efforts to enforce such requirements. Even with mandatory quotas for employing persons with disabilities, it is nearly impossible to enforce such quotas and they often become token features of companies' personnel policies or are totally disregarded.

Finally, when implementing mandatory affirmative action quotas, it often is very difficult to collect baseline data about the prequota numbers of persons employed with disabilities. Without such data, it is even more difficult to evaluate accurately the impact of new employment practices and/or policies. In addition, one of the major barriers to collecting such data is the definition of disabilities.

Confusion About the Definition of Disability

Defining what constitutes a disability has been an ongoing point of contention in many policy-making bodies in federal and state legislatures, business and industry, education programs, human services agencies, and organized labor groups. With such a diversity of opinions about disabilities, it is not surprising that many people are often apprehensive about supporting any of the specific points of view. In addition, many employees with mild disabilities consciously attempt to hide the existence of their disabilities or simply do not disclose their disabilities to their employers. Such problems are primarily trust issues, trust of a system that, in many ways, is too cumbersome and is often mismanaged. The system that seeks employment for persons with disabilities is often perceived to be a threat to self-sufficiency rather than an effective tool to promote the wholesome integration of persons with disabilities into the workforce.

Discrimination Against Persons with Disabilities

It seems ironic that after almost three decades of civil rights activism and legislation, *discrimination* continues to be a major issue limiting employment of persons with disabilities. Discrimination has been dealt with in the areas of gender, age, and race by means of relatively effective affirmative action legislation. Recommendations by forum participants suggest that mandatory affirmative action procedures requiring staff development training within business and industry may represent an effective means to destroy many of the myths that obscure facts and inhibit the examination of management and supervision methods affecting the employment of persons with disabilities (Brown & Wotruba, in press). An activist philosophy from the 1960s seems appropriate here; "You can't legislate morality. However, if you can control the way people act long enough, their values will eventually begin to change."

A number of Fortune 500 companies have been cited for their efforts to employ or reemploy workers with disabilities. If a variety of similar initiatives can be rewarded throughout business and industry, it may be possible to enhance this success by adapting a model applied effectively by the Veterans' Emergency Jobs Training Act. That act provided a maximum of $10,000 to corporations for each Vietnam and Korean War veteran hired. The money for hiring veterans was assigned directly into hiring supervisors' budgets. This served not simply as a hiring credit but also as an actual monetary reward. A similar policy could be implemented for the employment of persons with disabilities and could directly influence efforts by supervisors or managers who hire and supervise employees with disabilities (Brown & Wotruba, in press).

Incentive systems affect yet another area of concern—the need for coordination of efforts between businesses and industries when developing effective incentives, legislation, and policies. Joint initiatives could eliminate many personnel policy barriers as well as enhance compensatory approaches now being used in regard to employees who become disabled *after* being employed.

Concerns About Productivity

The belief that productivity will always be a major employment-related factor has seldom been questioned. Supported work programs that employ persons with disabilities, where work site counselors or job coaches are made available to employers or first-line supervisors to assist in accommodation, planning, and supervision efforts, represent one effective means to enhance the employment of persons with disabilities. However, private sector business personnel sometimes complain because the counselors and job coaches involved in such activities are not considered to be members of internal management teams. Fortunately, work site counselors and job coaches also learn how to do the jobs assigned to workers with disabilities, and they can then help these workers to interpret and master job-related tasks while continuing to function as valuable resources for first-line supervisors and managers.

Skills Necessary

In business and industry, persons with disabilities usually are required to possess two types of skills: (1) skills necessary to complete required work tasks within a specified period of time, that is, "productivity," and (2) skills, often not clearly defined, consisting of necessary social and employability skills that enhance interpersonal relationships in work environments. It is not uncommon to find persons who "fit" the technical qualifications for jobs but who continue to encounter serious problems because they are viewed as acting strangely or having inappropriate social behaviors. In these cases job coaches can often have a strong positive impact. Indeed, a forum participant from a major corporation suggested that special educators and vocational educators should ". . . provide employers with workers who have effective social skills and the ability to relate interpersonally as part of work teams. Industry personnel will then train those workers with disabilities to develop the needed technical skills'' (Brown & Wotruba, in press).

Demographic Trends Among Persons with Disabilities

The struggle to educate students with disabilities is often as difficult as is the task of finding meaningful employment for them. Students learn that they are part of a population that has been disenfranchised from the mainstream of life. Since the implementation of the Education for Handicapped Children Act (P.L. 92–142) in 1975, increasing numbers of children have been identified as being disabled, and the proportion of the student population that is classified as being handicapped seems to be increasing. Such information suggests that society should focus more closely on the life-long needs of persons with disabilities.

Responsibility to Provide Long-Term Support to Disabled Workers

When they are in school, students with disabilities are often referred to as "special needs learners." Upon graduation, these students become potential members of the work force who may continue to need one or more forms of special assistance or support. After they enter the work force, these same people are no longer considered to be students. However, as workers with disabilities, many will continue to require special accommodations in order to become productive workers. Prior to this point in their lives, persons with disabilities have received special assistance designed to help them succeed in education programs. When they leave their school environments, they no longer are eligible to receive much of the special assistance and the resources that were available to them in education programs. In addition, the common assumption that workers with disabilities do not function as well as other employees often causes serious discrimination against job applicants with disabilities.

Special needs students receive assistance from education specialists, and upon completing high school or reaching age 21, these students are often aided by specialists from vocational rehabilitation agencies. Soon after entering the work force, however, they often are on their own, with little or no ongoing support from community agencies. These individuals then must face society and their potential employers without the personalized assistance they have experienced throughout their elementary and secondary school careers. Our society seems to assume that the foundations of work and daily living skills are successfully developed during the school years and that each individual student is solely responsible for making the transition into a self-sufficient life as a productive member of the work force.

Surprisingly, society sometimes labels certain people as being disabled or handicapped, indicating limitations on what these people can be expected to do, yet society also expects such people to function successfully without the assistance that was deemed necessary while they were attending school. Several questions should be answered: Are school programs providing training that will enable persons with disabilities to solve problems that may emerge after they leave their sheltered school environments? Have appropriate education programs been provided to enhance the transition of students from school to postschool lives as meaningfully employed adult members of society? Have adequate counseling services been provided to enable students to examine their interests and abilities in relation to their transitions into the work force and into life styles that will enable them to be independent from their parents?

Benefits of Employers Filling This Role

Many of the benefits that result when employers assume long-term support roles for workers with disabilities are depicted in Figure 8.1. Many business and industry personnel are in positions to accommodate employees with disabilities for specific jobs within job-related settings, thus assuring that such employees are adequately trained to meet the needs of their employers. Consequently, the likelihood of having to retrain these employees diminishes, as do training costs and the negative impact on production levels. When training curricula and activities are adapted specifically to the unique needs and resources of employers, to the learning abilities of employees, and to the nature of job environments, training times are likely to be minimized and success rates maximized.

Employees also tend to be more comfortable when provided with "in-house" assistance to learn job-related skills and tasks since this approach helps them to understand how their jobs fit into broad work-site environments. As a result, job coaching or training processes tend to be more efficient when employees are trained for the actual types of jobs to which they will be assigned rather than for a broader range of jobs, as might be necessary in other types of training programs. For example, when employees are trained to operate only the equipment that they will need to do their jobs, training experiences tend to be less confusing and, typically, minimize employees' training times. Also, when employers provide employees with long-term job-related support, there is less chance that employees will be unsuccessful and have to be fired. When employers are committed to do so, it often is relatively easy to tailor jobs to the needs and abilities of individual workers and to match those workers to specific jobs that are more appropriate and/or that can be modified to accommodate specific workers' characteristics—making successful job performance and retention more likely (see Figure 8.2). Without long-term commitments from employers, disabled workers' production rates and satisfaction levels with their jobs are likely to diminish. In situations where employers are providing long-term support and employees encounter problems on their jobs, employers can select from three options. As shown in Figure 8.2, employers

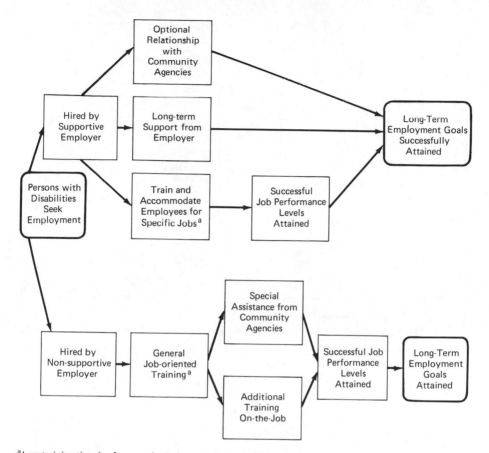

ª Less training time is often required when employers provide appropriate support services for workers with disabilities

Figure 8.1 Employers' Support for Employees with Disabilities and Job Training Time.

have options other than terminating poorly performing employees. Accommodation of employees (e.g., tailoring jobs to the traits of specific employees) is a possibility, as is attempting to find alternate jobs that are more appropriate for a specific worker.

Thus, long-term commitments by key business and industry personnel to successfully employ disabled workers can increase the likelihood that such workers will succeed in their jobs and that they will achieve long-term careers. Employers' long-term commitments can also enhance cooperation between employers and school and agency personnel who are directly involved in on-the-job training efforts for students with disabilities. As the number and nature of such relationships evolve, schools' training programs are likely to be-

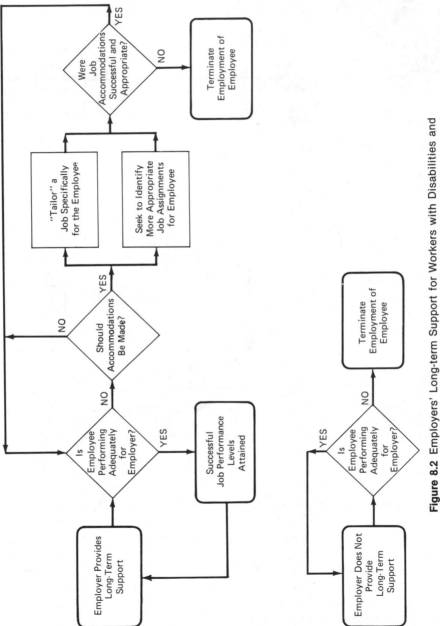

Figure 8.2 Employers' Long-term Support for Workers with Disabilities and the Employers' Efforts to Assure Workers' Job-Related Successes.

come more transition-oriented and to develop a wider array of useful job-related skills for students before they enter the work force. As a result, differences between academic skills and job skills in secondary schools, higher education institutions, vocational-technical institutes, and employer-provided training programs are likely to become less distinct.

Reasons to Hire Workers with Disabilities

Even though the merits of the model in Figure 8.2 seem apparent, it may not be obvious why employers should seek to develop long-term employment relationships with disabled workers. For instance, many members of society seem to reflect the following sentiment: "Why worry about placing workers with disabilities on jobs? Aren't sheltered workshops already established and capable of meeting disabled individuals' needs?" Such attitudes are serious problems when combined with Harris' findings that two-thirds of all disabled Americans between 16 and 64 were *not* working.

In today's work force, persons with disabilities are considered for placement not only in segregated workshops but also in an increasingly wider range of community employment opportunities. These jobs, in contrast to sheltered work activities, tend to offer higher pay and greater self-esteem, have more diverse working conditions, include fringe benefits such as health care insurance, and can lead to career advancements. Meaningful, productive jobs can contribute to our country's tax base, enhance business and industrial production, and significantly reduce the costs of social services (Phelps et al., 1982; Walls, Zawloki, & Dowler, 1986). Whereas productive jobs cost our society nothing, sheltered and/or supported work programs sometimes cost far in excess of $12,000 annually and are usually paid for by tax dollars (Phelps et al., 1982). Thus, as Table 8.4 summarizes, there are numerous advantages that result from including disabled individuals within the work force and that justify employers' efforts to manage and assist disabled workers to succeed in a wide range of competitive job settings.

Employers' Assumption of Greater Levels of Responsibility

The need to improve the use of business and industry resources to accommodate disabled workers highlights the fact that many trainers and supervisors are inadequately trained to implement such efforts. First-line supervisors and trainers need to recognize that many workers with disabilities are potentially good workers and that they have generally good attendance and safety records when *properly assigned and trained* in their jobs. For attendance, work performance, and safety, the records of workers with disabilities often are equal to or better than those of able-bodied workers. Disabled workers also tend to have lower job turnover rates than their nondisabled counterparts, and insur-

TABLE 8.4. A Comparison of the Nature of Sheltered and Competitive Employment

	Levels Typically Attained	
Issues Compared	Sheltered Employment	Competitive Employment
Salary levels	Very low	Low to high[a]
Fringe benefits	Typically nonexistent	Usually provided [a]
Career advancements	Seldom occurs	Yes[a]
Contributions to the tax base	Low	High[a]
Contributions to production capacity	Low	Low[a]
Costs to society	High	Low[a]
Costs to taxpayers	High	None[a]

[a]Competitive employment settings consistently exhibit advantages over sheltered employment settings in all areas compared.

ance rates generally are no higher when compared to those for nondisabled employees (Dupont study, 1981; Everett High School, 1985).

Properly Assigning Workers to Jobs

Increased numbers of trainers and supervisors should also become aware of accommodation strategies that are appropriate and feasible within their working environments. Furthermore, they should assist other personnel to learn these techniques. This knowledge could enable appropriate job-related changes that will assist disabled workers to perform successfully in a wider range of jobs. Employers should also identify community agencies and organizations that can offer advice, assistance, support, and other services after workers with disabilities are hired.

After personnel have developed appropriate skills for training and supervising disabled workers, they should be able to (1) analyze job tasks in order to make appropriate modifications that will enhance workers' performance levels, (2) communicate effectively with disabled employees, (3) understand and use effective job training strategies, and (4) supervise with insight and understanding in order to cope with disability-related problems as they occur (see Figure 8.3). The on-the-job successes of workers with disabilities depend heavily on attributes of employees and their supervisors and trainers. In combination, these personnel represent key forces that will influence the success or failure of workers with disabilities. Thus, if supervisors and trainers or their employees lack appropriate levels of knowledge, skills, and attitudes, employees' performance levels are likely to diminish.

As indicated in Figure 8.3, supervisors and trainers should enhance their

THE WORK ENVIRONMENT

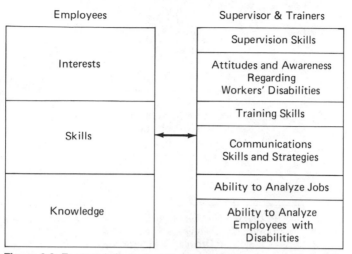

Figure 8.3 Factors Influencing Employees' Success on Their Jobs.

interests, knowledge, and skills in ways that will help them to assist workers with disabilities. They should be sensitive to and aware of how to cope with issues such as poor attitudes (e.g., discrimination) among co-workers and potential interpersonal problems caused by employees with disabilities. These goals suggest that supervisors and trainers should be willing and able to address co-workers' unfavorable attitudes and to conduct special training for co-workers to prepare them to interact with disabled workers.

Supervisors and trainers can also serve as role models, in the belief that attitudes of acceptance can be contagious. For example, job supervisors should not openly criticize and subject employees to name calling or disability labels. In addition, trainers should be aware that some disabled employees require extended learning periods and that they are often unable to organize their thoughts effectively. In other words, supervisors and trainers need ample amounts of knowledge about disabilities to help them to understand why certain problems occur. At the same time, it is crucial that employees with disabilities not be overprotected by supervisors.

Although this may seem like an impossible juggling act, it can be simplified by keeping three basic ideas in mind (see Figure 8.4). First, supervisors should *identify* the roots of job-related problems. Second, *changes should be made* that will minimize the probability that these problems may occur. Third, *attention should be focused on* (1) effective communications, (2) conflict management, and (3) appropriate supervisory skills that can be used to avoid or minimize these problems.

A list of suggestions that can be used to avoid problems when assisting

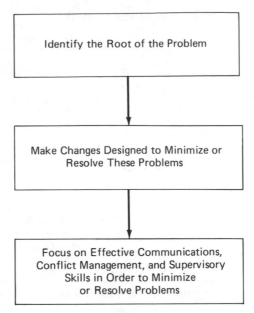

Figure 8.4 A Strategy Model for Accommodating Problems Encountered by Employers and Their Employees with Disabilities.

workers with disabilities within their job environments has been developed (see Table 8.5). Although this list is incomplete and grossly oversimplified, it encourages supervisors and trainers to monitor their behavior in terms of what they can do for employees, how they should respond to employees, and how they can communicate effectively with employees. In addition, other suggestions focus on how to monitor employees' performance levels and behaviors. Table 8.5 organizes these suggestions into broad guidelines that can be used to reduce problems among a wide variety of employees, both disabled and nondisabled. It should also be noted that these suggestions focus on the skills of supervisors and trainers, as well as employees, reinforcing the belief that both parties and their interactions contribute to the job-related successes of workers.

Supervisors and trainers should also be aware of factors that tend to preclude the employment of individuals with disabilities. The unusual appearance and/or behavior of *some* disabled workers and the fact that co-workers often have irrational fears that disabilities are contagious can seriously reduce the likelihood that workers with disabilities will be employed. For example, during job application and interview processes it is easy for people to emphasize what employees *cannot* do instead of what their abilities are. Another inhibiting factor is related to employers' unjustified fear that once employees with dis-

TABLE 8.5 SAMPLE STRATEGIES FOR AVOIDING OR OVERCOMING PROBLEMS WITH WORKERS WHO HAVE DISABILITIES

Monitor Yourself

1. Assign workers to appropriate job tasks.
2. Examine your own tolerance levels and reactions to workers.
3. Act in ways that facilitate employees' acceptance of each other.
4. Put aside myths and fears about individuals and focus on the facts.
5. Involve employees in decision-making processes, as is feasible.
6. Avoid labeling employees in terms of their disabilities.
7. Establish realistic goals for employees.

What You Can Do for Employees

8. Show employees where to find restrooms, lockers, equipment, supplies, and other key locations.
9. Establish "buddy" systems that pair able-bodied workers with workers who are disabled.
10. Make appropriate job accommodations when needed.

When Responding to Employees

11. Demonstrate your confidence in employees.
12. Attempt to make employees feel welcome.
13. Be emphathetic.
14. Be consistent in your behavior, expectations, and standards.
15. Give appropriate support.
16. Talk to individuals in private.
17. Listen to what employees have to say.
18. Offer a friendly, supportive working relationship.
19. Encourage and help employees to try to do their best.
20. Provide help when asked.

When Interacting with Employees

21. Be concrete and specific.
22. Describe (ahead of time) exactly what is expected of employees.
23. Speak to employees as adults.
24. Introduce one new idea at a time.
25. Realize that a nod of agreement doesn't always mean that employees understand; request specific responses.
26. Talk directly to employees.
27. Do not talk to employees while doing something else at the same time.
28. Be aware of what you may be communicating indirectly.
29. Don't be sarcastic.
30. Develop two-way communications with employees.
31. Explain why things are done.
32. Do not interrupt employees to finish sentences for them.

(continued)

TABLE 8.5   CONTINUED

Monitoring Employees

33. Make sure employees know all prerequisite skills necessary for each job-related activity.
34. Maximize the number of successes that employees experience.
35. Help employees succeed.
36. Use employees' learning strengths to attain job goals.
37. Let workers demonstrate their levels of proficiency.
38. Make sure the pace for training activities is not too fast or too slow for each employee.

abilities have been hired, it will be extremely difficult to fire them if that should ever become necessary and appropriate. All employers' concerns and fears should be evaluated as they emerge: Are individuals refused employment because of employers' fears? Are individuals ranked at the bottom of hiring priority lists because they haven't been given a chance to show what they are capable of doing? Are employers more concerned about workers' appearance than their potential work performance? Are employers unwilling to hire persons because of their own misconceptions of what people with disabilities are like?

Of course, as noted in Figure 8.5, employees should be monitored in terms of several considerations: Are employees capable of doing their jobs? Are accommodations being overlooked that could be implemented to enable individ-

MONITORING SYSTEM

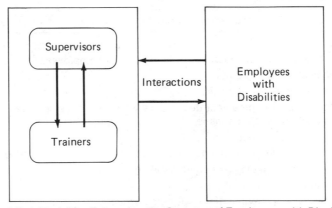

Figure 8.5 A Model for Enhancing the Success of Employees with Disabilities by Monitoring How They Interact with Job Trainers and Supervisors.

uals to do their jobs with the skills they already possess? Is too *little* expected from potential employees? Have employees been consulted in terms of their reactions to employers' decisions and actions? In addition, employers should monitor the skills of their supervisors and trainers and those of potential employees, as well as the interaction of these two sets of individuals.

WORKERS WITH DISABILITIES: "IDEAL" EMPLOYEES?

So far, we seem to have painted a portrait of disabled individuals as being perfect employees who *always* succeed on jobs if their employers adequately analyze and accommodate their needs. Of course, this is not true. In fact, as a group, individuals with disabilities are very similar to nondisabled people. The number of successes and failures among workers with disabilities is, potentially, very similar to the total population of workers. Some advocates of disabled employees tend to describe their clients as being "superhumans" who almost always succeed. These claims are just as unfair as the tendency to discriminate negatively against workers with disabilities. Obviously, most employers want employees who are rarely absent, who always get along with other employees, and who always go beyond the call of duty to get their jobs accomplished. Instead of being "ideal" employees, newly hired employees with disabilities do periodically get sick, miss work occasionally, and typically get no more work done than other workers. As a result, employees with disabilities should not be expected to perform better than any other employee. Surprisingly, some employers may be disappointed by the lack of above-average worker performance, but why?

Employers' expectations are sometimes inflated inappropriately and their disabled employees perform below expected levels. This situation has become known as the "super cripple" phenomenon and is associated with situations in which it is assumed that (1) workers with disabilities act happier on their jobs, (2) they love repetitive tasks and never tire of them, (3) they never get sick, (4) they never miss a day of work, or (5) their jobs always come first. In reality, however, disabled workers exhibit human frailties like all other workers. All people tend to get sick occasionally, have unexpected emergencies, get bored, and make mistakes. No worker is perfect, and employees with disabilities should not be expected to be better than nondisabled workers. Supervisors and trainers should acknowledge that workers tend to differ widely in terms of their knowledge and skill levels, their performance speeds, and their attitudes toward work and the people around them. Disabled individuals can be good workers, but we should not expect more (nor less) of them than of other employees.

STRENGTHENING TRANSITION FACILITATORS
WITHIN OUR SOCIETY

Upcoming labor trends that will influence the employability of persons with disabilities encourage the identification of change agents operating within our society. This group of power brokers includes middle managers and chief executive officers (CEOs) in our nation's business community. Unfortunately, although many of these persons tend to be strongly supportive of policies related to the employment of persons with disabilities, their mandates often are not effectively implemented at or below the middle-management level (Brown & Wotruba, in press).

State and federal legislators represent another potentially powerful group of change agents that could support efforts to employ persons with disabilities. Legislators could create incentives that would improve employment opportunities, for example, the inclusion of workers with disabilities under mandates established by affirmative action employment guidelines and the revision of social security regulations.

The education system's efforts to enhance the transition of all students into the work force also represent a very powerful force for bringing about change. Programs that focus on helping students to prepare for adult lives as productive citizens and that offer early interventions aimed at coping with the transition from school to the work force could greatly reduce many transition problems that occur after students leave secondary school.

Collaborative efforts among change agents represent strategies that, potentially, can implement highly effective mechanisms for identifying and overcoming barriers to the employment of persons with disabilities. Perhaps a national task force should review and evaluate data on the efficacy of current transition-related efforts for this sector of the labor force. Resulting recommendations for appropriate legislative action might focus on major problems and result in significantly enhanced employment opportunities.

Finally, cooperation should be increased among organizations and agencies representing or advocating for persons with disabilities. Obviously, individual lobbying efforts by various special interest groups for increased funding levels have been effective. However, more efficiently coordinated efforts by these groups would probably enhance greatly the quality of life for a broad range of workers (and would-be workers) with disabilities. For a more in-depth discussion of this issue, see the chapter on interagency collaboration in this text.

PREPARING EMPLOYERS TO TRAIN
AND SUPERVISE WORKERS WITH DISABILITIES

Recent efforts by the Universities of Minnesota and Washington to assist employers to accommodate disabled employees have emphasized effective communications, conflict management, and supervision strategies. The concepts stressed while training persons to communicate effectively were designed to emphasize (1) communicating nondefensively and (2) becoming aware of the interpersonal issues encountered during efforts to enhance the transition of persons into the work force and meaningful adult lives. Conflict management training emphasizes the needs of managers, supervisors, trainers, and other human service providers to use structured processes for avoiding and resolving conflicts within work environments. Efforts of this nature encourage specific, open commitments to improve interactions between workers and trainers or supervisors. Conflict management efforts also tend to specify clearly what should be expected of both workers and their supervisors and trainers as they seek to resolve conflicts within work environments.

These communications and conflict management strategies may initially appear to be oversimplified prescriptions for addressing complex interpersonal issues and problems. However, past experiences have verified that the effectiveness of these models is due to the fact that they are easy to understand and are relatively simple to implement. Such strategies also provide effective tools that enable supervisors, managers, and trainers to overcome many of the anxieties experienced when they first encounter workers with disabilities. These activities can also help business and industry personnel to realize that people with disabilities (like almost everyone else in our society) want to have a sense of belonging to their society and to be productive members of the work force. Most workers with disabilities expect no special considerations and appreciate receiving fair and honest appraisals of how well they are doing their jobs. All they want are reasonable opportunities to use their abilities productively.

Critical Issues

Although employers tend to vary greatly in terms of their training needs, motivations, and interests, recent training development activities for employers have increasingly focused on the seven following areas:

1. Critical issues involved when hiring people with disabilities
2. Supervising workers with disabilities
3. Appropriate incentives, disincentives, and barriers that apply to the employment of workers with disabilities
4. Disabled workers' "characteristics"
5. Strategies for accommodating workers' disabilities in their work environments
6. Effective communication strategies
7. Conflict management strategies

Employers want not only *specific information* about workers with disabilities but also information about strategies that will help them address *specific issues* that emerge when training and/or supervising workers with disabilities.

Employer training workshop participants often want to discuss both effective and ineffective training and supervision strategies and processes, that is, what works and what doesn't work. Employers also value knowing *both* the strengths and weaknesses of workers with disabilities and how to cope with their fears about hiring and firing such employees. After developing a better understanding of key issues and processes, workshop participants tend to become more willing and able to employ increasing numbers and types of persons with disabilities.

By discussing both the strategies needed to accommodate workers with disabilities and the major issues related to such activities, workshop presenters can (1) instill participants with a greater understanding of the complexities of workers and work environments (2) help participants avoid becoming discouraged by the failures they may encounter when working with employees who have disabilities, (3) teach participants how to confront effectively and accommodate disability-related problems, and (4) help participants to recognize situations in which individual workers may not have been appropriately matched to job requirements. In addition, participants need to hear about the benefits that result from the employment of persons with disabilities from employers who have actually experienced success (as well as failure) with workers who have disabilities. The impact on participants of such discussions often is greater and longer lasting than comments from persons less directly connected with business and industry.

Society strongly values the ability to appear "normal," and many employers seek to employ persons who look and act in ways that allow them to fit unobtrusively into their work environments. It is important to find out if potential employees can do the job—in spite of their physical appearance and their mannerisms. In addition, co-workers and trainers or supervisors should be encouraged and helped to understand and accept these characteristics. Otherwise, co-workers may feel threatened when disabled workers successfully master jobs similar to their own and may find ways to sabotage disabled workers to protect their own egos. If not watched, "we versus they" attitudes can emerge, and employees with disabilities (or any workers who appear and/or act differently from other workers) become isolated from the "normal" workers and labeled as being different; then widespread dissatisfaction and unrest can overwhelm work environments. Far too often, workers with disabilities are assumed to be dirty, dumb, slow, and/or unreliable because they are feared and/or *misunderstood* by the people around them.

Many employers hesitate to hire people with disabilities because they fear that they cannot do the job, but many also fear that they will never be able to get rid of such employees if they do not perform adequately. Employers should not be afraid, however, both to hire *and* to fire people with disabilities—keeping in mind that disabled workers will not do a better job, nor any worse, than nondisabled individuals. However, supervisors need enough knowledge about workers' disabilities to be flexible and to know how to help employees use their skills successfully. For example, supervisors and trainers can provide extra learning time, memory aids, adaptive devices, and flexible work hours. Thus, knowledge about disabilities, the ability to match workers with appropriate jobs, and knowledge about ways to make jobs and their working environments more suitable greatly increase the probability that employees with disabilities will be successful.

Supervision

At the same time, supervisors need to know the characteristics of a good supervisor and manager and what kinds of related skills are necessary when dealing with workers who are disabled. They also need to appreciate the value of regularly critiquing their own behavior. It is important to encourage synergy in the workplace, using feedback and suggestions from all employees in all areas of the business to get the job done in the best manner possible; thus supervisors' managing styles are important for promoting success on the job for any employee.

Incentives, Disincentives, and Barriers

Few laws and regulations encourage hiring people with disabilities; thus hiring them may not appear to be feasible for the business. However, barriers to the employment of people with disabilities are slowly disappearing as more and more businesses are discovering benefits that result from the employment of workers with disabilities.

Typical Characteristics and Accommodations

Knowledge about people with disabilities, and about their limitations and strengths, is important to match appropriately workers to jobs and to enhance success on those jobs. If employers are not knowledgeable about disabilities and are not able to identify workers' capabilities, employers are more likely to fear hiring such employees. Once employers better understand their employees with disabilities, those employers' anxieties about such workers will be reduced, and the two can work together more successfully. To enhance employees' job-related successes, changes may be necessary, and supervisors should know what types of accommodations are feasible or know where to get such information. Luckily, employers will find that most accommodations are made at little or no cost.

Accommodation processes are relatively straightforward: Employees have useful skills, and supervisors can arrange for job accommodations that should be made. But if successfully employing persons with disabilities is so simple, why aren't more of them employed? Far too many persons with disabilities are unemployed or working parttime, although many would prefer to be working in meaningful full-time jobs. Obviously, this problem is very complex and many factors must be considered.

Effective Communications and Conflict Management

During and after initial employee screening interviews, managers', supervisors', and trainers' communication skills can contribute greatly to the success of new employees. In addition, since conflict tends to occur periodically in all work settings, effective communication and conflict management skills are valuable. Supervisors, managers, and trainers need to know that their duties involve being good listeners as well as being good at the technical aspects of their jobs. Thus, the interactions between each supervisor, manager, and trainer and their employees contribute to the working climate and to workers' job success.

Economic and Cultural Trends

Employers should be cognizant that there will be a worker shortage by the mid-1990s and that the ability to evaluate carefully all job applicants' probability of success on the job will soon become even more important. Those businesses that are able to establish such practices will have a competitive advantage in the years to come. Employers and advocates for disabled persons should find ways to encourage qualified disabled individuals to apply for positions and to encourage cooperation between schools and employers to help make the transition from school to the work force function smoothly. This process can be partially enhanced by teaching students appropriate job-related skills before they leave school. Employer assistance activities should be designed to show employers that the benefits of hiring disabled workers far outweigh the additional time and resources sometimes needed to train them, to enlighten other employees about their co-workers who have disabilities, and to make job accommodations (as needed).

These training experiences should offer practical discussions of ideas (and sometimes, frustrations), useful applications of those ideas to specific work environments, and information about where to find additional help if unexpected problems should arise. The successes of such efforts will depend heavily on (1) open-minded attitudes and useful information about disabled workers, and (2) access to accommodation strategies that have succeeded in similar situations elsewhere or the ability to generate such strategies within local work environments.

Strategies for Accommodating Employees

Two forms have been developed to assist employers to accommodate workers with disabilities. The first form systematically identifies mismatches between employees and required job skills, and the second form guides efforts to make appropriate accommodations to alleviate mismatches. The Employee and Job Profiles form (see Figure 8.6) compares broad categories of employees' skills and skills required to perform most job tasks successfully. When workers are found to be in need of assistance (to allow them to succeed on the job), their

EMPLOYEE AND JOB PROFILES	EMPLOYEE'S ABILITY TO DO THIS TASK			FREQUENCY OF TASK DURING JOB ACTIVITIES		
Tasks rated:	Good	Poor	Unable to do	Often	Seldom	Never
1. Learning job tasks						
2. Reading						
3. Understanding written instructions						
4. Performing basic arithmetic tasks						
5. Understanding verbal instructions						
6. Conversational skills						
7. Use of a telephone						
8. Writing with a pen or pencil						
9. Use of grammar & spelling						
10. Typing/keyboard skills						
11. Hearing clearly and accurately						
12. Seeing clearly & accurately						
13. Attention span						
14. Reasoning skills						
15. Memory skills						
16. Organizing information						
17. Use of grammar & spelling						
18. Transferring skills to new tasks						
19. Motivation and persistance						
20. Interpersonal skills						
21. Stress management						
22. Manual dexterity						
23. Eye-hand coordination						
24. Lifting or carrying						
25. Reaching						
26. Standing						
27. Bending						
28. Walking						
29. Sitting						
30. Working at a standard desk or bench						

Figure 8.6 Form for Analyzing Employee Abilities and Job-Related Tasks.

deficits are transferred to the Job Accommodation Analysis form (see Figure 8.7), where workers and their job task weaknesses are evaluated in terms of what accommodations are needed and the feasibility or desirability of implementing them.

EMPLOYEE: _____

JOB TITLE: _____

ANALYST: _____

DATE ANALYZED: _____

JOB ACCOMMODATION ANALYSIS FORM

Which abilities or skills should be accommodated?	With this employee in mind, how can appropriate job accommodations be made?	At what cost?	Must the job be restructured so the worker's disabilities will not limit job performance?	Are these modifications feasible?
			Yes No	Yes No If NO, why not?
			Yes No	Yes No If NO, why not?
			Yes No	Yes No If NO, why not?
			Yes No	Yes No If NO, why not?

Figure 8.7 Job Accommodation Analysis Form

Employers can use the Employee and Job Profiles form to rate employees in terms of these tasks by deciding if the individual has a high skill level (good), if employees can do these tasks only with difficulty (poor), or employees cannot do the tasks (unable to do). Ratings are recorded as marks in the appropriate locations and are connected with a line to form a profile of employees' skill levels.

Similarly, corresponding jobs are evaluated according to the tasks that are required for them. Each job task is rated according to whether or not it is typically required (often), is occasionally required (seldom), or not required (never). Again, marks are placed on the rating scale and a line is drawn to connect them to form a profile of each job's required tasks. These two side-by-side profiles can identify worker-job matches where problems may develop if appropriate accommodations or other changes are not arranged.

Please note that the "never" column is highlighted on the job profiles rating scale, indicating that there is no need to worry about inadequate worker skills not required by a job. However, if a skill is necessary or sometimes necessary, analysts should look at the corresponding ratings of the employee's rating profile.

Accommodation Analysis

After identifying job tasks in which employees have inadequate skill levels, analysts should answer questions in the form's other columns to determine the feasibility of providing effective accommodations. The form's second column focuses on ways in which accommodations can be made for a particular employee (e.g., displaying job-related activities in either printed or pictorial form). The third column requests information about the cost of accommodations, and the fourth column asks if the job should be modified or restructured to ensure the employee's performance of job tasks.

The fifth column asks analysts to evaluate the feasibility of these modifications within the specific work environment. After completing this analysis form, the analyst can review the resulting information to obtain an initial indication of the type(s) and cost(s) of accommodations needed to assist specific employees with disabilities to succeed on their jobs and the feasibility of those changes. At this point specific plans should be made in terms of *who* will provide *what* services, at *what cost,* and *when* those accommodations will be provided.

CLOSING COMMENTS

These forms and analysis procedures do not make critical decisions for employers. However, they can organize information about individual workers and prospective jobs so that workers' skills can be analyzed in relation to job activities and processes. After pinpointing workers' strengths and potential problem areas with the Employee and Job Profiles form, employers can systematically analyze information and use the Job Accommodation Analysis Form (other forms or processes focused on similar facts could be equally effective) to make appropriate decisions about training workers or about employing additional employees with disabilities in the future. As our society moves toward the drastically different job market of 1995 and beyond, strategies like this one will offer tools for humane and cost-effective solutions for many employees and employers alike. Once employers realize the potential importance of workers with disabilities and how they can contribute meaningfully to the financial well-being of businesses, the use of such strategies will probably become commonplace. However, workers and employers have many hurdles to pass before such hopes can become a reality.

REFERENCES

Beckman, L. J. (1976). Attribution of teachers and parents regarding children's performance. *Psychology in the Schools, 13*, 213–218.

Bowe, F. (1984). *Employment trends: 1984 and beyond. Where the jobs will be.* Fayetteville: Arkansas Rehabilitation Research and Training Center, Arkansas University.

Brandt, R. (1985). On teaching and supervising: A conversation with Madeline Hunter. *Educational Leadership, 42*(5), 61–66.

Brolin, D. (1978). *Life centered career education: A competency based approach.* Reston, VA: The Council for Exceptional Children.

Brown, J., & Field, S. (1983). *Enhancing the transition of mildly mentally retarded and learning disabled vocational students into meaningful related employment* (a grant proposal submitted to the U.S. Office of Special Education and Rehabilitative Services). St. Paul: University of Minnesota and University of Washington.

Brown, J., & Wotruba, J. (Eds.). (in press). *The employment of persons with disabilities forum.* Proceedings of a Forum Sponsored by Minnesota Research and Development Center, University of Minnesota, St. Paul.

Brown, J. M., & Kayser, T. F. (1982). *The transition of special needs learners into post secondary vocational education.* St. Paul: Minnesota Research and Development Center, Department of Vocational Technical Education, University of Minnesota.

Bruininks, R., Thurlow, M., Lewis, D., & Larson, N. (1987). *Post-school outcomes for special education students and other students one to eight years after high school.* Unpublished manuscript, University Affiliated Program on Developmental Disabilities, University of Minnesota.

Collignon, F. (1980). *Policies of private sector employers toward the disabled: A review of current programs and relevant literature.* Berkeley, CA: Berkeley Planning Associates.

Education Amendments of 1976. (October 1976). Title II, Vocational Education, Public Law 94-482.

Education for All Handicapped Children Act Amendments. (1983). Public Law 98-199.

Education for Handicapped Children Act of 1975 (November 29, 1975). Public Law 94-142, 20 U.S.C. 1412.

E. I. Du Pont de Nemours and Company. (1981). *Equal to the task.* Wilmington, DE.

Everett High School. (1985). *Provisions for information to employers.* Everett, WA.

Fardig, D. B., Algozzine, R. F., Schwarthz, S. E., Hensel, J. W., & Wostling, D. L. (1985). *Exceptional Children, 52*(2), 115–121.

Hasazi, S. B., Gordon, L. R., & Roe, C. A. (1985). Factors associated with the employment status of handicapped youth exiting high school from 1979 to 1983. *Exceptional Children, 51*(6), 455–469.

Hasazi, S. B., Gordon, L. R., Roe, C. A., Hall, M., Finck, K., & Salembier, G. (1985). A statewide follow-up on post-school employment and residential status of students labeled "mentally retarded." *Education and Training of the Mentally Retarded, 20*(4), 222–234.

Holman, J. E., & Bruininks, R. H. (1985). Assessing and training adaptive behaviors. In K. C. Lakin & R. H. Bruininks (Eds.), *Strategies for achieving community integration of developmentally disabled citizens* (pp. 73–104.). Baltimore: Paul H. Brookes.

Johnson, D. R., Bruininks, R. H., & Thurlow, M. L. (1987). Meeting the challenge of transition service planning through improved interagency cooperation. *Exceptional Children, 53*(6), 522–530.

Jones, E. (1973). What it's like to be a black manager. *Harvard Business Review,* pp. 108–117.

Kiernan, W. E., McGaughey, M. J., & Schalock, R. L. (1986). *Employment survey for adults with developmental disabilities* (Contract No. 03DD0135). Washington, DC: U.S. Department of Health and Human Services, Office of Human Development Services, Administration on Developmental Disabilities.

Klauda, P., & Byrne, C. (1987a, May 3). Baby boom delivered well-educated diversity. *Minneapolis Star and Tribune,* pp. 12A–13A.

Klauda, P., & Byrne, C. (1987b, May 3). Time to prepare for aging of baby boomers is now, analysts say. *Minneapolis Star & Tribune,* pp. 1A, 12A.

Louis Harris and Associates, Inc. (1986). *The ICD survey of disabled Americans: Bringing disabled Americans into the mainstream.* New York: International Center for the Disabled.

Louis Harris and Associates, Inc. (in press). *The ICD survey II: Employing disabled Americans.* New York: International Center for the Disabled.

Mithaug, D. E., Horiuchi, C. N., & Fanning, P. N. (1985). A report of the Colorado statewide follow-up survey of special education students. *Exceptional Children, 51*(5), 397–404.

National Council on the Handicapped. (1986). *Toward independence: An assessment of federal laws and programs affecting persons with disabilities—with legislative recommendations* (Publication No. 85–082605). Washington, DC: U.S. Government Printing Office.

Phelps, L. A., Blanchard, L. C., Larkin, D., & Cobb, R. B. (1982). *Vocational programming and services for handicapped individuals in Illinois: Program costs and benefits.* Springfield: Illinois State Board of Education.

Revell, W. G., Jr., & Arnold, S. M. (1984). Role of the rehabilitation counselor in providing job-oriented services to severely handicapped mentally retarded persons. *Journal of Applied Rehabilitation Counseling, 15*(1), 22–27.

Russell, G. (1985). Economy & business: A maddening labor mismatch. *Newsweek.*

Stodden, R. A., & Boone, R. (1987). Assessing transition services for handicapped youth: A cooperative interagency approach. *Exceptional Children, 53*(6), 537–545.

U.S. Department of Labor. (1977). *Dictionary of occupational titles.* Washington, DC: U.S. Government Printing Office.

Vocational Rehabilitation Act of 1973 (September 26, 1973). Public Law 93–112, 87 Stat. 355, 29 U.S.C. 722.

Walls, R. T., Zawlocki, R. J., & Dowler, D. L. (1986). Economic benefits as disincentives to competitive employment. In F. Rusch (Ed.), *Competitive employment issues and strategies* (pp. 317–329). Baltimore: Paul H. Brookes.

Wehman, P., & Barcus, J. M. (1985) Unemployment among handicapped youth: What is the role of the public schools? *Career Development for Exceptional Individuals*, 8(2), 90–101.

Wehman, P., Hill, M., Hill, J. W., Brooke, V., Pendelton, P., & Britt, C. (1985). Competitive employment for persons with mental retardation: A follow-up six years later. *Mental Retardation*, 23(6), 274–281.

Will, M. (1985). *Transition: Linking disabled youth to a productive future*. (Vol. 1, No. 1, Autumn). Washington, DC: Office of Special Education and Rehabilitative Services, U.S. Department of Education.

Ysseldyke, J. E., Christenson, S., Pianta, B., Thurlow, M. L., & Algozzine, B. (1982). *An analysis of current practice in referring students for psychoeducational evaluation: Implication for change* (Research Report No. 91). Minneapolis: Institute of Research on Learning Disabilities, University of Minnesota.

Zigmond, N., & Thornton, H. (1985). Follow-up of postsecondary age learning disabled graduates and drop-outs. *Learning Disabilities Research*, 1(1), 50–55.

EPILOGUE

Analysis and Synthesis of Transition Issues

Janis Chadsey-Rusch, Frank R. Rusch, and L. Allen Phelps*

Employment for youths with disabilities continues to influence this country's educational and rehabilitation efforts. Indeed, recent legislation continues to support efforts focused on persistent problems, including those associated with transition issues. This text is an important contribution to our better understanding of transition issues. In this final chapter we reexamine the issues discussed in each of the preceding chapters and suggest possible directions for future research. It is in the context of this epilogue that we attempt to synthesize some of the most pressing issues and problems in transition, including the context of transition, collaboration processes, and employment component.

CONTEXT FOR TRANSITION

The introductory chapter frames a number of definitional, historical, philosophical, and operational perspectives on assisting youths with disabilities in the transition from school to work. At the outset Berkell and Gaylord-Ross

---

*Frank R. Rusch is director of the Secondary Transition Intervention Effectiveness Institute at the University of Illinois and professor of special education. Professor Rusch received his Ph.D. from the University of Washington. He has published over 100 books, chapters, and journal articles in instructional research and program evaluation.

Janis Chadsey-Rusch is an assistant professor of special education at the University of Illinois at Urbana-Champaign. She completed her doctorate at the University of Illinois. Her research interests relate to social interactions, communication, and ecological psychology.

Alan Phelps is professor and head of the Department of Vocational and Technical Education at the University of Illinois at Urbana-Champaign. Phelps received his BS and MA in Education from Central Michigan University and his Ph.D. in Vocational and Special Education from the University of Illinois. His major area of interest is public policy as it relates to education for special-needs youths and adults. He is involved in national organizations, including the President's Committee on Employment for the Handicapped. Phelps also served as vice president of the American Vocational Association, Special-Needs Division.

endorse the principle that school-to-work transition should be a carefully orchestrated process that involves special educators, parents, and a host of other
school and adult service providers to plan and provide individualized education, training, and initial employment experiences. Acceptance of this definition provides the basis for embracing a number of related principles that focus
on the right to work, a functional analysis of disability, cooperation and program articulation among educators and other service providers (e.g., rehabilitation counselors, prevocational coordinators, and vocational educators),
placement of students in the least restrictive and most responsive educational
settings, and consideration of a full range of adult employment options. Each
of these principles is formulated in light of an initial analysis of the recurrent
patterns of high unemployment, low earnings, and poor educational attainment experienced by youths in our nation. The authors appropriately point out
that in our contemporary society, a successful transition through this period is
crucial for all youths, but it is of paramount importance to those with disabilities, who experience academic and social difficulties in school.

In the context of transition, it is imperative to consider the economic factors that affect youths with disabilities; an analysis of these factors is perhaps
the most important social science element of school-to-work transition theory.
The analysis of how individuals, employers, and our society choose to allocate
scarce resources to enhance the employability of disabled youths is indeed one
of the most basic and overriding considerations in transition. As Passmore
clearly suggests, such choices should be viewed at the macro level as policy
choices and at the micro level as individual choices. To inform both kinds of
choices, Passmore argues convincingly that theory and research results need
to be applied more rigorously if prospects for employment are to improve for
youths with disabilities.

Several important issues appear when transition is considered within economic and social contexts; these issues include the importance of work to human development; the nature, causes, and consequences of youth unemployment; and the interaction of disability and youth unemployment. From a
philosophical perspective, work is of central importance because we are often
defined by the work that we do. Further, work is essential to human existence
because it provides opportunities for each of us to be purposeful, responsible,
creative, compassionate, and useful. Because in most industrialized societies
there are constraints placed on opportunities for individuals (especially disabled individuals) to find fulfilling work, the economic aspects of work have
become highly interrelated with the capacity of individuals to realize their hu-
manness.

Although the causes of youth unemployment are diverse and poorly
understood, the consequences of joblessness are indeed profound in terms of
their impact on the development of youths and human potential. Citing other
studies on youth unemployment, Passmore notes that unemployment among
youths tends to be highest among those generally regarded as less able or those

with clearly recognized limitations in their present status—Hispanics, blacks, those living in inner cities or rural settings, those in communities with depressed economies, and those who are disabled. The social and private costs of youth joblessness are also significant. A 1 percent increase in the unemployment rate can account for significant annual increases in federal outlays, for example, up to 64 percent in some programs such as job training.

The transition of youths to work should also be viewed within the structure of labor markets and the forces of supply and demand that operate in those markets. For example, careful analyses of the supply structure for various occupations must be made. In addition, the decisions of individuals to enter the labor market will be influenced significantly by the potential loss of income from social security programs—specifically, SSDI and unemployment compensation. Passmore reports that most studies of income transfer programs find that these programs serve as a disincentive for individuals to pursue employment (Walls, Zawlocki, & Dowler, 1986) and that the causes for such individual choices are very complex. Citing Levitan and Taggart's (1977) analysis, Passmore reinforces the importance of developing informed social policy choices by the need to examine critically the tradeoffs to be made in providing either income transfer programs or rehabilitation services to individuals with different types and severities of disability, especially in an era of intense competition for scarce public resources.

When examining the demand side of the economic equation, Passmore notes that industries in the United States are highly interdependent and driven by the material needs for goods and services through personal consumption expenditures, investments, imports, exports, and government expenditures. It is possible to link labor costs and employment needs to current and projected demand. In describing the industry and occupation employment projection system used by the U.S. Bureau of Labor Statistics, Passmore notes that it is possible to link data on the mental and physical requirements in occupations to employment trends. Because training individuals with disabilities involves a significant investment, Passmore urges that training be provided in occupations that are relatively immune to fluctuations in the economy (e.g., bookkeeping).

Passmore also discusses employment discrimination and employer incentives. He suggests that the reduction of stereotypes regarding the abilities of disabled individuals will not only improve employment opportunities for this group but also probably increase the productivity of the entity. Although they are predicated on the assumption that they offset some of the higher costs for employing disabled workers, employer incentive programs appear to have paperwork requirements that significantly discourage employers' participation.

In addition to economic factors, the context of transition should be viewed from a lifelong perspective. Brolin and Schatzman provide a comprehensive historical and developmental analysis of the emergence of career education and its importance to youths and adults with disabilities. The authors draw significantly from the career guidance and work adjustment literature to identify key elements of a curriculum that leads toward the development of the work personality. The work personality consists of a full complement of appropriate work habits, values, interests, and other employability-oriented skills.

The Life-Centered Career Education (LCCE) curriculum contains competencies that contribute to work personalities. Twenty-two learner competencies in four major domains (academic, personal-social, daily living, and occupational) have been validated through student follow-up surveys as central to successful adjustment to adult life. The lifelong career development approach is also described in reference to 12 important implementation propositions. Among the most salient propositions are those that view the curriculum as (1) needing to be infused into most subject areas; (2) requiring active partnerships among the school, parents, business and industry, and community agencies; (3) capitalizing on hands-on experiential learning; (4) employing both formal and informal career and vocational assessment, and (5) requiring programmatic leadership from an identified transition resource coordinator.

Brolin's Life-Centered Career Education curriculum, which has focused on serving mildly disabled youths in high schools (and more recently in postsecondary settings), continues to provide a framework for instruction that transition-oriented programs serving this population find useful, functional, cost-efficient, and comprehensive. Teachers and curriculum supervisors working in special programs as well as in mainstream settings have adopted the curriculum widely.

Areas for Future Research

It is clear from the chapters discussing the context of transition that improving the school-to-work process for disabled youths is not a new issue or a new societal problem. Since the early 1960s, the fields of special education, vocational rehabilitation, mental retardation, employment training (CETA and JTPA), and vocational education have devoted considerable attention to the needs of individuals with disabilities who are successfully completing high school, gaining appropriate further education, and entering the labor market. Since 1980, the investment of federal funds alone in these programs has exceeded $1 billion every year. Yet recent studies point to the paucity of data-based research that distinguishes between effective and ineffective policy and practice (Flynn, 1982; Phelps, 1986). Specifically, Phelps (1986, pp. 11–77) noted, "While vocational education has been seriously engaged in the business of serving special populations since 1968, the field lacks a comprehensive knowledge base of effective practices."

Although vocational education (along with other federal and state programs) has invested heavily in launching new programs and providing a broader array of related services, program evaluation requirements are often minimal or incomplete. Without serious and sustained testing and evaluation of various program models, alternate instructional designs and materials, and different forms of interagency cooperative arrangements, vocational educators can only speculate when making decisions regarding these issues. Without better-informed perspectives on what happens to youths with disabilities as they proceed through these programs and seek to enter the work force, we cannot develop sound programs of teacher training, adopt appropriate funding policies, or provide guidance for interagency collaboration. Although at present there is an intense demand to provide services for workplace-bound disabled youths who gained access to public schooling as a result of Public Law 94–142, practitioners, policy makers, and researchers clearly need to adopt better collaborative strategies for evaluation and research on the present enterprise.

From the theoretical and planning perspective, there is a continuing need to improve interdisciplinary and interagency collaboration. Recent research on career development and work patterns of all workers, as well as of those who are disabled, should be analyzed carefully to identify new employment trends, such as job sharing; the use of technology in certain jobs; and supported employment. Studies by labor economists can provide educators with information about the appropriate types of competencies, skills, and attitudes that youths with disabilities need to enter and compete successfully in the labor market. Research in psychology, social work, and human development will help educators provide experiences for these youths that will in turn help them to cope with such issues as divorce, transportation, discrimination, and other issues affecting their capacity to live and work independently.

Research is also needed that examines labor supply and demand variables from the macro and micro perspectives. The interaction between the individual and societal views of variables influencing decisions and behaviors relative to the labor market is a critical issue. Can social and economic policies be implemented to cause individual behavior to change? Or to what extent do patterns of individual choice and behavior generate an essential prerequisite to new policy? Another corollary proposition is, should our government create more powerful incentives for hiring and appropriately employing disabled individuals in the public and private sectors (with the goal of reducing public transfer programs and expenditures)? Or should government respond only when the economic and social plight of the disabled community is sufficiently serious to cause significant social concern? Additional studies of labor market behavior and participation of youths with different disabilities are needed to examine these questions more closely. Leaders of transition programs at the state and local levels should initiate studies of the costs and benefits of alternative policy options that concern social and education programs for the population with disabilities.

Although analyzing economic and employment difficulties is enlightening, it also illustrates several significant limitations of the work in this field to date. The analyses of the labor market performance of youths with disabilities is needed for several reasons. First, longitudinal studies have failed to collect useful data on other youths or adults with disabilities, particularly those with inapparent disabilities such as learning disabilities and emotional disturbances. Second, once individuals exit the special education or rehabilitation systems and become employed, they often are not anxious to be reidentified as having disabilities. Finally, relatively few smaller, focused studies, such as case studies, have been undertaken to examine the employment difficulties encountered by other groups of disabled individuals in particular industries or companies. It appears that the field will continually be faced with a complicated morass of privacy considerations for former students and clients, difficulties in collecting useful data about the nature and stability of some disabilities, and problems associated with the complexity and nonuniformity of employment situations. These ambiguities clearly suggest that additional case-study-oriented research should be conducted on the economics of transition in order to better understand this complex and rapidly changing phenomenon.

FACILITATING TRANSITION
THROUGH COLLABORATION

Collaboration is a key element in the transition process. Through collaboration, youths can receive planned, appropriate, and nonduplicated services. Many individuals are likely to participate in the transition process, including individuals charged with identifying persons in need of transition assistance, educators, clients, families, and service providers.

Greenan discussed issues related to identifying, assessing, and placing persons with handicaps into appropriate services. The description of these procedures is likely to be familiar to most professionals involved in the delivery of vocational services. For example, Greenan discussed the identification of children at the preschool, elementary school, and secondary school levels. He also discussed the role of postschool agencies in the identification process. Essentially, at the preschool and elementary school level, many children with special needs are likely to have been identified by either regular or special education personnel. In accordance with the mandates of Public Law 94–142, prescribed procedures are followed to identify students in need of services.

At the secondary level, some students who have not been identified as having special needs may be placed in vocational programs. Vocational teachers who feel that these students need specialized help may refer these students to special education staffs and often participate in review processes via the rules and regulations from Public Law 98–524 (Carl D. Perkins Act), which are similar in intent to Public Law 94–142.

Once students graduate from the public schools, it is likely that special educators and/or vocational educators will refer those students who may need postschool services to vocational rehabilitation. Rehabilitation personnel will begin the identification process by determining client eligibility for services. In addition, employment and training program personnel such as those persons affiliated with the Job Training Partnership Act (JTPA) and social service agencies (e.g., Goodwill) may also identify individuals needing transition services.

In terms of assessment, Greenan again discussed many of the options and procedures that are likely to be familiar to personnel involved in providing vocational services. He described instruments that can be used to assess ability, achievement, aptitude, work behaviors, attitudes, interpersonal skills, and interests. It is important, however, to recognize the strengths and weaknesses of many of these assessment procedures. Assessment should be viewed as an ongoing process that is used not only to place students into programs but also to plan and monitor student progress.

It is clear that when students have been identified as needing special services, the field of education will become involved in the transition process. Retish viewed transition from a broad perspective; it is a process that begins at birth, continues throughout one's life, and encompasses more than the transition from school to work. The education system plays a predominant role in the transition process, the first transition occurring when one leaves home and enters school for the first time. Subsequent transitions occur when one goes from elementary school to secondary school and when one leaves the secondary school for work or further postsecondary school experiences.

Retish also described schools from a broad perspective; he did not focus on special education or vocational education but instead discussed education in general and the impact it has had on students with disabilities. In particular, Retish pointed out that the education system itself is undergoing a period of transition; this transition period has been fueled by the Carnegie, Holmes, and *High School and Beyond* reports. It is clear from these reports that as the world changes, so must the education system.

Several education issues were described by Retish, including curricula, job development, program and student evaluation, parent and support services, and teacher preparation. Retish, a strong proponent of evaluation, suggested that curricula and job development should be restructured based on data from student and program evaluation. Evaluation data, such as high school follow-up reports (e.g., Mithaug, Horiuchui, & Fanning, 1985), will help to define the roles schools should play in the transition process.

Parents and their relationship with the schools are an integral component of the transition process. As Retish pointed out, many parents are fearful of the transition that their children must make when they leave the safe confines of public school systems. Students currently leave a fairly well-organized education system of instruction and enter into a massive disorganized array of potential human services. Clearly, educators need to work closely with parents to help alleviate their fears.

In the end, much of the responsibility for the transition process will belong to the teachers. Yet most teachers have not been prepared to facilitate the transition process. As Retish indicated, teachers will need to be aware of the community and the skills students should have to be successful in the community. Teachers also will need to know about jobs, support systems, leisure and integration activities, and cultural differences.

Although Greenan and Retish primarily discussed many of the players in the transition process at the local level, collaboration also can occur at the federal and state level. Tindall and Gugerty discussed collaboration at three levels: (1) federal, (2) state, and (3) local. Federal level collaboration can have a definite impact on state and local level policies. The most influential federal departments that can affect the transition of youths with handicaps are the Office of Special Education and Rehabilitative Services (OSERS), the Office of Vocational and Adult Education (OVAE), the Social Security Administration, and the U.S. Department of Labor. Although these departments stress the need for collaboration, little actual collaboration exists among them. As Tindall and Gugerty suggested, collaboration at the federal level is probably the most difficult to achieve. However, federal agencies can play an important role by creating new and improved legislation related to transition and providing guidelines for a collaboration approach that can be used at the state and local levels.

If state agencies collaborate effectively, they can provide a good model for local service providers to follow. In addition, through collaboration, services can be implemented more quickly and resources can be used more efficiently. The likely outcome of this collaborative process is a smoother transition for individuals with handicaps. States can collaborate through the mandates of several pieces of legislation, for example, Public Law 94–142, the Carl Perkins Act, and the Job Training Partnership Act. Interestingly, Tindall and Gugerty suggested that at the state level, anyone can initiate the transition process. However, someone should take the lead, or collaboration will be unlikely.

Tindall and Gugerty stated that legislation is not enough to foster collaboration at the local level. Variables that seem to contribute to effective collaboration at the community level include (1) the continued involvement of key individuals; (2) commitments to shared goals that focus on the education and training needs of individuals with disabilities and on activities that show that "tangible progress" is being made to meet those goals; (3) clearly stated and implemented processes for collaboration between service providers and advocacy groups; and (4) formal agreements (e.g., Individual Transition Plans) that document transition processes, including goals, time lines, activities, and responsibilities.

The primary measure of outcome for the collaborative process has been

employment. In their chapter, Tindall and Gugerty also discussed leisure activities and their role in transition. There is more to adult life than employment,
and effective collaborative processes need to be evaluated with more than just
employment as the primary outcome measure.

Areas for Future Research

There is a myriad of research issues related to facilitating transition through
collaboration. In terms of identifying persons in need of transition assistance,
we should use more effective procedures than the ones currently being used to
identify and classify individuals with disabilities. Information is needed that
will pinpoint *specific* youths needing transition services. If we view transition
from the model developed by Will (1984), it is probably wrong to conclude
that all students labeled as having disabilities will need transition services. That
is, some individuals will not need "special services" to make the transition
from school to work, whereas others will need ongoing services throughout
their employment.

There are two approaches that may potentially be helpful in the identification of students in need of transition services. One approach would be to assume that all students with IEPs should also have individualized transition
plans (ITPs) (McDonnell & Hardman, 1985). Then, personnel would decide
on an individual basis which students actually needed transition services.

The other approach would be more empirical in nature. Data could be
collected on various subject variables (e.g., level of handicapping condition,
socioeconomic status, and prior education), program variables (e.g., vocational experiences while in school), home variables (e.g., parental attitudes),
and outcome variables (e.g., employment status) so that predictions could be
made about the types of persons who would probably need transition services.

Clearly, effective strategies are needed to identify those individuals who
require help to make the transition from school to work. Traditional identification procedures that are being used to identify students with special needs
may not be the most appropriate measures to identify students who need transition services.

It is also important to identify or develop instruments that can be used to
assess skills related to transition. There is little information related to the types
of procedures and instruments that can best be used to measure directly the
most important subject characteristics associated with successful transitions.
For example, some studies (e.g., Menchetti, Rusch, & Owens, 1983) have suggested that traditional approaches to vocational assessment such as psychological tests, motor measurement tests, and work sample tests are not very useful
for persons with mental retardation, especially in terms of identifying training
needs or pinpointing appropriate jobs. Similarly, in their review of all of the
OSERS-funded secondary transition projects, DeStefano, Linn, and Mark-

ward, (1987) found that instruments judged to be the most useful were measures of social and daily living skills.

Future research may reveal that persons needing transition assistance should be identified at an early age. Certainly, no one would deny that transitions occur throughout many periods of our lives. In addition, few would deny that transition from school to the work force or the adult community is influenced by educational experiences that occur before entry into secondary schools. However, it may behoove educators (at least in the near future) to focus many of their efforts on the secondary school and the transition process from school to the community. This particular time in a child's life—from approximately 16 to 21 years of age—has been targeted for change by the federal government (Will, 1984).

What is the role that teachers, parents, and educators in general are likely to play in the transition process? To answer this question, we should not ignore the findings and the potential impact of the education reform movement. Also, we should recognize the fears of parents and the fact that many teachers lack the knowledge needed to prepare students adequately to adapt to and accommodate the adult world. However, the time may have come to leave generalities behind and focus on specifics. It is time to define the roles of educators, to evaluate these roles, and to redefine them as necessary. For example, several authors have specifically described the roles and competencies of the various persons that are likely to be involved in the transition process (e.g., Everson & Moon, 1987; Gillet, 1985; McDaniel, 1986; Wehman et al., 1987). In fact, Everson and Moon (1987) listed individual responsibilities for administrators and direct service staffs from the fields of special education, vocational rehabilitation, and vocational education. They also listed the roles that parents can assume in the transition process. Finally, other authors (e.g., McDonnell & Hardman, 1985) have described a vehicle (Individualized Transition Plan) that can be used to facilitate and coordinate this process.

Many might argue with these roles and refer to these "lists" as a simplistic solution to a complex problem. However, these identified roles and responsibilities provide a natural starting point for research. Through research, the effectiveness of these roles and responsibilities for enhancing the transition process can be evaluated, changed, and refined.

Finally, we should conduct research on collaboration issues that affect more than just the transition from school to work. The concept of transition needs to be broadened to include community adjustment as well as employment. A number of variables could be used to measure the effectiveness of transition from school to community, including level of integration, quality of life, social skills, and daily living skills. An important area for future research will be to determine which outcome measures account for the largest proportion of variance in the transition process.

Although research has suggested many of the successful components associated with effective collaboration, the process of bringing people together, and keeping them together, seems to warrant future research. For example, a case study examining this interactive process could provide useful information. Answers to questions such as "How do groups break down turf barriers?" and "How do groups pool dollars and resources?" would help the collaborative process.

THE EMPLOYMENT COMPONENT OF THE TRANSITION PROCESS

Although the concept of transition needs to be more broadly defined so that it includes adjustment to the community, employment is still the critical component that receives the most emphasis in transition programs. Traditional preplacement services (e.g., work adjustment training, work experience, and prevocational training) have not successfully prepared students for employment. Johnson and Warrington suggested that job development and follow-up services have begun to identify an emerging placement process that has been shown to be effective with individuals who have diverse disabilities, including severe mental retardation. During the past decade our understanding of what constitutes good practice in this area has developed immensely. These practices have been influenced by special education and rehabilitation alike.

Job development is essential in the transition process, and employers should be viewed as "partners" in the process of finding new jobs and adopting a marketing approach to placement. Partnerships among education, rehabilitation, and industry are new. Forming these partnerships is important because business places certain demands on future employees and expects education to prepare these employees adequately. Education, in turn, asks questions about the expectations that businesses have and changes its curricula to prepare students to meet those expectations.

Increasingly, schools and adult service agencies have identified potential jobs for students by studying market labor trends, contacting employers, and structuring the actual placement of their graduates. This new focus is an important trend in education programs because the outcome of education is intended to benefit the student as well as business.

Most recently, matching potential employees to jobs has developed to the point where traditional methods of assessing students also are being challenged. Johnson and Warrington pointed out that "the location of the job in the community, availability of transportation, [student] interest in the work, job skills and ability levels required, time of the day and week [that] work is scheduled" are important factors in job matching. When the level of analysis begins to focus on individuals as potential employees and specific target jobs as potential placement sites, several strategies are relevant. For example, restructuring targeted jobs, streamlining work routines, and job sharing are discussed. These strategies represent important developments in the field.

Providing follow-up services to persons with disabilities is relatively new, and our understanding of what constitutes good practice is still emerging. Although several authors have written about how they have provided extended follow-up services to persons with handicaps (cf. Rusch, 1986; Wehman, 1981), much remains to be studied, particularly in light of recent federal legislation that requires extended services to be provided to all persons who receive support services from rehabilitation.

Job development, placement, and follow-up services are primarily the responsibility of local service providers. However, the roles of employers are also crucial to the transition process. In their chapter, Brown, Joseph, and Wortruba suggested several ways that employers' roles can be enhanced to facilitate the transition of learners with disabilities. One way to increase employers' involvement would be through federal and state policy initiatives. In particular, federal and state incentives that encourage private sector businesses and industries to employ persons with disabilities should be continued. In addition, federally mandated minimums or quotas attached to existing affirmative action legislation and policies might also encourage involvement.

Many personnel within business and industry have misconceptions about the work abilities of persons with disabilities. Brown and his colleagues suggested that information, in the form of staff development training seminars, could reduce the myths and stereotypes often held about individuals with disabilities. For example, employers need to be aware that workers with disabilities tend to be equal or better than workers without disabilities in many aspects of work performance, attendance, and safety records. In addition, employers need to know that there are many strategies that can be used to increase the likelihood of effectively matching workers with their jobs. For example, personnel within business and industry can be trained to analyze job tasks in order to make appropriate modifications that will enhance worker productivity levels.

If individuals within business and industry were to participate in staff development seminars, a number of benefits could be realized. Employers would be less likely to become discouraged by difficulties they might encounter when working with persons with disabilities, they would have a better understanding of the complexities of workers and the work environment, and they could develop a trained labor force from which to choose future employees.

Areas for Future Research

Employment is a crucial component of the transition process, and future research should ensure that employment is a reality for all persons with disabilities. With changing legislation, new employment outcomes have emerged. In particular, supported employment, which includes the expectation of long-term supervision, will challenge rehabilitation, special education, and vocational education to reallocate existing resources (capital and human) to develop complementary services. Supported employment should draw on existing job development and placement, job matching, and follow-up research literature. The expectation that we place students in integrated settings that pay wages for competitive work with necessary support services will result in our asking new questions. Although studies exist, we will need to become more aware of how several different disciplines should work together to abate a long history of unemployment among this nation's youths with disabilities.

In light of recent legislation such as Public Law 99–506, rehabilitation's role in providing job-specific services for a period of up to 18 months for *all* persons with disabilities, including those with severe handicaps, will require that schools make early financial and human commitments to students who are approaching graduation from high school. This early commitment will include actually placing students in targeted job settings and providing follow-up services. Consequently, secondary and postsecondary transitional models that result in job retention should be explored.

Research is also clearly needed to determine the best methods to ensure employment for persons with mild disabilities. At the present time it is unclear what kind of job development and placement services will best serve this population. Clearly, the supported-work model is not appropriate for these youths; however, best practices that ensure continued employment for this population are sorely lacking.

Finally, research is needed that further explores ways to enhance employers' involvement in the transition process. Methods need to be formulated that effectively change employers' attitudes and increase their receptivity toward hiring individuals with disabilities. In addition, strategies are needed to teach employers how to train disabled workers on the job as well as to foster their acceptance into the workplace.

CONCLUSION

Transition should be viewed as a dynamic process involving a partnership of consumers (i.e., students), school services (e.g., vocational education and special education programs), postschool services (e.g., rehabilitation), parents, and local employers that results in all youths being able to live and work in natural communities. Critical variables that are likely to contribute toward facilitating this process include schools that provide community-based training and work experiences, formalized student transition plans, and interagency collaboration and involvement. In addition, all these variables should be considered in terms of their relationships to labor and economic trends and forecasts.

Although the delineation of these variables is not new, questions still remain regarding how best to operationalize them. For example, little is known about the effect that the excellence movement will have on the transition process. If students, particularly those with mild disabilities, do not have the opportunity to take vocational education courses or to participate in work experience programs in the community because they need to fulfill more stringent academic requirements, what effect will this have on their transition adjustment? Although it is clear that students with severe disabilities need to be involved in functional curricula, the curricula issue for students with mild disabilities is more obscure.

Clearly, planning and collaboration are essential to the transition process, and the addition of a transition plan, attached to a student's IEP, could help facilitate this process. However, more information is needed on how best to ensure that all the participants know that certain behaviors are essential to collaboration (e.g., commitment to planning for individual students and role release), but this will not always guarantee that collaboration will occur. Thus, additional studies should document this process.

Inherent to the transition process are the personnel involved. It is important to develop both effective preservice and inservice models that best prepare individuals to participate effectively in the transition process. These models should consist not only of coursework but also involve closely monitored practical experiences that teach personnel the instructional technology needed to facilitate transition, the administrative components associated with transition, and program evaluation skills.

Finally, all transition programs should continually be evaluated for their effectiveness. Follow-up studies of high school graduates will provide valuable information concerning transition practices. Care should be taken, however, when selecting outcome measures. Although quantitative variables such as wages earned and hours worked are important indicators of program success, qualitative variables such as satisfaction with friends and quality of life are also important.

Even though many components of the transition process still need to be operationalized, the process of transition is clear. With today's knowledge and continued research and development, a smooth transition from school to work is feasible for all of our nation's youths.

REFERENCES

DeStefano, L., Linn, R., & Markward, M. (1987). *Review of student assessment instruments and practices* (rev.). Urbana-Champaign: Transition Institute at Illinois, University of Illinois.

Everson, J. M., & Moon, M. S. (1987). Transition services for young adults with severe disabilities: Defining professional and parental roles and responsibilities. *Journal of the Association for Persons with Severe Handicaps, 12*(2), 87–95.

Flynn, R. J. (1982). Effectiveness of conventional and alternative vocational education with handicapped and disadvantaged youth: A research review. In K. P. Lynch,

W. E. Kiernan, & J. A. Stark (Eds.), *Prevocational and vocational education for special needs youth*. Baltimore: Paul H. Brookes.

Gillet, P. K. (1985). Transition: A special education perspective. In R. N. Ianacone & R. A. Stodden (Eds.), *Transition: Issues and Directions* (pp. 113–119). Reston, VA: Council for Exceptional Children.

Levitan, S. A., & Taggart, R. (1977). *Jobs for the disabled*. Baltimore: Johns Hopkins University Press.

McDaniel, R. (1986). Preservice implications for delivering effective transitional services in vocational rehabilitation. In J. Chadsey-Rusch & C. Hanley-Maxwell (Eds.), *Enhancing transition from school to the workplace for handicapped youth: Personnel preparation implications* (pp. 193–211). Urbana-Champaign: University of Illinois.

McDonnell, J., & Hardman, M. (1985). Planning the transition of severely handicapped youth from school to adult services: A framework for high school programs. *Education and Training of the Mentally Retarded, 20*, 275–286.

Menchetti, B. M., Rusch, F. R., & Owens, D. (1983). Assessing the vocational needs of mentally retarded adolescents and adults. In J. L. Matson & S. E. Breuning (Eds.), *Assessing the mentally retarded* (pp. 247–284). New York: Grune & Stratton.

Mithaug, D. E., Horiuchi, C. N., & Fanning, P. N. (1985). A report on the Colorado statewide follow-up survey of special education students. *Exceptional Children, 51*, 397–404.

Phelps, L. A. (1987). Evaluating the special populations and equity provisions of federal vocational education legislation. In *Design papers for the national assessment of vocational education*. Washington, DC: National Assessment of Vocational Education, U.S. Department of Education.

Rusch, F. (Ed.) (1986). *Competitive employment issues and strategies*. Baltimore: Paul H. Brookes.

Walls, R. T., Zawlocki, R. J., & Dowler, D. L. (1986). Economic benefits as disincentives to competitive employment. In F. R. Rusch (Ed.), *Competitive employment issues and strategies* (pp. 317–329). Baltimore: Paul H. Brookes.

Wehman, P., Moon, M. S., Everson, J. M., Wood, W., & Barcus, J. M. (1987). *Transition from school to work: New challenges for youth with severe disabilities*. Baltimore: Paul H. Brookes.

Wehman, P. (1981). *Competitive employment: New horizons for severely disabled individuals*. Baltimore: Paul H. Brookes.

Will, M. (1984). Let us pause and reflect—but not too long. *Exceptional Children, 51*, 11–15.

Index

Page numbers in *italics* indicate illustrations. Page numbers followed by *t* indicate tables.

Vocational Rehabilitation Act of 1920, 11
Vocational samples in vocational assessment, 82–83
Volunteer work, 16–17
V-Tecs Curriculum, 88

Wage incentives for employer in job development, 174–175
White House Conferences on Handicapped, career development and, 25–26
Work
importance of, 44–45
right to, 2
Work force, diverse, management of, concerns related to, 194

Work routines, compartmentalizing, in job development, 178
Work samples in vocational assessment, 77, 81–82
Work stations, paired, in job development, 178
Work Study (WS) programs, 100

Youth employment
disability and, 47–49
patterns of, 45–47
problem of
causes of, 46–47
consequences of, 47
nature of, 46
Youth organizations, vocational programs in, 100–101
Youth unemployment in context of transition, 228–229